Bodybuilding
A Realistic Approach

How You Can Have A Great Body!

BY FRANK A. MELFA

2nd Edition

Power Writings
New Brunswick, New Jersey

Bodybuilding
A Realistic Approach
How You Can Have A Great Body!

BY FRANK A. MELFA

Published by:

Power Writings
P.O. Box 11320
New Brunswick, NJ 08906-11320

Copyright ©1998 by Frank A. Melfa
Second Edition 1998

Publisher's Cataloging-in-Publication
(Provided by Quality Books, Inc.)

Melfa, Frank A.
    Bodybuilding, a realistic approach : how you can have a great body / Frank A. Melfa. -- 2nd ed.
    p. cm.
    Includes bibliographical references and index.
    Preassigned LCCN: 97-95132
    ISBN: 0-9641640-7-8

    1. Bodybuilding. 2. Bodybuilding for women. I. Title.

GV546.5.M45 1998   646.7'5
                        QBI98-230

Exercise photographs by Marcelo S. LaRosa unless otherwise credited.
Illustrations by Timothy P. Cilurso

Printed by Command Color Press

Warning Disclaimer

Before you start any exercise program, it is highly recommended that you consult with a physician first, especially if you have a history of medical problems or are currently taking prescribed drugs.

No Liability

The views expressed in this text are the author's opinions. Factual information is cited. This book is designed to provide information in regard to the subject matter covered. It is sold with the understanding that the publisher and author are not engaged in rendering legal or professional services. This book does not provide medical advice. Any medical advice should be obtained from a medical professional. The nutritional information may not be applicable for everyone.
You should consult with a licensed nutritionist before starting a new diet.

The information included about anabolic steroids is not intended to promote, encourage, or advocate their use or any other illegal substance.

Frank with brother-in-law, photographer, and friend, Marcelo S. LaRosa.

Acknowledgments

Bodybuilding is my *passion*, even though I don't compete anymore. It has changed my life completely. Through bodybuilding, I have written and published this book, and developed a lust for art, writing, and life.

I dedicate this book to my family and friends who supported me through my entire bodybuilding and book writing experiences.

Thank you Vincent Burke for teaching me how to pose, driving me to my contests, oiling me up back stage, and carrying my bags. Thank you Tim Cilurso and Bill DeJianne for buying me my first Gold's Gym membership. You guys lived and breathed bodybuilding with me. I have no idea how you put up with me.

Thank you mom for cooking me special meals and putting up with my grouchiness. Thank you Francesca & Josephine, my two beautiful sisters, for attending and cheering for me at my contests. Thank you Marcelo for all the contest pictures and your contribution to this book.

Thank you Rich Tuite, for your editing efforts and the great book signing party!

Thank you Judy and Bruce Van't Groenewout for your help and confidence. It's still the most difficult thing I have ever asked anyone!

A special thanks is given to everyone who contributed to this book: Louis Csabay, Bill DeJianne, Elisabeth King, Daniel Lapinski, Lori Rocker, Richard J. Tuite, and Al Winters.

I express my gratitude to the following bodybuilders who agreed to appear in this book: Scott Baumann, Vincent Burke, Luke Cantestri, Diana Cimato, Gina Delaney, Jeannine M. Paratore, Amy Ginsburg, Denise Marsh, and all the Mr. & Ms. Rutgers Competitors.

Promotional gratitude goes to Diane Simowski and Carol Curren from Barnes & Noble. You are two of the most sincere people I have ever worked with.

Thank you Ed Halper from New York Sports Club in East Brunswick, NJ and Kevin and Tammy Freeman from Xtreme Fitness in Edison, NJ for allowing me to use your gyms.

Thanks to Linda Henry and Muscle & Fitness® Magazine for their permission to include excerpts from what I feel is the most comprehensive fitness magazine.

This book would never have been possible without the sincere dedication of my good friend, Tim Cilurso, who designed the entire book from cover to cover.

Sincere thanks to Roger Young and Stan Zwier of Command Color Press for their assistance and guidance throughout the manufacturing process of this book.

About The Author

The words *dedication* and *discipline* are often times misused or misinterpreted. As you embark on your reading of the following pages, keep in mind that this book has been written by someone who lives and embodies the very definitions of *dedication* and *discipline*.

Frank A. Melfa was born in Paterson, New Jersey in 1967. He grew up competing in organized football, wrestling and track. In junior high school,

 Frank began lifting weights seriously in an effort to improve his athletic performance. At the age of 12, he was already bench pressing 225 pounds and squatting close to 400 pounds! He continued to train regularly through high school, excelling in football and wrestling.

In 1988, as a sophomore at Rutgers University, Frank decided to dedicate his time and energy to compete in the largest and most prestigious college bodybuilding contest in the country, The Mr. & Ms. Rutgers Bodybuilding Contest. After only months of preparing for his first bodybuilding contest, he placed second in the middleweight class. In 1989, after a year of attending nutrition courses, applying smarter training techniques, and gaining more experience, Frank not only won his weight class, but won the overall Mr. Rutgers title. From there, he went on to win the middleweight class at the AAU Mr. New Jersey, and placed second in the middle-weight class at the prestigious and highly competitive NPC Mr. New Jersey.

In addition to his experience as a successful bodybuilder, Frank formed his own personal training business, amassing a diverse clientele of over 100 clients. From 1990 to 1992, Frank trained four overall winners of The Mr. & Ms. Rutgers Bodybuilding Contest. His impressive and dedicated following of clients sparked the interest of Johnson & Johnson, the largest health care company in the world. Frank managed the Personal Training Program at Johnson & Johnson's World Headquarters in New Brunswick, NJ. There, he and a team of trainers provided individualized training to over 160 employees. Johnson & Johnson provided Frank and his team with comprehensive and world-class training to safely and professionally conduct personal training sessions.

At Johnson & Johnson, Frank's communications skills were applied when he wrote for the company newsletter, *For the Health of It*. He began by writing about the success of the Personal Training Program and eventually expanded to fitness articles.

Currently, Frank manages his own Publishing Company and continues to build his career selling pharmaceutical products for Wyeth-Ayerst Laboratories. He also has his M.B.A. in pharmaceutical and chemical studies from Farleigh Dickinson University.

by William J. DeJianne, Friend and Free Lance Writer

PHOTO BY AUGUSTO F. MENEZESE

Table of Contents

CHAPTER 1

A Realistic Approach to Bodybuilding

A Realistic Approach to Bodybuiding_____

Many of today's bodybuilding books and magazines portray professional bodybuilders with monstrous physiques. It's unrealistic for most of us to build that kind of muscle, even with the use of steroids. Some of the men portrayed in bodybuilding books and magazines weigh anywhere from 200 to 300 pounds. Some of the women look just as muscular as the men! This book portrays amateur bodybuilders, including myself, that have competed in bodybuilding contests with more realistic physiques. We built our bodies with hard weight training and excellent eating habits.

In the cover photographs, I weigh less than 170 pounds. Hard muscle and low bodyfat can look very deceiving. Some people thought I weighed 200 pounds or more. Jeannine M. Paratore, also portrayed on the cover and the internal photographs, proves that women can compete in bodybuilding contests and still maintain a feminine physique.

The message of this book is that everyone can have a great body using realistic training methods and eating right. I'll educate and hopefully motivate you by providing the right exercises, the right workouts, and the right eating plans to help you reach your fitness goals. As far as I'm concerned, the only type of exercise that will help change your physical appearance is weightlifting. We can call it weightlifting, bodybuilding, bodyshaping; call it what you want, but they all require resistance exercises. The best resistance exercises are performed with weights.

Setting Realistic Goals:

The first thing I will say about a goal is to have one! The book, *The One Minute Manager,* states, "Goals begin behaviors." Changing your behavior starts with sitting down, thinking about your goals, and writing them down. Know what you want to accomplish. Do you want to build muscle? Tone up? Lose weight and shape up? Quantify your goals; be specific. Do you want to lose 10 pounds in two months? Do you want to gain 10 pounds of muscle in two months? Do you want to get into shape for summer or vacation?

The second thing about goals is to be **realistic!** Trying to get into shape one week before vacation is not realistic. It takes time, planning, and hard work. Setting unrealistic goals results disappointments that lead to failure. If you work hard, put in the time, and change your eating habits, you will succeed.

Speaking of unrealistic goals, I read an article in a magazine where a professional bodybuilder recommended performing 40 sets of shoulder exercises in one workout and consuming 30,000 calories a day! This is a perfect example of what I'm talking about. I do not recommend performing 40 sets for the entire body, let alone shoulders. Consuming 30,000 calories in a week is difficult, doing it in one day is close to impossible.

Once you have set your realistic goal, know how you are going to get there. The only way to do this is by having a plan. If you don't have a plan, don't plan on reaching your goal. Your plan will break your goal up into mini goals. Don't just think you are going to wing it and it's going to happen by itself. Reading this book is a good start. It will show you what to do, but it can't do it for you. Read chapter 16. It includes a section on planning for a bodybuilding contest. You may not want to compete in a contest, but it gives good examples on planning and why it's so important.

- First, get a planner and log everything that I'm about to tell you in the "things to do" part of your planner.
- Second, join a gym. Pick a day in your planner to visit some gyms in your area. You may even want to consider a personal trainer.

- Once you have joined the gym set a goal on the number of days you plan to workout. Be realistic. I would not recommend starting with five days. Maybe start with three days. Use your planner to determine the specific days you plan to go to the gym. Try to be consistent with the days and the times. Consistency is a key to reaching your goals, including consistency in your workouts, food intake, and attitude.
- Next, go to the supermarket and buy good, healthy food. Make a list in your planner of the foods to purchase. If you need help with this, see the Nutrition section of this book.
- Set your goals and log them in your planner.
- Read the rest of this book.

In order to reach your goals, you will need to change the way you eat. Eating right and lifting weights is the best combination to tone, shape, or build your body. Genetics do play a role in your appearance, so it is important to set realistic goals. For example, if you are five feet two inches tall, you cannot expect to look like someone who is five feet nine inches tall. We all have different body types. Identifying your body type is important when setting goals.

Understanding Your Body Type

Identify your body type from the three basic types of physiques:

- Ectomorph
- Mesomorph
- Endomorph

I used Arnold Schwarzenegger's book, (*The Encyclopedia of Modern Bodybuilding, Firestone Books, Simon & Schuster, 1985)* to help me write part of this section on body types. At the time, I think Arnold referred more to male bodybuilders that wanted to build large muscles and excluded women who want to shape and tone their bodies. He gives great examples on how these three different body types can build muscle on those types of frames. I want to do the same in my book. I also want to show how anyone that just wants to shape and tone and not necessarily want to build huge muscles, can benefit from learning about these body types. I include three other body types specifically for women, the hourglass, pair, and apple shape, that I describe later in the chapter.

An **ectomorph**, characterized by a long physique, is not only tall, but has long arms, legs, hands and feet, narrow waist, narrow shoulders and chest, and has low body fat.

A **mesomorph**, characterized with a medium build, is not tall or short, but has a solid physique, large chest, long torso, wide shoulders, and short arms and legs.

An **endomorph** is characterized by a short, soft, muscle structure, stocky, more body fat than a mesomorph, and usually thicker around the waist and hips.

It's difficult to describe any one person, male or female, to be *exactly* one of these body types. For the most part, the body types are vague. Most people are a combination of any two or a combination of all three. This classification of body types is simply a way of identifying your body and setting realistic goals. I wouldn't get too caught up with it. As far as goals are concerned, have one. You can't achieve what you don't set out to do. Whether you are an ectomorph, mesomorph, or endomorph, you can achieve your body's fullest potential. Once you have identified your body type, you can then choose a role model with whom to identify and then set a goal.

Mesomorphs can pack on muscle easier than ectomorphs. Short arms and legs make it easier to lift heavy weights. Ectomorphs with their long arms and legs find it difficult working heavy weights through a full range of motion. For example, they have a farther distance to travel when squatting. How many tall people do you know with thick, muscular legs? This can be a problem because their egos can get in the way. They want to impress people by using heavy weights and as a result, they don't work through a full range of motion. Performing partial squats or not touching the chest with the bar during bench presses can lead to minimal results.

An ectomorph can increase muscle size *(if this is a goal)* by lifting moderate to heavy weights using very basic exercises and working through a full range of motion. Even if their goal is to tone or shape, they should still use moderate weights working through a full range of motion. They should target the major muscle groups using basic exercises such as, barbell bench presses, dips, rows, pullups, overhead presses, barbell curls, squats, and deadlifts. Ectomorphs with long torsos would benefit greatly from deadlifts to add thickness to the middle and lower back, and pullups to add width to the upper back.

The positive part of being an ectomorph is the capability of attaining an aesthetic physique because of their long and sleek muscles and very low bodyfat. Arnold describes himself as more of an ectomorph with mesomorph characteristics. He's tall and lean, but yet found it easy to build massive muscles. Who had a better physique than Arnold?

Jeannine, portrayed on the cover, is about as close to a pure ectomorph as you can get. She's tall, lean, with long arms, legs and fingers. I never quite noticed the length of her feet though. Even Jeannine with her great physique told me that she finds it difficult keeping fat off her stomach area. Only through strict dieting and vigorous weight training is she able to maintain her admirable physique.

Mesomorphs can vary their exercises and weightlifting programs and still find it easy to build muscle. They may have a more difficult time keeping off bodyfat compared to an ectomorph.

I have a mesomorph-like physique. I'm about five feet eight inches tall. I have relatively low bodyfat. I was never over-weight. As you can see from the photographs, I do have a solid physique, wide shoulders, but short arms and legs. The high placement of my lattisimus dorsi and my long torso put me at a disadvantage when I competed. Simply, I had a small back compared to other middleweight bodybuilders. I was also tall compared to the other middleweights. The stockier middleweights had no problem packing muscle on their back because they had short torsos, more characteristic of the endomorph. This did not discourage me. I performed a lot of pullups, deadlifts, and rows to help build the best back possible for me. My legs, shoulders and chest made up for my lagging back. Now that I don't compete anymore, my goals have changed. I just want to maintain a very muscular and lean physique. I'm not too concerned about building a huge back, but I still perform lots of pullups and other back exercises.

Endomorphs usually have the most difficulty reducing bodyfat to actually see their muscles. On the other hand, they may be able to build large muscles because of their stocky build. In this case, endomorphs should use light to moderate weights performing multiple repetitions. They should concen-trate heavily on consuming low-fat, low-calorie meals and incorporate some type of aerobic exercise.

Women can identify themselves with the three body types as well as men, but as I mentioned above, they can also fall into more descriptive shapes:

- Hourglass
- Pear
- Apple

The **hourglass** figure, considered the ideal shape, is characterized by strong shoulders, full breasts, narrow waist, and shapely hips.

The **pear,** is characterized by being "bottom-heavy" storing fat in the buttocks and hips, with narrow shoulders, and not as full breasts as the hourglass.

The **apple** shape is round, characterized by a "big" waist, hips, and thighs, and a full upper body.

What I have done below, is combine the previous body types explained earlier with the hourglass, pear and apple, to describe body types and recommend how to use weights to reach fitness goals.

Body Shape: Endomorph, Apple

Here we have a someone who is hypothetically, big and round. Lifting weights can strengthen and tighten muscles, but won't do much as far as losing weight. Through my experience as a personal trainer, I have trained every body type known to humanity. I have trained endomorph, apple-shaped women. I found that unless they lost weight, lifting weights did little to improve their physical appearance. In some cases, some women had complained that lifting weights was making them look even bigger! This can be true. They may have had big, flabby arms to start. From lifting weights and not losing weight, their arms were now big and tight rather than big and flabby. The idea here is to incorporate weightlifting, aerobics, and a low-fat, low-calorie diet.

Exercise and eating right work synergistically. Lifting weights without proper eating won't work that well. The idea here is lifting weights two or three times per week consistently, using light weights, performing multiple repetitions, combining some type of aerobic activity, in addition to eating well.

Exercising two to times per week consistently and improving eating habits would work much better than exercising five to six times per week and not changing eating habits.

Lifting weights can help you lose weight because the body uses more energy and calories to sustain muscle than fat. A pound of fat contains 3,500 calories and burns two calories a day to sustain itself. A pound of muscle contains 700 calories and burns 75 calories to sustain itself, about 37 times more than fat. Then again, these numbers are insignificant if someone is consuming 100 grams of fat or more per day.

Body Shape: Mesomorph, Pear

A small upper body on a pair-shaped woman can make her lower body appear bigger. By lifting weights, a person with this type of body can strengthen, build and shape her upper body and make her lower body look smaller. The idea here is to broaden the shoulders and strengthen the back. We often see women's clothing with shoulder pads. That's because broader shoulders makes the waist look narrower, giving it that hour glass look. Working with weights on the lower body can help tone the hips and legs and lose weight faster and easier. Diet alone decreases the actual size of the hips!

Body Shape: Ectomorph (with high body fat, lacking muscle tone)

If I had to choose any of the three body types to improve, this would be it. Here is one of the rare times a woman can look better by gaining weight, that is losing body fat and gaining muscle. Once again, muscle does weigh more that fat. To really drive this point home, remember that a pound of muscle is about the size of your fist, while a pound of fat can fill several large food containers.

Tall, long women can appear to look thin, but have high body fat and lack muscle tone. I know, because I have conducted bodyfat measurements on these types of women. All it takes to improve is some modifications in diet and hitting the weights. I can still remember a successful client her goal who fit this body type, coming up to me and asking me to feel her biceps muscle. She would always say, "Do you remember when it was soft, when there was nothing there but fat?" Then she showed me her thighs: "Come here, feel this, feel how hard this is!" She saw results because she stuck with what I taught her. She came to the gym about three days per week consistently. She used moderate weights working through a full range of motion and performed the basic exercises that I taught her. I remember her telling other women to stop wasting their time on leg machines and start squatting and lunging instead. We'll get into the right of exercises later in the book.

To compliment the theory on body types, I used an article that appeared in the August 1994 issue of *Shape Magazine* to further help defined body types:

- Hourglass
- Pyramid
- Inverted Pyramid

The hour glass described similar characteristics as discussed above. The pyramid shape is similar to the pair shape. That is, a small upper body and wide hips. The inverted pyramid characterized wide shoulders and narrow hips. The article made similar recommendations in respect to lifting weights as I have suggested, to improve the overall appearance of your particular shape.

Women & Bodybuilding & The Fear of Getting Too Big

Women's bodybuilding is synonymous with the names of Rachel McLish, Carla Dunlap, and of course, Cory Everson. What do these women have in common? They are all past Ms. Olympia winners and have GREAT BODIES!

Initially, when Rachel McLish made her bodybuilding debut in 1980, everyone had reservations about women having muscles. *"I was very aware of how new and controversial the sport was when I first decided to get into competition."* Rachel expressed in a 1992 interview with *Muscle & Fitness*.* *"The women competitors themselves were often unsure about what kind of development to strive for. A lot of them associated muscles with looking like a man and were afraid to fully develop their physiques. I liked my body and I liked it even more with a lot more muscle on it so I was able to concentrate 100% on creating the best bodybuilding physique my genetics would allow, with no doubts or fears to get in my way."*

Upon seeing her physique at the first Ms. Olympia in Philadelphia in 1980, the judges recognized the real beauty of a muscular woman. She was radiant and charming on stage and grasped the hearts of both men and women in the bodybuilding world. In no time, Rachel became the epitome of women bodybuilding appearing in several magazines and movies and reformed most qualms about women having muscles.

Rachel says, *"I'm really pleased that I helped set a certain standard when I was competing. I tried to train and diet to be as muscular as possible when I went on stage, but I worked just as hard on developing quality and aesthetic balance."* Following in her footsteps was Cory Everson. Cory, a six-time Ms. Olympia champion, was much more muscular than Rachel, but just as beautiful and aesthetic.

* *Reprinted with permission of Muscle & Fitness Magazine, August 1992*

The Fear of Getting Too Big

Getting **too big** is a great fear for women just starting with weights. Most women do not want to build big muscles, and find other women who are too muscular unattrac-

Jeannine Fisher, left, and Gina Delaney prove that women can be muscular and not look too big.

tive. What most women fail to realize is that many of these women are using steroids and compete in bodybuilding for a living. Being realistic about your goals also means understanding the growth potential of your muscles through weight training. Lifting weights in most cases will help you tone, strengthen, and enhance your physi-cal appearance. Only in extreme

PHOTO BY BOB GOLDMAN

cases, where your goal is to get big, will lifting weights get you big. Unless you drastically increase your caloric intake, you won't get any bigger.

Increasing muscle mass is very difficult even for men to achieve. Women should not worry about getting too big. Rachel McLish, explains, *"Once upon a time women were very apprehensive about weighttraining. They were afraid of getting too big and looking too masculine. But they know better now."*

Your goal can be to have an attractive figure by using light weights without the goal of getting big.

Most amateur, women, bodybuilders have great, feminine physiques, because they don't lift weights for a living and don't take steroids. Most of these women compete in regional contests and have full time occupations. Like most women, they lift weights to stay in shape. Some take it a step further and compete. The photographs on the previous page of Gina Delaney and Jeannine Fisher, prove that women of different body types can have muscles, compete in bodybuilding, and maintain a feminine figure.

Gina compliments the mesomorph, pair-shape, body type described earlier. She stands at only five feet two inches. Her lean, sleek muscles give her the appearance of an ectomorph. Jeannine, who is characterized as an ectomorph, shows her wonderful physique at a regional bodybuilding contest.

Rachel McLish started bodybuilding in 1970 when only a few knew about the sport. Today, women of different occupations, ages and physical goals fill the gyms. They train hard with weights to chisel their physiques. Women want to be fit, and using weights is a great way of accomplishing that goal.

The optimum plan is to increase muscle and lose fat. This can be accomplished by following a realistic eating plan, lifting weights, and incorporating some type of aerobics plan.

Firm Thighs, Hips, & Buttocks

You want firm thighs, hips, and buttocks? Then start squatting and lunging! Squats and lunges are the only exercises you will ever need to perform to tighten up your lower body. They will target every muscle, including your inner and outer thighs. In the first edition of this book, I included cable exercises for inner and outer thighs and buttocks. I thought about it and decided to exclude those photographs. They just don't match up to what squats and lunges can do. Believe me. Try these exercises and I'll bet that you will feel every part of your lower body.

Squats: *(See Chapter 3 for squatting tips and proper form.)* Squats are great for toning your thighs and buttocks. In the photographs, Jeannine squats using a light barbell. She also uses five pound plates under her heels for balance.

Lunges *(See Chapter 3 for form and instruction.)* Lunges are probably the most effective exercise to tone the buttocks. You can either alternate legs or continue with the same leg for consecutive repetitions.

Side Lunges with a broom stick: If you want to target your inner thighs, then nothing is more effective than side lunges. Hold a broom stick held behind your neck. This will help you  with balance. Start by stepping to the right. Bend the right knee and point your right foot in the same direction. Keep your left leg as straight as possible. Don't bend your left knee. Keep your body straight and do not lean forward or to the side. Push off your right leg and return to your original position. After pausing and resetting yourself, step with your left leg following the same form.

Women & Osteoporosis

Osteoporosis is a condition that occurs when there is a decrease in bone density. This condition occurs gradually and eventually leads to severe hip and spinal fractures. It affects about half of all post menopausal women. According to the National Osteoporosis Foundation, nearly 25 million people (80% women and 20% are men) have this disease. Osteoporosis causes 1.5 million fractures annually. People over the age of 35 have a 2 to 100 times greater chance of fracturing a bone than younger people.

Research has shown that lifting weights can prevent the loss of bone mass. The decrease of activity and stress on the bones lead to the decrease of bone density. Increasing stress to the bones by weightlifting, can result new stress lines where the bones are less susceptible to breaking. The National Osteoporosis Foundation suggests that weight-bearing or impact-loading appears to be important in the prevention of osteoporosis.

Calcium is another important factor for preventing osteoporosis. Women need about 800 to 1,200 mg of calcium a day to sustain strong bones. Most women consume much less than what is recommended. Dairy products and vegetables are rich in calcium and should be consumed on a regular basis. Studies have shown that an increase in calcium in either food or supplemental form can increase bone density in the lumbar spine area up to 15%.

Alcohol and coffee have shown to decrease bone density. Limit alcohol and coffee intake to one drink or cup a day.

CHAPTER 2

Getting Started

Getting Started _____

A lot is written about beginner bodybuilding and weight training and too often articles and books contain exercises and programs that are too complex for a beginner. If you are just starting out on a bodybuilding or weight training program, or just looking to tone up using weights, remember to keep it simple.

Keeping your workouts simple entails "sticking with the basics." Basic exercises are essential for building a strong foundation which includes strengthening the major muscle groups:

- Chest
- Back
- Shoulders
- Arms
- Legs
- Abdominals

Be sure to include basic exercises for all body parts. Too often we see people performing the same exercises everyday for the same body parts which can result in an overdevelopment of these parts. A proper balance is needed to create a strong foundation. Chapter 3, *Body Part Training*, includes photographs and detailed instructions on how to properly perform basic exercises for each body part mentioned below:

Chest:
- Bench press
- Flye

Back:
- One-arm row
- Lat pulldown
- Pullups

Shoulders:
- Overhead press
- Upright row
- Lateral raises

Biceps:
- Barbell biceps curl
- Dumbbell biceps curl

Triceps:
- Dumbbell triceps extensions
- Kick backs
- Lying barbell triceps extensions

Legs:
- Squats
- Lunges
- Leg curls
- Leg extensions
- Calf raises

Crunches are the most basic exercises for the stomach *(see Chapter 3, Body Part Training Using Basic Exercises, for a variety of stomach exercises).*

Once you know how to properly perform the basic exercises, you need to identify your goals. Do you want to tone up or increase muscle size?

Your goals will determine the answers to the following questions that are most commonly asked:

- How much weight should I use?
- How many repetitions should I perform?
- How many sets should I perform per body part?
- How much time should I take between sets?
- How many days a week should I lift weights?
- Will using weights make my muscles too big?

Before we begin to answer these questions, let's define some "gym" terminology:

A repetition or *rep* is how many times you perform a certain exercise consecutively. The number of consecutive repetitions you perform will make up a *set*. For example, if you perform a biceps curl ten times and rest, and perform another ten repetitions, you will have performed two sets of ten repetitions. I also use the word *plate* to refer to weights, ie. 25-pound plate, 45-pound plate. *One plate* is equal to a 45-pound plate. In a *supinated* grip, the palms are up, as in a biceps curl. In a *pronated* grip, the palms are down, as in a reverse wrist curl.

How much weight should you use?

If your goal is to tone up and increase your overall strength, use a weight that will allow you to perform at least 12 to 15 repetitions. If you are just starting out, gradually work your way up to a heavier weight. Starting out with heavy weights could result in injury.

Someone who wants to increase muscle size should train at a range of 4 to 12 repetitions, pyramiding the weights for each set. For example, suppose you want to increase your chest size. Start with a weight that will allow you to perform 10 repetitions, following with eight reps for the second set, six reps for the third, and so on.

An example of pyramiding weight for muscle size:

Weight	Reps	Sets
100	10	1
120	8	1
130	6	1
140	4	1

Your goal will determine the amount of weight to use. Choosing the proper weight to perform your range of repetitions comes down to trial and error. Forget these complicated formulas and percentages of bodyweight calculations. Keep it simple! If your goal is to increase muscle tone, then try a weight that will allow you to perform at least 15 repetitions. If you can only perform three repetitions, the weight is too heavy. On the other hand, you might choose a weight that is too easy, where 15 repetitions are performed effortlessly. Your last few reps should be challenging. Remember, you must work hard to see results!

A rule of thumb—if your goal is to increase muscle tone, the range should be 12 to 15 repetitions. If your goal is to increase muscle size, your range should be 4 to 12 repetitions.

	Sets	Reps	Rest *(time between sets)*
tone	4-6	12-15	20-30 seconds
size	6-10	4-12	90-105 seconds

How many sets and how much rest between sets will also be determined by your goals. If your goal is to increase muscle tone, you do not need to perform multiple sets per body part. A range of four to six sets per body part is sufficient: six sets for large muscle groups *(chest, back, shoulder, legs)* and four sets for small muscle groups *(biceps and triceps)*. Not much time is needed between sets when toning is your goal, since you are not lifting heavy weights. Since the muscle does not need the extra time to recover, 20 to 30 seconds between each set is sufficient.

If your goal is to increase muscle size, then you need to perform more sets for each body part. For large body parts a range of eight to ten sets is recommended and six to eight for smaller body parts.

Since you will be using heavier weights, a longer rest is needed between sets—between 1 minute, 30 seconds, and 1 minute, 45 seconds, is sufficient time for muscle recovery between sets.

When performing abdominal exercises, limit your rest time to about ten seconds, unless you are using weights.

How many sets you do will also be determined by how many days and how much time you have in your workout session to devote to weight training. You want to include all body parts no matter how many days you decide to weight train. If you can devote three days to weight training, you could then train the entire body within those three days. For example:

Monday	Wednesday	Friday
chest/biceps abs	back/triceps abs	shoulders/legs abs

You do not have to take a day rest between your workouts if you are not training the same body parts. For example:

Monday	Tuesday	Wednesday
chest/biceps abs	back/triceps abs	shoulder/legs abs

If you can only devote two days to weight training, you could then train the entire body in two days. For example:

Monday	Wednesday
chest/back/biceps abs	shoulders/triceps/legs abs

What you are actually doing in these examples is training each body part only once a week. Each workout should not take more than 45 minutes to 1 hour.

Abdominal exercises could be included in every workout. The abdominal muscles recover faster than any other muscle in the body. They tighten and contract every time you sneeze, laugh, talk, exercise and during other activities we all take for granted. Three days a week for abdominals is sufficient. A washboard stomach can be accomplished only through strict dieting *(see Chapter 6, Nutrition)*.

If your time is limited, you can train the entire body in one workout within 20 minutes by performing one or two sets for each body part without taking a rest between sets. For example, you can start with an exercise for the chest, immediately perform one for the back and then go to the shoulders, triceps, biceps, and finish with a leg exercise. Return to chest and go through once again. The concept here is that while one body part is working, the other is resting, so there is no need for a rest between sets. This is a great aerobic workout as well as one for toning, because you are constantly moving from one exercise to another with an accelerated heart rate.

When using this total body workout, a one-day rest between workouts is recommended because the muscles need at least 24 hours to recover. How intensely you train each muscle will also determine the rest time. If you are only performing one or two exercises per body part, then 24 hours is plenty of rest time. If your muscles are still sore, wait until they fully recover before training them again.

There is a lot to remember, especially if you are just starting out. Keeping track of your exercises, workouts, weights, reps, sets, and days, can be very difficult. That is why it is very important to keep track of all this information using an exercise log. I have made available the *Exercise Log & Food*

Diary™ to help you keep track of your fitness goals *(see the order form in the back of this book).* Ask any bodybuilder about the importance of logging your progress in order to reach your goals *(see Planning is Everything in Chapter 16, Contest Preparation, regarding the importance of logging your workouts and food intake).*

The following two charts show good examples of a two-day toning workout, training chest, legs and abs on Day 1, and back, shoulders and abs on Day 2, with the basic exercises discussed earlier. The exercise log in the *Exercise Log & Food Diary*™ is used for the following examples:

Day 1: Toning

Date: _10/1/94_

Exercise Log			DAY I

Aerobic Activity: Bike

Calories Burned: 400

Distance: 6 miles

Time: 40 min

Weight Lifting			

Muscles Worked: Chest, Legs, ABS

Exercise	Wt	Reps	Sets
Bench Press	45	15	4
Flye	15	15	2
Squats	50	15	2
lunges	25	20	2
leg Curls	40	15	3
CALF RAISES	45	15	2
Crunches		20	3
Side Crunches		20	2
Curlups		15	2

25

Day 2: Toning

Date: 10/2/94

Exercise Log			DAY2

Aerobic Activity: STEP CLASS

Calories Burned:

Distance:

Time: 45 minutes

Weight Lifting

Muscles Worked: BACK, Shoulders, Arms, Abs

Exercise	Wt	Reps	Sets
One arm Row	15	15	3
Lat Pulldown	60	15	3
Overhead Press (dumbbells)	10	15	3
Upright Row	25	15	3
Dumbbell Biceps Curl	12	16	3
Dumbbell Triceps Ext	8	15	3
Crunches		20	2
Knee Raises		20	2

Shown on the following three pages are building examples of a three-day split routine using the *Exercise Log & Food Diary*™.

Day 1: Building Muscle

Date: 9/15/94

Exercise Log			
Aerobic Activity: Bike			
Calories Burned: 400			
Distance: 6 miles			
Time: 40 min			
Weight Lifting			
Muscles Worked: Chest / Biceps			
Exercise	**Wt**	**Reps**	**Sets**
Bench Press	135	10	1
	225	10	1
	275	6	1
	300	4	1
Dips (with weight)	45	10	1
	60	8	1
	70	6	1
Flyes	40	10	1
	45	10	2
Barbell Curls	95	10	1
	105	8	1
	115	6	1
Preacher Curls	65	12	1
	85	10	1
	95	8	1
Dumbbell Curls	40	10	3

Day 2: Building Muscle

Date: 9/16/94

Exercise Log		DAY 2

Aerobic Activity: STair Master

Calories Burned: 450

Distance: 4.8 miles

Time: 30 Minutes

Weight Lifting

Muscles Worked: BACK / Tries

Exercise	Wt	Reps	Sets
Pullups *using a belt For DumBBell	25lb	10	1
	45lb	8	1
	55lb	6	1
	NO WT	12	1
Dumbbell One Arm Row			
	70	10	1
	80	8	1
	90	6	1
Lat Pull down (Behind)	120	10	1
	130	8	1
	140	6	1
Lying Dumbell Tri Ext	65	10	1
	75	8	1
	85	6	1
Kick Backs	20	10	3

Day 3: Building Muscle

Date: 9/17/94

Exercise Log		DAY 3	
Aerobic Activity: Bike			
Calories Burned: 300			
Distance: 4.5 miles			
Time: 30 minutes			
Weight Lifting			
Muscles Worked: Shoulders / Legs			
Exercise	**Wt**	**Reps**	**Sets**
Overhead Press (Barbell)	100	12	1
	125	10	1
	135	8	1
	145	6	1
Upright Rows (Barbell)	95	10	1
	125	8	1
	135	6	1
Dumbbell lateral Raise	20	10	1
	25	8	1
	30	6	1
Squats	135	15	1
	185	12	1
	225	10	1
	275	8	1
Lunges	95	16	1 each leg
	115	16	1
	125	16	1
Leg Curls	80	12	1
	90	10	1
	100	8	1
	110	6	1

For those of you who are worried about getting "too big," stop worrying. Increasing muscle size is a very difficult thing to do. It requires lifting very heavy weights and performing numerous sets of exercises several days a week. Also, unless you drastically increase your caloric intake, you will not gain weight. If your goal is to tone, use very light weights with very few sets, only two to three days per week.

Once you have gotten started and have become familiar with these basic exercises discussed in Chapter 3 and training concepts, read about other training techniques and exercises in Chapters 12 and 16.

Proper Breathing

The most important part about breathing when lifting weights is that you do just that: *breathe*. We always breathe during exercise, but some people tend to hold their breath when lifting weights.` You want to avoid holding your breath because your muscles need oxygen in order to perform. You run the risk of cutting oxygen to the brain which could cause you to pass out.

Should you breathe out on the way up or down when pushing or pulling a weight?

The optimum way to breathe during weightlifting is to inhale during the negative movement and exhale during the positive movement. Depending on the exercise, that can be either up or down. For example, when bench pressing, inhale as you lower the weight to your chest, and exhale when pushing the weight back up. When performing a lat pulldown, inhale on the way up and exhale on the weigh down. The rule of thumb is to exhale on exertion.

Some people get too caught up with how they should breathe and get confused. As long as you are breathing, it doesn't really matter. It's better to concentrate on the exercise and breathe naturally than to lose concentration deciding how to breathe.

Weightlifting Belts: Do We Really Need Them?

Weightlifting belts are recommended for individuals with muscle- building goals that perform squats, bentover rows, and deadlifts using heavy weights. For those using light to moderate weights with toning goals, weightlifting belts are usually not needed.

The theory behind the use of weightlifting belts is that when you exert force while squatting and bending as in the exercises mentioned above, your stomach protrudes, developing pressure against your belt. This pressure acts as leverage that stabilizes and protects the lower back and spine. It can also enable you to lift heavier weights. Powerlifters are known to have huge stomachs and wear monstrous size belts around their waists. This combination helps them create more pressure, allowing them to lift heavier weights. Powerlifters rely on their belts and would never attempt lifting those record-breaking weights without them.

Basic upper body exercises, such as bench presses, flyes, lateral raises, and upright rows, do not require the use of a belt, especially when light weights are used. Exercises performed lying on your back, such as bench presses and flyes, do not create pressure because rather than the stomach protruding, it flattens in the lying position. Heavy overhead presses may require the use of a belt because they place great pressure on your lower back.

Some weightlifters and bodybuilders claim that the constant use of a belt weakens the lower back. They claim that muscles that are usually used without a belt are weakened. This theory sounds very logical. Use a belt only when needed unless you have a lower back problem. The use of a belt may add some extra support for those that suffer from lower back pain. Performing the exercises mentioned above, even with light weights, will help develop your stomach to build pressure that may relieve some stress from your lower back.

Injuries from Weightlifting Belts

Fracturing ribs is a common occurrence from misusing weight belts. This results from wearing a belt too tight and too high on your torso. You do not need to tighten a belt to the point where your internal organs get crushed. Once you start to lift, abdominal pressure develops and the belt automatically tightens around the waist. Even though the belt may not seem tight enough when not exercising, remember that the pressure develops during exercise.

Machines vs. Free Weights

The argument of whether to use machines or free weights should be exercise-specific rather than general. The focus should be on machines that mimic free weight exercises. For example, a machine bench press versus a free weight bench press, a machine overhead press versus free weight overhead press, machine biceps curl versus free weight biceps curl.

The exercise-specific argument should be made because some machines are necessary to target certain muscles. For example, leg curls on a leg curl machine are necessary for the hamstrings because it is one of the few exercises for hamstrings. There is no specific free weight exercise that mimics the leg curl machine. There are free weight exercises that can be performed for the hamstrings, but some machines are safer and more effective. For example, a free weight alternative for hamstrings is a stiff-leg deadlift, an exercise not recommended for someone with lower back problems because of the tremendous strain it places in that area. Why risk an injury when you can safely work the hamstrings with leg curls?

I prefer and recommend free weights for any goal, but I also enjoy machines. Some machines that do not mimic free weight exercise are great for variety. For example, I use a cable crossover machine to perform pushdowns for triceps. There are many other triceps exercises that can be performed using free weights, but why limit yourself?

So What's Better for You, Machines or Free Weights?

The answer depends on your goals. If you want to increase muscle size, use free weights. If you want to tone your body, you can use both. Does this mean that you cannot increase muscle size with machines? No, you can, but you would see faster and better results with free weights.

Advantages and Disadvantages

The main advantage of free weights is that more muscles are required for balance and control. This can lead to stronger, bigger, and well-balanced muscles. Machines provide the balance and control, eliminating a major part of lifting.

Free weights allow for a better range of motion. Barbells and dumbbells allow you to lift and lower weights where muscles fully contract and elongate. For example, bench pressing with free weights allows you to lower the bar to your chest. Conversely, some machines such as Nautilus® and Body-Masters®, do not include a bar, but have an arm mechanism that never touches the chest. Dumbbells allow for an optimum range of motion that can never be achieved with a machine. For example, dumbbell flyes allow a wide and circular motion that a machine would never allow.

Any exercise with free weights can be modified to allow a pain- free range of motion. For example, lateral raises can hurt your shoulders. With dumbbells, the exercise can be modified by raising the dumbbells slightly forward. Bench presses have been known to hurt the shoulders. With free weights, a slight change of the bar's direction by lowering it closer to your stomach can relieve pressure from the shoulders.

With machines, you would possibly need to eliminate the movement all together. You can not modify the direction of machines because they are designed to travel a specific path.

Another big advantage with free weights is that you can perform *any* exercise. Most machines are limited to one exercise. 100 machines would not equal the capability of a bar and dumbbells.

With free weights, a grip is your own personal preference. A barbell or dumbbell allows a wide or narrow grip to target different muscles. For example, a close grip on a bench press works more triceps, where a wide grip works the chest. Most machines do not allow this flexibility because they have designated places for grips.

Setting a machine to fit for your body can be time consuming and challenging as well. With free weights, there are no adjustments. Anyone can grip a bar or dumbbell, or lie or sit on a bench.

The only disadvantage of free weights is that they can be dangerous, so a spotter is recommended. There is a better chance of injuring yourself with free weights than with machines. There have been instances where people have dropped weights on themselves, causing permanent damage and even death. Machines do not require a spotter and are much safer than free weights. You do not have to worry about balancing, controlling, or dropping weights.

Some machines have adjustments to intentionally limit your range of motion. Those with certain types of injuries should not be using a full range of motion. For example, certain leg extension machines limit the range of motion to protect a person with bad knees. The last three inches of the exercise may cause pain. The machine can still be used effectively by blocking the last three inches of the machine's range of motion by adjusting a lever.

Weight Stack Machines and Weight-Loaded Machines

Machines mainly come with a weight stack where you select a weight by placing a pin in the stack. Other machines need to be loaded with weight such as leg press. Most weight-loaded machines are very useful and effective such as:

- Leg press
- Hack squat
- Smith Machine
- Seated calf raise

Useful Weight Stack Machines:

- Lat pulldown
- Cable crossover
- Leg extension
- Leg curl

Training Partners

There are several advantages and disadvantages to having a training partner.

Advantages:

- Getting to the gym
- Staying motivated
- Varying workouts
- Having a spotter

The first advantage of having a training partner is that your chances of getting to the gym are much better. How may times have you planned on going to the gym and then decided against it? Your chances of making it to the gym are much better knowing your training partner is waiting and relying on you to be there.

Motivational advantages of a training partner:

- Competitiveness
- Completeness of workouts
- Respect and bonding

Having a training partner immediately implies that you will train harder with increased motivation. If your partner is slightly stronger than you, it will give you that extra incentive to lift heavier and go that extra mile to try and keep up with your stronger partner. Even if your partner is not as strong as you, chances are you will train harder than you would normally just because of his or her presence. If your training partner's physical strength is almost equal to yours, a workout can become a battle. Every set and rep is executed at maximum effort, both trying desperately to out-perform the other. This unspoken but healthy competition can result in a more intense workout.

With a training partner, workouts are usually completed as planned. Without a partner, workouts sometimes get cut short for various reasons. I can recall training legs with Tori Masonis, a national womens competitor that squatted and deadlifted over 500 pounds. We started our workout performing five sets of squats using 315 pounds for 20 repetitions. After the fifth set, I was ready to call it quits. Thanks to my training partner, I finished the workout as planned. I also might not have pushed myself to that level on my own.

Having a training partner can help develop an empathetic relationship. The pain and fatigue that you both experience can lead to mutual respect. Bonding develops when you share the rush and accomplishment of finishing a tough workout. You push each other to perform that last rep or set and motivate each other to increase weights. This special bond can be very reassuring, knowing your partner will push you through the entire workout.

Variety is a core component to staying motivated. Having a training partner means never getting bored with the same old routine. By combining different training techniques, new exercises are incorporated stimulating novelty and other muscles to be worked.

Training partners are great spotters. Besides the fact that you will always have a spot when you need one, your partner knows exactly how much to help in order to perform those last effective repetitions. Your partner can hand you heavy dumbbells that can otherwise be very difficult to lift yourself. For example, heavy dumbbells are difficult to manage when trying to lie on a bench to perform presses. Your partner can assist you by handing you the dumbbells as you properly position yourself on the bench.

Disadvantages:

Partners that are:

- Tardy
- Inconsiderate
- Inexperienced
- Lacking in training intensity
- Talkative

No one enjoys waiting. Waiting for a partner can lead to a discouraging workout and harsh feelings. Rather than starting a workout with a passion to attack the weights, you instead start by being angry at your partner.

Consideration during a workout involves:

- Handing weights
- Providing safe and effective spots
- Using supportive statements such as, "great set," "good form," and "way to go"

Training with an inexperienced partner can be frustrating and time consuming. For example, how many times have you found yourself squeezing out that last rep when your partner prematurely hoists the bar back to the rack? Inexperienced partners tend to ask too many questions during workouts. This wastes valuable training time and slows the progression of the workout.

Some training partners lack intensity—they can not train as hard as you. I discovered this problem when people tried to train back or legs with me. Most never made it past the first exercise. Some needed to take 20 trips to the water fountain while I was ready to start the next set.

Choosing a Partner

Choosing a partner is like interviewing a candidate for a job. You want to find out as much about them as possible:

- Goals
- Training experience
- Training habits including:
  - *duration*
  - *philosophies*
  - *intensity*
  - *favorite exercises*
  - *strengths and weaknesses*
- Schedule
- Flexibility

Choose a partner who has similar goals. If your goals are to build muscle using heavy weights, your partner's should be the same. Most relationships prosper when mutual goals are shared.

Pick a partner who has good gym experience. A good candidate should be familiar with most types of machines and free weight equipment. Their experience should help you as much as yours helps them.

Find out about their training habits and philosophies. They should also be similar to yours. Some people like spending more time in the gym, taking more time between sets and allowing for conversation. Others move quickly through workouts, allowing little time and minimal conversation between sets. Their thoughts on how much weight to use and number of sets and reps to perform will also help you make a decision.

Check to see if your schedules are compatible. Do you both get off from work at the same time? How far is work from the gym? How often will work interfere with workouts? If your potential partner has many miles to travel and you are located near the gym, problems may arise. Choose days and times that are mutually convenient. Limiting a training partner to weekends may be an alternative. This can decrease the likelihood of conflicting schedules.

Flexibility in training techniques is essential. Is your partner as receptive to your training techniques as you are to his or hers? This should be a give-and-take relationship where sacrifices are made and compromises are reached. Combining two training philosophies can be mutually beneficial.

Training Partners of the Opposite Sex

Your training partner does not have to be of the same sex. I find that women make great training partners. I have trained with Tory Masonis, one of the strongest women in the country. She outlifts most men and trains with an intensity that is hard to measure.

Since most women lack equal strength, changing weights can be a small inconvenience. Finding a compatible workout partner with the qualities mentioned above is more important than their sex and strength.

Through my experience, I have found that women train hard with maximum intensity to keep pace with men. I have also found that most men train harder with women because of their macho instinct to impress. They would never allow a woman to outperform them in any part of the workout. For example, some men do not perform squats because they are difficult and require a tremendous amount of energy. If a woman suggests performing squats, the man will accept the challenge to protect his pride, regardless of his distaste for the exercise.

CHAPTER 3

Body Part Training Using Basic Exercises

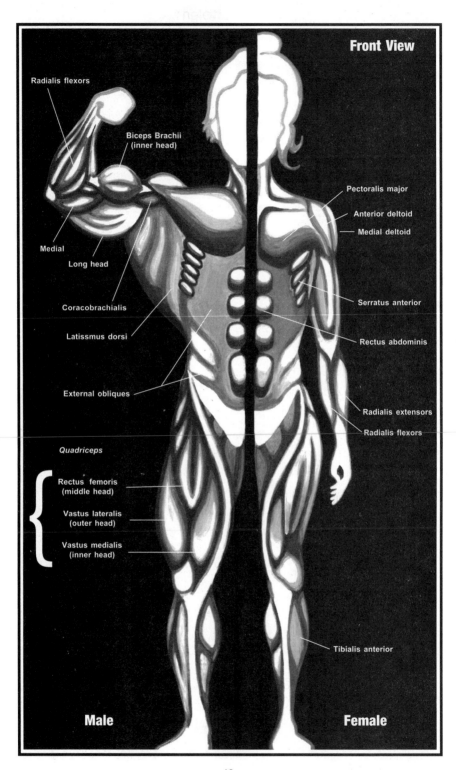

Front View

Radialis flexors

Biceps Brachii
(inner head)

Pectoralis major

Anterior deltoid

Medial deltoid

Medial

Long head

Coracobrachialis

Serratus anterior

Latissmus dorsi

Rectus abdominis

External obliques

Radialis extensors

Radialis flexors

Quadriceps

Rectus femoris
(middle head)

Vastus lateralis
(outer head)

Vastus medialis
(inner head)

Tibialis anterior

Male

Female

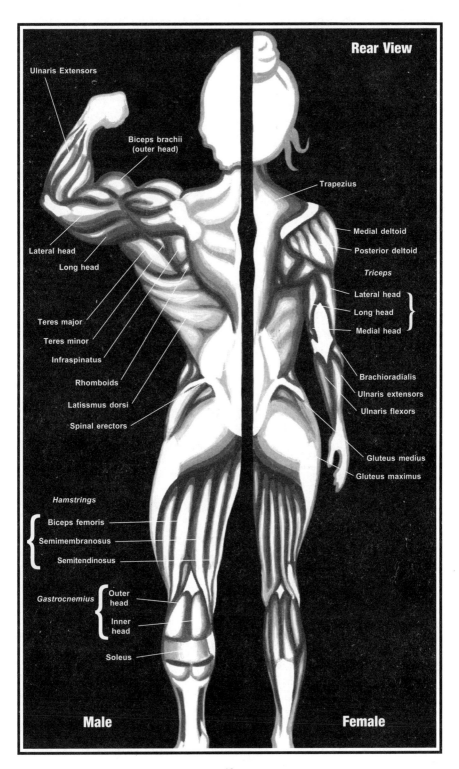

Rear View

Ulnaris Extensors

Biceps brachii
(outer head)

Trapezius

Medial deltoid

Posterior deltoid

Lateral head

Triceps

Long head

Lateral head

Long head

Medial head

Teres major

Teres minor

Infraspinatus

Brachioradialis

Rhomboids

Ulnaris extensors

Latissmus dorsi

Ulnaris flexors

Spinal erectors

Gluteus medius

Gluteus maximus

Hamstrings

Biceps femoris

Semimembranosus

Semitendinosus

Gastrocnemius { Outer head

Inner head

Soleus

Male

Female

43

Chest

Muscles of the Chest:

- Pectoralis Major
- Pectoralis Minor

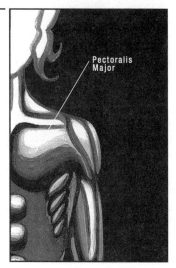

The **pectoralis major** forms the front wall of the chest. It attaches to the front of the humerus, along the chest cavity and the clavicle.

The **pectoralis minor** is not visible and lies deep beneath the pectoralis major. It attaches to ribs three, four, and five on the rib cage.

Chest Exercises

The bench press is a basic and very effective chest exercise. It can be performed using a barbell or dumbbells, on a flat, incline, or decline bench.

Barbell Bench Press *(on a flat bench):* With a shoulder-width grip, slowly lower the bar across the middle of the chest keeping the elbows out. Keeping your elbows out as shown in the photograph will ensure you are using more chest and less triceps. Once you reach your chest, be sure to pause for a second and then push the weight up, keeping your elbows out and squeezing your chest at the top.

A shoulder-width grip will assure maximum effort from all areas of the chest. A close grip will put more stress on the triceps. A wide grip will decrease the range of motion and bring the back into action. Keeping the elbows out will ensure that the chest is working, not the triceps.

Incline 1

Incline 2

Incline & Decline Barbell Bench Press: When performing either two of these exercises, the most important thing to remember is to lower the bar across the top of your chest, especially with decline presses. With incline presses, you don't have much of a choice because of the position of your body on the bench. The bar automatically crosses the top of your chest. I see too many people lower the bar to their stomach when performing decline presses. This inhibits a full range of motion, resulting, minimal gains.

Because of the awkward position of your body on the decline bench, this exercise can be difficult and dangerous to perform for a beginner. If you do decide to perform this exercise, be sure to have a spotter.

Decline 1

Decline 2

Smith Machine Incline Press: I really like performing incline presses on a Smith Machine. I feel almost total isolation of my chest and get a great stretch as well. Notice how the bar crosses the very top of my chest in the photo. The only disadvantage is dragging an incline bench under the smith machine and finding the right position. This takes some time and I usually like to perform exercises that require minimal set up time, like the dip or incline dumbbell presses.

Dumbbell Incline Presses: Hold two dumbbells together over your chest with your palms facing away from you. Slowly lower the dumbbells keeping your elbows out. Get a good stretch in your chest by pausing at the bottom for a split second. Press the dumbbells back to their original position keeping your elbows out. Squeeze your chest at the top. The path the dumbbells travel when performing this exercise is important. When lowering the dumbbells, be sure the initial movement is out and away from your chest rather than straight down. The dumbbells should not hit your chest at the bottom. They should be even and a couple of inches away from the outside part of your chest. Push the dumbbells through the same path on the way up as on the way down.

Dips are one of my favorite chest exercises. Although this is one of the most effective chest exercises, I rarely see it performed. That 's good for me, because I love doing them and never have to wait for the dip station. I don't ever remember waiting to use the dip station. The reason why dips are rarely performed is because they're hard. Like I always say, if it's hard, it must be effective. If you find these very difficult to perform, get a spotter to help you. Eventually, you will be able to perform some quality reps on your own.

Notice that the parallel bars are narrow at one end and wide at the other. For best chest results, grip the middle. For best triceps results, grab the narrow end. A wide grip will limit your range of motion.

With a medium grip, lower yourself by bending at the elbows. Be sure to go down as far as possible. Lead with your chin and chest and try to get your legs out, rather than going straight down. This will increase the range of motion and ensure a great stretch throughout your chest.

Once you can perform 10 to 15 dips with good form, try adding weight by using a weight belt. I sometimes add three 45 pound plates and bang out some hard reps. My form suffers a little, but what the hell. You can deviate from good form, **occasionally**. If your gym doesn't have a weight belt, slip a dumbbell in your own belt. This works just as well.

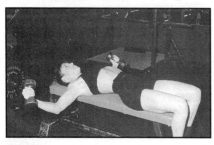 

Flyes: Jeannine demonstrates the standard flye on a flat bench shown above. Start with the dumbbells held together over your chest with palms facing each other. Lower the dumbbells in a wide circular motion, even with your chest, keeping a slight bend in the elbows at all times. Pause at the bottom and then take the same circular path up, with the same bend in the elbows, squeezing your chest at the top.

Flyes off end of bench (*pullover flyes*)**:** Flyes can be performed on a flat bench, incline bench, or decline bench. My favorite way to perform flyes is off the end of a bench. I also call these *pullover flyes*, because the body position is almost similar as with a pullover. I perform these mainly because of the tremendous stretch I feel throughout my entire upper body. With incline flyes, your hips are also low, but not as low compared to this technique. You can perform these off the end of any bench. So if all the regular or incline benches are being used, you now have a good alternative. When performing flyes on a bench, remember to:

- Keep your feet together and flat on the floor.
- Keep your hips down low. When lowering the dumb-bells, push your hips down.
- Shoulder blades across the very end of the bench. Use a wide circular motion on the way down and up as if hugging a tree.

Pullovers: I usually finish off my chest workouts with either pullovers or flyes or both.

Having the right body position during this exercise is crucial:

- Shoulder blades across the bench
- Head hanging over the bench
- Feet together and flat on the floor
- Hips low
- Buttock two to six inches from the floor depending on height of bench

From this position, start with a dumbbell held over your chest with a slight bend in the elbows. Overlap your hands around the rod of the dumbbell, with your palms up. Slowly lower the dumbbell back and down maintaining a *slight* bend in the elbows. If you bend your elbows too much, your triceps will be doing most of the work. After reaching back as far as you can, *pull* the dumbbell back over your chest maintaining the same bend in the elbows. When lowering the dumbbell, be sure to keep your hips down. This will ensure a great stretch throughout the entire upper body.

Back

Muscles of the Back:

- Latissimus Dorsi
- Rhomboids
- Trapezius
- Spinal Erectors
- Infraspinatus
- Teres Major
- Teres Minor

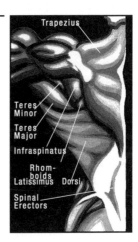

The **latissimus dorsi**: Latissimus means widest and dorsi means back. This massive muscle group covers a great area of the middle and outside of the back. It is responsible for both width and thickness.

Rhomboids are very powerful muscles located in the middle of the back used for any pulling action.

The **trapezius** is a long flat sheet of muscle that runs from the top of your neck and down the middle of your back.

Spinal erectors are the muscles of the lower back and do exactly what the name indicates—keep the spine erect. They also protect nerves in the lower back.

The **infraspinatus** and the **teres minor** are two of the rotator cuff muscles that lie on the scapula *(see Shoulder Injuries in Chapter 14, Overtraining and Injuries, for more details about the rotator cuff muscles).*

The **teres major** stabilizes the head of the humerus during movements to the side of the body.

Back Exercises

The **Pullup** is
my favorite back
exercise that I
usually include in
all my back
workouts. I
perform them
religiously be-
cause they are
very effective in

developing the upper back, especially the latissimus dorsi. If
you're looking for that "V" shape, then pullups are for you. I also
like them because they require no set up time. That means no
looking for a bar or machine to use. No adding weight. No
adding collars. No changing weight. No putting weights back.
Just grab and go!

Like dips, pullups are difficult to perform. As a result, most
people don't perform pullups, which means I never need to wait
to perform them. You make the choice: Wait on line to use the
pulldown machine or maximize your time and effort performing
pullups.

If they are really difficult for you to perform, then get someone to help you. Have someone hold your feet and boost you
up, even if you can only get about four reps on your own and
another four with a spotter. This applies to both men and
women. Naturally, women don't have equal upper body
strength as men, but the women I see performing pullups are
the ones with the best physiques. I'm sure when they first
started they could only manage one or two reps. They had to
work their way up to 10 or more reps. I've seen guys that
could bench press 300 pounds, but can't do more than one or
two pullups. Remember that balance and symmetry of the
musculature is important. If you currently don't include pullups
in your back workouts, then now's the time to start.

Several grips can be used when performing pullups: overhand, underhand, close, wide, shoulder width....Start with a shoulder-width, overhand grip *(pronated grip)* as shown in the previous page. This will limit work from the arms and target the back. Next to the shoulder width grip, I also like using a close grip as shown below. These are a little easier to perform, but I get a better squeeze up top and feel more of a stretch in my lats.

Close Grip 1   **Close Grip 2**

Regardless of your grip, do them right! That means pulling your chest up to the bar. Notice in both sets of photographs, that my chest is up facing the bar. This ensures that every muscle of the upper back is working with little assistance from the arms. It's obvious when someone is using too much of their arms to pull themselves up. Their shoulders shrug and move forward and their back hunches and convaves out. The shoulders should be pulled back and the lower back should be arched.

Pulldowns are effective for developing the upper back, more particularly the latissimus dorsi, but you should not rely on this exercise alone. Too many people wait on line to use the lat pulldown machine when they can be performing other exercises such as pullups. Do not wait for equipment! Have a contingency plan ready. Waiting for equipment will only delay and interrupt your workout.

Pulldowns can be performed by pulling the bar to your chest or behind your neck. Perform pulldowns to your chest using the same form as with pullups. With pulldowns, you are pulling the bar to your chest on an angle rather than straight down. With pullups, you are pulling your chest to the bar on an angle. With both exercises, you need to,

- ■ Arch your back.
- ■ Keep your elbows out.
- ■ Don't shrug your shoulders.
- ■ Squeeze your shoulder blades together.

Pulldowns behind the neck require pulling the bar straight down behind your neck. This works more of the muscles of the middle back. Be sure to lean forward when pulling behind your neck. This will assure a greater contraction of the back muscles. I prefer pulldowns to the front, because I sometimes feel shoulder pain when performing pulldowns behind the neck. Whatever hurts, I don't do! *(See Overtraining and Injuries.)*

- Squeeze your shoulders back and down.

- Avoid shrugging your shoulders.

- Flare out your elbows.

- Bull your chest.

- Arch your back.

Step 1   **Step 2**

Bent-over Rows: This was once one of my favorite basic back exercises. It's a great mass builder, but sometimes painful on the lower back. The bent-over row requires excellent form that I wouldn't recommend to a beginner.

Take a shoulder-width grip with your feet about six inches apart. Pull the bar up between your chest and stomach maintaining a bent position over the bar and floor. During this pulling action, your lower back needs to be arched, your chest *bulled*, knees bent, and buttocks out. And most importantly, pull with your back, not your arms. Once the bar reaches your midsection, squeeze your shoulder blades together. This contracts your entire back.

After squeezing your shoulder blades together, slowly lower the bar down towards the floor. Be sure to flare your lats out and get a good stretch. This ensures a full range of motion. Also, on the way down, you can round your lower back. You don't have to keep it arched. This will also help you stretch your back and fully extend your arms. Once you start to pull up again, arch your back again.

As you can see, a lot is involved. But there is an alternative, T-Bar rows.

T-Bar Rows are just as effective as bent-over rows, but much less taxing on the lower back. The long bar between your legs and the weight in front, give you more leverage and make it easier to maintain a bent position.

Follow the same instructions as bent-over rows. Most gyms provide a T-bar station. If not, position a regular bar in any corner of the gym as shown in the second set of photographs. As you can see, the bar is between my legs. You can either grab the bar hand over hand as if grabbing a baseball bat, or preferably use a handle as shown in the photographs.

Step 1   **Step 2**

One-Arm Row (using a bench): The one-arm row is probably one of the most basic back exercises. It's fairly easy to
perform, but unless you pull with your back and not your arm,
you're mainly going to be working your arm. You got to remember to squeeze both shoulder blades together, even
though you're only working one side at a time. You need to
think of your arm as an attachment from the dumbbell to your
shoulder blade. If you had no arm, this exercise would still be
possible to perform, by attaching something from the dumbbell
to your arm. All you would do is pull from your shoulder blade
and all the muscles of your upper back would do all the work.

Jeannine is shown using a bench, working her right side first.
Her left knee and hand*(that are both slightly bent)* are on the
bench, while her right foot is flat on the ground. Her right
hand of course is holding the dumbbell. Also notice that her
lower back is arched and her head is straight. From this
position, pull the dumbbell up and slightly away from your
body squeezing both shoulder blades up top. Be sure to use
the hand that's on the bench, in this example, the left hand,
for leverage. Don't over pull by turning your torso. Keep
your back in line or parallel to the floor. If you pull both
shoulders back and stick your chest out, you won't over pull
to one side. Slowly lower the dumbbell and get a good
stretch by fully extending your arm.

One-Arm Row (standing): I prefer to perform this exercise standing, leaning on anything that will support me. In the photo I'm leaning on a weight stack. I prefer this method because it makes, pulling both shoulders back, arching my back, and "bulling" my chest, all easier. When I pull, I use the weight stack, or whatever I'm leaning on for leverage. I almost throw myself forward as I pull. Also, I have a better range of motion. I have more room to pull and lower the dumbbell. You can actually compare step one in Jeannine's photo to my step one. Notice the better stretch in my back.

Seated Row: I usually finish my back workout with seated rows using the low pulley. Because of the leverage that's generated by my feet pressed against the foot rest, and the cable, I get the best stretch and contraction in my back with seated rows than the other back exercises. As I discussed with one-arm row, the biggest mistake people make with this exercise is they pull with their arms and not their back.

Tips for Step 2:
■ Sit up straight at the end of the pull.
■ Hold and squeeze for a full second.
■ Keep both shoulders down and back.
■ Keep your chest out.
■ Keep your knees slightly bent.

Pretend that you have no arms, they are merely extensions from your shoulders to the handle. Pull by squeezing your shoulder blades together. Do not shrug your shoulders. Use your arms only to finish the exercise by pulling the handle to your stomach and squeeze. Be sure to *bull* your chest, arch your back and squeeze your shoulder blades together. On the way down, slowly let your body move forward and flare your lats and fully extend your arms. Be sure to get a good stretch.

Lower Back Exercises

Back Raises help isolate the muscles of the lower back. They can be performed on a hyperextension chair as shown in the photos, or anywhere you can lock the back of your legs and raise your upper body. You do want to be careful when performing this exercise. You don't need to completely hyperextend the lower back. Raise your torso enough to where it is parallel to the floor as Jeannine shows in the second photo.

Deadlifts: This is a tough exercise to perform, but very effective for developing the entire back. Although it is mainly a lower back exercise, it also helps develop the latissimus dorsi and trapezius muscles. I describe the use of this exercise in Chapter One specifically for ectomorphs with long torsos who want to add thickness to their back. If your goal does not include adding thickness to your back, then this exercise is not necessary.

Deadlifts require the use of excellent form to be effective and safe. If not performed properly, serious lower back injury is unavoidable.

Tips for Lowering the Bar:

- Keep your back arched.
- Squat the bar down bending your knees.
- Keep your head up.
- Flare your lats.

From a squatting position, with your feet under the bar and your body over the bar, take a shoulder width grip. In the photos, I'm gripping the bar with an underhand grip with

Tips for Lifting the Bar:

- Arch your back.
- Keep your head up.
- Slightly bend your elbows.
- Keep your chest out.

one hand, and an overhand grip with the other hand. This grip will help you pull the bar up and get a good squeeze up top. As with most back exercises, I usually use wrist straps to prevent the bar from slipping out of my hands.

From this squatting position, lift the bar remembering to keep your back arched, chest out, elbows slightly bent, and head up. Once you are standing, flare your lats as if flexing them for a bodybuilding contest. (If you don't know what this means, go to the posing chapter and look for a back or front lat spread.) Be sure to slowly lower the bar and remember to keep your back arched and knees bent. You want to squat the bar back down; don't lower it with your back. Flare your lats on the way down.

Trapezius Exercises

You can train traps with either back or shoulders. If I train traps with back, I usually perform shrugs between sets of pullups, better known as staggered sets (see chapter 12). So I would perform a set up pullups and then immediately perform a set of shrugs. Shrugs can be performed with either a barbell or with dumbbells.

Barbell Shrugs: Standing barbell shrugs are the most basic. Hold the bar with a shoulder-width grip with your arms fully extended in front of you. With your knees slightly bent, shrug your shoulders up towards your ears. Notice the slight bend in my elbows. You don't want to bend your elbows too much, where you start performing upright rows instead of shrugs. Be sure to hold and squeeze at the top before lowering the bar. Before I lower the bar, I sometimes pull my shoulders back for a fuller range of motion. Once I lower the bar, I flex my traps as if performing a most muscular pose (see the Posing chapter).

You can also perform this exercise holding the bar behind your back. This automatically brings your shoulder together. You don't need to pull your shoulders back. I don't expand too much on this exercise because I want you to stick with the basics. Remember, keep it simple.

Smith Machine Shrugs: As you can see, you can use the Smith Machine to perform shrugs. Like I mentioned in Chapter Two, you can perform almost any exercise on a Smith Machine as you can with a barbell. Just follow the same instruction as barbell shrugs. The first photo shows a good example of flexing the traps when lowering the bar.

Dumbbell Shrugs: I like to mix up barbell and dumbbell shrugs. Depending on my energy that day, I sometimes do them both. I get a slightly different feel with dumbbells because the weight is now at my sides rather than in front as with a bar. It's easier to pull the shoulders back with dumbbells. Just be sure to get your shoulders up first before pulling your shoulders back.

Shoulders _____

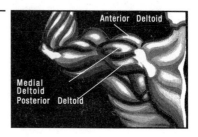

Major Muscles:

- Anterior Deltoid
- Medial Deltoid
- Posterior Deltoid

The **anterior deltoid** is the front of the shoulder, the **medial** is the side, and the **posterior deltoid** makes up the rear.

Shoulder Exercises

The most basic and effective shoulder exercise that hits all three heads is the overhead or military press. The overhead press performed with either a barbell or with dumbbells is usually performed seated for lower back protection. I sometimes perform barbell overhead presses to the front, standing. I even like to cheat a little to push out the last few reps. For the most part, I use strict form.

Behind The Neck Military Presses: This used to be my favorite shoulder exercise. I was once able to press 245 pounds for six or seven reps! But one day it finally happened: I heard and felt my shoulder pop. I really thought it was over for me. *It*, meaning ever lifting a weight again. Luckily it turned out only to be a strain. When the bar is behind your neck, it puts your shoulders in an awkward position. A slight awkward movement can really do damage to the shoulders.

I still enjoy performing this exercise behind my neck because I get a good stretch in the shoulders and it limits the use of the anterior delts. The anterior delts get a lot of work from bench presses and other exercises. I just don't use nearly as much weight as I once did. When I do, I use a very light weight. That means no more 245 pounds! I now use the Smith Machine to perform this exercise.

Smith Machine Behind-the-Neck Presses are just as effective and safer than regular behind-the-neck presses. Even though your shoulders are still in a vulnerable position, the machine inhibits any awkward movements because it stabilizes the bar. The bar won't move to the right or to the left or farther back, putting your shoulder in a bad position.

When performing this exercise, be sure to lower the bar slowly behind your neck. I like to lower the bar almost to my traps for a better stretch as shown in the photos, but it's not necessary. Just lower the bar like the exercise says, *behind the neck,* right before the vertebrae of your spine. And please remember, if it hurts, don't do it. You can always perform dumbbell overhead presses.

Dumbbell Overhead Presses: I have been performing more dumbbell overhead presses because they're easier on the shoulder joint. They are still very effective for developing the shoulders if done properly. You can perform regular over-head presses or Arnold presses, as Jeannine demonstrates on the following page. For regular dumbbell overhead presses, start with the dumbbells held at ear level with your palms facing away from you. Slowly press the dumbbells overhead until your arms are almost fully extended. You want to maintain a slight bend in the elbows at the top. Be sure to push the dumbbells towards each other. You don't have to bang them together. This adds a fuller range of mo-tion, since the dumbbells have to travel a little longer distance. This also allows you to squeeze your delts up top.

Arnold Presses: For a fuller range of motion, try performing Arnold Presses, *(Yes, they are named after Arnold Schwarzenegger).* With the dumbbells held in front of your chest with your palms facing you, *(this grip is called a supinated grip)* push the dumbbells up towards the ceiling gradually turning your wrists until your palms are facing away from you. Try not to push straight up. Instead, use a more circular motion while turning your wrists allowing for a greater range of motion. Jeannine is shown performing this exercise in a three-step process to emphasize the full range of motion. Just remember it's all one motion.

Barbell Upright Rows: Another effective exercise for the shoulders is the upright row which can be performed with a barbell or dumbbells. I usually perform these with a barbell because I like to use heavy weights, but dumbbells are a great alternative. When using a barbell, take a thumb-width grip from the center of the bar with your arms fully extended. Your heels can be either together or slightly apart. I prefer to have my heels touching with my toes about three inches apart. From here, slowly pull the bar up and slightly away from your body and up to your chin, keeping your elbows out. Pulling the bar slightly away from your body rather than straight up will increase your range of motion and will work the shoulders more effectively.

When the weight is too heavy, I see people limit their range of motion by pulling the bar straight up to the chin rather than slightly away from the body and up to the chin. Also, when the weight is too heavy, I see people leaning back, hoisting the bar up, cheating big time. This could also result in serious lower back injury. So if you're one of these people, either lighten up the weight or try Smith Machine upright rows.

Smith Machine Upright Rows: Performing upright rows on the Smith Machine is almost like using a bar. But as I mentioned above, it won't let you cheat. You will find that you won't be able to use nearly as much weight using the Smith Machine as you can with the regular upright rows. You will also feel a better burn in your shoulders because you have to guide the bar down slowly. This means that there is constant pressure on your shoulders.

Important Tips for Upright Rows:

- Maintain a slight bend in your knees.
- Keep your elbows out on the way up.
- Avoid leaning back.
- Keep your back arched.

Dumbbell Upright Rows: When using dumbbells, be sure to keep your elbows out on the way up as Jeannine clearly shows. Of all the different ways to perform upright rows, dumbbells allow for the fullest range of motion. Does that mean to limit this exercise to dumb-

Dumbbell Upright Rows

bells? No, it's just another way of doing them. They are also an alternative if you feel shoulder pain with a bar. Dumbbells usually are less taxing on the shoulder joint regardless of the exercise.

Whenever performing any standing exercise such as: upright rows, biceps curls, or squats, stand with your back arched. There has been some controversy regarding this issue. The back is in a very strong position when arched by complimenting the natural curvature of the spine and protecting the low back from hyper-extending. Too often we see people injure themselves by leaning back and straining the lower back during a biceps curl or upright row. Will performing standing exercises in this position guarantee no injuries to the lower back? The answer is no, but a lot depends on how much weight you use, how properly you perform your exercises, and if you have had any past lower back injuries.

Lateral Raises: Lateral or side raises are probably one of the most improperly performed exercises. It looks simple: Raise two dumbbells to your sides, but yet difficult. The idea here is to isolate the side of your shoulders. Most people I see performing this exercise use too much weight and raise the dumbbells between the side and the front of their body. They do more of a *front/side* raise, rather than a strict side raise. I strongly suggest using light weight. Overhead presses and upright rows take care of your heavy work. Now it's time to *lighten* it up and do it right!

When performed properly, lateral raises can help develop the outer part of the shoulders, known as the medial deltoids. I view this exercise as a hammer and chisel to sculpt the outside sweep of the medial delts.

With two dumbbells at your sides, slowly raise your arms to your sides until your arms are parallel to the floor. Keep the elbows slightly bent with the palms of your hands facing the floor.

Important Tips for Lateral Raises:

- Keep your shoulders back.
- Slightly bend your elbows.
- Keep your wrists down and your palms facing the floor.

Keeping your shoulders back will also keep pressure on the medial deltoids. Only a slight bend in the elbows is needed to perform this exercise. Anything greater than a slight bend will work the anterior deltoids. Pretend to be pouring water from two pitchers by keeping your wrists down and palms facing the floor. This will target the medial deltoids rather the anterior and posterior deltoids. Keeping the wrists down will also prevent assistance from the forearms.

Lateral raises with one arm: Lateral Raises can also be performed one arm at a time. Here you need to hold on to something with one hand such as the side of a squat rack and perform a lateral raise with the other hand. I slightly lean my body towards the working arm for leverage.

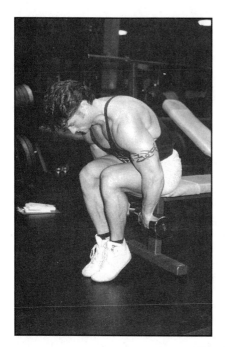

Seated

Reverse Flyes: This exercise isolates the rear deltoids, probably the most neglected muscles of the upper body. Reverse flyes can be done from a seated position or lying face down on an incline bench using two *light* dumbbells. I wouldn't recommend performing this exercise from a standing, bent-over position. This could really hurt your lower back.

I emphasize the word *light*. For most people, anything heavier than 15 pound dumbbells is too heavy. I use a maximum of 25 pound dumbbells. The rear delts are small muscles that do not require heavy weights to see results.

Tips Seated on Bench:

- Sit on the very end of a flat bench holding two light dumbbells under your thighs.
- Stay up on your toes.
- Raise the dumbbells to your sides, with a slight bend in your elbows.
- Hold and squeeze your shoulder blades together before slowly lowering the dumbbells.

On Incline Bench

I usually perform them on the incline bench as shown above, for lower back protection. Which ever way you choose, be sure to keep only a slight bend in the elbows throughout the entire range of motion. Raise the dumbbells to your sides or even slightly towards the front, forming a "Y" with your arms. Squeeze your shoulder blades together for one full second before slowly lowering the dumbbells. Try to stick your chest out as you squeeze your shoulders together.

Tips Using the Incline Bench:

- Start with your chest resting high on the bench. Notice I'm not sitting on the bench.
- Stay on your toes. This allows a high position on the bench.
- Keep your chest on the bench when raising the dumbbells. If you need to lift your chest completely off the bench, then the weight is too heavy.
- Hold and squeeze your shoulder blades together before lowering the dumbbells.

Triceps

Three Heads of the Triceps:

- Long Head
- Medial Head
- Lateral Head

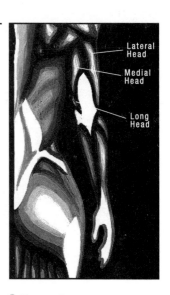

The triceps brachii is a three-headed muscle that makes up two-thirds of your arm. The triceps work anytime you push anything away from your body.

Triceps Exercises

The **French Curl** is one of my favorite triceps exercise that can be performed with a straight bar, curl bar, or a dumbbell, in a seated position.

Sitting on a bench, start with the bar held overhead with a thumb-width *grip (about three or four inches from the center of the bar).* Slowly lower the bar

Exercises:

Long Head

- *French curls*
- *Lying triceps Extensions*
- *One-arm triceps extensions*
- *Reverse-grip cable triceps pushdowns*
- *Close-grip bench press*

Lateral Head:

- *Pushdowns with a bar*
- *Kickbacks*
- *Dips*

Medial Head
(Lower triceps)

- *Pushdowns with rope*
- *Weighted dips*
- *Dips between two benches*

Be sure to see Precontest Training in Chapter 16, for the descriptions and photographs of additional exercises listed above that are not shown in this chapter.

behind your neck bending and keeping your elbows in towards your ears. From here, push the bar back over your head taking the same path as on the way down.

French Curl with a Dumbbell: This is what I call a no nonsense exercise. There's no need to find a bar, adding weight to it, or adding collars. You just pick up a dumbbell, sit somewhere and push it over your head. It's hard to mess this one up! I like using a heavy dumbbell to perform this exercise. It's a lot easier than using a bar because your hands are closer together and the range of motion is limited. But that's OK because this exercise never fails to give me a great pump in my triceps. Be sure to keep your back arched and your feet flat on the ground.

Close Grip Bench: When performed properly, this exercise could add some serious development to your triceps. The important thing to remember about this exercise is to keep your elbows in. Too often I see people use too much weight and flare their elbows out. As a result, the chest is doing most of the work. Also, lower the bar to the top of your chest, not your stomach! Lowering the bar to the top of our chest ensures more triceps action. Lowering the bar to your stomach decreases the range of motion.

Start with a thumb-width grip as shown in the close-up photo. Also notice my thumbs on the same side as the rest of my fingers. I like this grip because my thumbs don't get in the way. From here, slowly lower the bar to the top of your chest keeping your elbows in. Pause once you reach your chest and then press back up, keeping your elbows in.

Lying Triceps Extensions:
This exercise is similar to French Curls. Instead of sitting on a bench, you are lying on it.

Lower the bar to your forehead bending the elbows then push the bar back up keeping the elbows in towards the ears and even with your forehead. Do not push the bar towards your chest. This takes the pressure off the triceps and onto the chest.

Tips When Performing Pushdowns:

- Stand with your feet close together.
- Buttocks out.
- Back arched.
- Wrists curled forward .
- Thumbs aligned with the rest of the fingers all on one side.
- Palms facing the floor.
- Bar and cable close to your body as possible.
- Bar never moves past your chest on the negative movement.
- Elbows back on the way down.

Pushdowns: This is another commonly used triceps exercise performed using a cable machine or a lat machine with any type of a bar.

Start with the bar held directly under your chest with a thumb width grip from the center. With your elbows clamped to the side of your body, push the weight directly towards the floor and squeeze the triceps. Return the bar back under your chest keeping your elbows in close to your body. Various gadgets can be used to perform pushdowns. To start, use either a straight short bar or an inverted triceps bar. *(See Precontest Training for more details on pushdowns.)*

Dumbbell Triceps Extensions: Sitting on a bench, hold a dumbbell over your head with your palm facing the back of your head. Slowly lower the dumbbell behind your head bending the elbow. From here, press the dumbbell back over your head squeezing the triceps.

Kick Backs: These are performed in a similar position as with the one-arm row. If your left knee and hand are on the bench, hold a dumbbell in the left hand. Start with the left elbow positioned high past your torso. From here, extend the arm and squeeze the triceps. When lowering the dumbbell, be sure to keep the elbow up. Another important pointer is to keep the wrist straight. Too many people curl the wrist when extending. As a result, the forearm comes into play, taking stress off the triceps.

Biceps

The biceps brachii is a two-headed muscle that works anytime you pull toward your body.

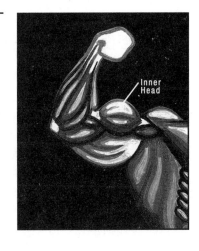

Inner
Head

Biceps Exercises

Standing Barbell Curls: This is the most basic and probably the most effective biceps exercise. When I was competing in body-building contests, this was an exercise I would usually perform with heavy weights. Now, I like to decrease the weight and increase my range of motion.

Notice in the photos how I increase my range of motion by raising the bar out and away from my body rather than just straight up. The bar travels a longer distance, placing more emphasis on the biceps. I purposely exaggerated step two so you can see the biceps in action. Step three is also slightly exaggerated where I'm squeezing the biceps up top rather than resting. Be sure to take the same path on the way down. Slowly lower the bar getting the negative benefit as well as the positive movement. When I lower the bar out and down, I slightly lean back. I don't let the weight of the bar force my torso forward. This ensures for a good stretch of the biceps during the negative movement.

Also notice my grip: My thumbs are on the same side as the rest of my fingers. This also places more emphasis on the biceps. Rather than *choking* the bar with my fingers, the bar rests on the meaty part of my palms. This is a more direct link from the bar to my biceps. Also, this grip puts the biceps in a more supinated position, where my palms are fully facing up towards the ceiling. My wrists are now fully turned and in line with my arms, and my biceps are more contracted and *peaked* during the entire range of motion.

- Start by gripping the bar about a shoulder-width with your arms fully extended in front of you.
- Stand tall, with your feet about three inches apart, with your back slightly arched and your knees slightly bent.
- Curl the bar up towards your chest, squeezing the biceps at the top.
- Be sure to keep your shoulders down. Don't shrug them!
- Slowly lower the bar back down until your arms are fully extended.

Preacher Curls: This is my favorite biceps exercise. Because of the isolation that the preacher bench provides, emphasis is put on the lower part of the biceps, allowing very little room to cheat. You can use either a curl bar as shown in the photo, or a straight bar. Once again, I grip the bar with my thumbs on the same side as the rest of my fingers rather than wrapped around the bar. This is optional. If you feel comfortable gripping the bar with your thumbs around the bar, that's OK too.

Notice the position of my body: I'm not sitting on the seat. Instead, my pelvic is leaning into the seat with my legs slightly sprawled. My back is arched and I'm on my toes. This position allows for more leverage when curling the bar and a better stretch when lowering the bar. On the way up, I lean in towards the bar. On the way down, I move away from it.

You can either use a wide grip or a close grip for variety. You will probably find the wide grip to be more difficult. I like to mix my grip up, targeting different parts of the biceps for maximum development.

Once you choose your grip, curl the weight all the way up. For an increased range of motion, curl the weight over your head. From the top of the exercise, slowly lower the weight until your arms are fully extended and repeat.

Dumbbell Curls: Standing or seated, dumbbell curls are great for finishing a biceps workout.

Dumbbell Curls Standing: Start with dumbbells at your sides with your palms facing the sides of your legs. Curl one arm up gradually turning your wrist. Don't turn your wrist completely at the start of the exercise. It's a gradual process throughout the entire range of motion. Be sure to keep your shoulder back. At the top of the exercise, turn your wrist and squeeze your biceps. Slowly lower the dumbbell down. When **completely** finished with one arm, start the other. Don't use momentum to drive the other arm up.

Dumbbell Curls Seated: These can be performed seated, off the end of a flat bench, or using a bench with back support as shown in the photos. Start with dumbbells at your sides with your arms fully extended. Notice I'm on my toes. This adds some leverage to the movement and helps me sit up straight, rather than slouched. Slowly raise one dumbbell, gradually turning the wrist on the way up. Notice that my wrist is completely turned at the top. This helps me squeeze the biceps to a peak! Slowly lower the dumbbell down until your arm is fully extended. Once again, be sure to complete one arm before alternating.

Seated Tips:

- Alternate arms.
- Completely finish one arm before starting the other.
- Don't shrug your shoulders.
- Sit up straight, arch your back, and stay on your toes.

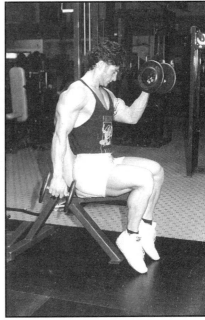

Forearms _____

Muscles of the Forearms:

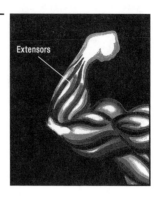

- Flexors
- Extensors

The forearms get a lot of work from biceps exercises, but direct forearm exercises should be performed for best results.

The **ulnaris extensors** and **flexors** are closer to your pinky finger and the **radial extensors** and **flexors** are closer to your thumb.

The extensors work when you curl your wrist up with your knuckles facing you and your palms facing the floor. The flexors work when you flex or curl your wrist up with your palms facing up.

Forearm Exercises

Barbell Wrist Curls: A variation of this exercise can be to work both the flexors and extensors.

To work the flexors, grip the bar with your hands in a supinated position *(palms up)* about three to four inches apart. Lower your wrists as far down as possible allowing the bar to roll down your fingers. Curl the bar with your wrists only, all the way up, keeping your forearms flat on your thighs.

Behind-the-Back Wrist Curls: Wrist curls can be performed holding a bar behind your back as shown above.

Reverse Wrist Curls can be performed with either a barbell or with dumbbells. They work the extensors or the top of your forearms. They are performed the same way as regular wrist curls, except that your hands are in a pronated *(palms down)* position. For more leverage, stay up on your toes. This brings our legs parallel to the floor increasing your range of motion.

Quadriceps _____

Major Muscles:

- Vastus Lateralis
- Vastus Medialis
- Vastus Intermedius
- Rectus Femoris

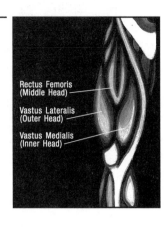

Rectus Femoris
(Middle Head)

Vastus Lateralis
(Outer Head)

Vastus Medialis
(Inner Head)

The **vastus lateralis** makes up the outside sweep of the thighs. The **vastus medialis** is located on the inside part of the thigh. The **vastus intermedius** lies between the vastus lateralis and the vastus medialis and deep beneath the rectus femoris. The **rectus femoris** makes up the middle of the thigh.

Quadriceps Exercises

Squatting Tips:

- Perform repetitions slowly.
- Maintain an arched back throughout the entire range of motion.
- Get your buttocks out on the way down.
- Keep your head straight and *do not* look down or lean forward.
- Pause at the bottom, then drive the weight upward.

Squats: Regardless of your fitness goals, squats are one of the most effective leg exercises. They mainly work the thighs, but also tie in the buttocks and hamstrings. When performed properly, squats can enhance leg development without injury.

Performing squats properly means working through a full range of motion using reasonable weight. If your goal is to build your legs, your first thought is to use heavy weights. But if you are not working through a full range of motion, your legs won't grow; I don't care how much weight you use. I have to admit, I used heavy weights, sometimes well over 400 pounds, but I always worked through a full range of motion. Now we need to define what a full range of motion is when squatting.

A big controversy about squats is whether you should go all the way down or not. Working through a full range of motion doesn't necessarily mean going all the way down where your buttocks almost hits the floor. In the photos, I'm squatting down where my legs are parallel to the floor. This is still considered a full squat. Unless you have a knee or lower back injury, you should perform full squats regardless of your goals. I used to squat down farther than parallel for an extra stretch and range of motion, but I don't anymore. It's not worth risking a knee or lower back injury.

Your Squatting Stance: When you normally stand, you don't stand with your feet completely straight, that is where your toes and heels are equi-distant. Your toes are usually farther apart than your heels. Unless you are pigeon toed, your toes normally point out. If you were to measure the distance from your left big toe to your right big toe, it will be anywhere from eight to twelve inches in distance. And your heels will be about four to eight inches apart. That is your squatting stance, the way you normally stand. I even measured my feet. My toes were about twelve inches apart and my heels were eight inches apart.

Bar Position: The bar should rest across your shoulders behind your neck. Be sure the bar doesn't rest on your vertebrae near your upper neck. From here, you can either grip the bar tightly or hold the weights as shown in the photos. I have to admit; I'm demonstrating using light weights. If I had heavier weights on the bar, I would grip the bar instead of holding the weights. When my shoulders were sore, I sometimes stretched out my arms holding the weights. But for safety purposes, grip the bar.

Once you got the right stance and the right bar positioning, slowly squat down remembering to always keep your head straight, your buttocks out and your back arched. Don't let your knees buckle. Keep the same distance between your knees throughout the entire range of motion. Once you reach the parallel position, come back up, once again keeping your back arched. Also keep your feet flat on the ground throughout the entire range of motion. Don't lift your heels off the floor.

Front Squats: Squats can also be performed with the bar across the front of your shoulders. Front squats target the front of your thighs. The position of the bar takes pressure off your buttocks and puts it all on your thighs.

- Cross your arms and hold the bar about four to six inches apart.
- Be sure the bar lies across the top of your shoulders.
- Point your elbows up so the bar doesn't roll off your shoulders.
- Squat using the same form as with regular squats.

Hack Squats: In addition to isolating the quadriceps, hack squats offer lower back support and are a little easier on the knees compared to regular squats. These can be used as an alternative or in combination to squats for developing the quadriceps. I really like performing them because of the incredible burn I feel in my quads.

It's pretty hard to mess these up. Grab the handles, position your feet as if performing regular squats, slowly squat all the way down and push back to the original position. I like to vary my foot positioning. Sometimes I use the regular stance as described with squats. Most of the times I position my feet closer, about three inches apart. With a closer stance, I feel even more isolation in my quads. If you want to target your buttocks, take a wide stance with your toes out.

Because of the knee and lower back support provided by the hack squat, I like to go down farther than parallel as shown in the photograph.

Leg Presses: As with squats, this exercise can prove to be a great leg developer, only if performed properly. I would have to say that people cheat most when performing leg presses, especially guys. No offense guys, but you know who you are. You load the leg press up with seven to ten plates on each side and go down a fraction of an inch, thinking you're really working hard. When all is said and done, look at your legs. Have they grown at all? Most people I see cheating with leg exercises have little leg development. Notice in the photos how far down I go. I have pretty good leg development from performing all my exercises properly.

Once again, this is an exercise that's pretty difficult not to do right. You can take just about any leg position, but as with hack squats, I prefer to take a close foot position. Once again this helps isolate my quads. A wider stance ties in the buttocks. Since I go all the way down, my heels tend to slightly raise off the platform, but that's OK. It's hard to keep your feet flat when working through a full range of motion in this position.

Notice that this is an inverted, weight loaded, leg press. A horizontal, weight stack, machine where you select the weight with a pin is not nearly as effective as a weight loaded unit. Be sure you're using the right leg press.

Lunges: If you want to target your buttocks in addition to developing your legs, then you have to start lunging. Lunges can be performed in a stationary position with either dumbbells or with a barbell. Jeannine is shown performing stationary lunges holding dumbbells at her sides.

From a standing position, take a step forward, bending the front knee to about a 90 degree angle, while sitting back on the rear leg. Be sure not to over step with the front leg, where your knee surpasses your toe. Notice the rear leg in the second photo: the knee is bent; the heel is up; and the toes are on the floor. Also notice in the photographs that Jeanine's back is straight. She is not leaning forward. Notice how I stick out my chest on the next page during traveling lunges. Holding the bar behind the back can help you stay straight and stick your chest out as apposed to holding the dumbbells at the sides.

After taking a step forward, push off the front leg back to your original position. From here, you can either alternate legs, or continue stepping with the same leg. I prefer to alternate legs. Before you step again, be sure your body is in a good position. Pause between steps. Don't get sloppy; take your time.

Traveling or Walking Lunges:
The toughest and most effective way to perform lunges is to travel across the gym floor. Rather than pushing off the front leg and going back to your original position and then re-stepping, continue lunging as if you were walking, taking deep steps across the gym. Be sure you have plenty of room to lunge. Try using a short bar so you don't bump into anything or anyone.

Have a destination in mind. Once you lunge to your destination, turn around slowly, and lunge back to your original spot. From here, take a short break and then repeat.

These are tough! They will take every ounce of energy from you. If you really want to shape your legs and work hard, give these a try. In addition to shaping your legs, they will improve your cardiovascular endurance as well. Your heart rate will shoot through the roof!

Hamstrings _____

Major Muscles:

- Biceps Femoris
- Semimembranosus
- Semitendinosus

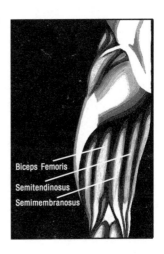

The **biceps femoris** is the largest of the three muscles located on the outer part of the hamstrings. The **semimembranosus** and **semitendinosus** make up the middle and inner part of the hamstrings respectively.

Hamstring Exercises

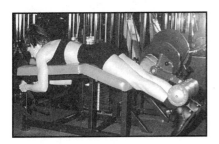 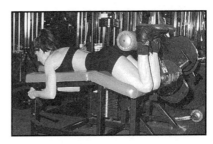

Lying Leg Curls: This is the most basic and safest hamstring exercise performed on a leg curl machine. Only a few things to remember: The pad should rest on the back of your ankles. It shouldn't roll up to your calves and it shouldn't rest on your heels. Curl your legs all the way up to your buttocks and squeeze for a full second. Be sure not to raise your hips off the bench. Slowly lower your legs until they are fully extended. You should feel a good stretch in the back of your legs on the way down. I usually sit on the bench between sets and stretch my hamstrings. This can easily be done by extending one leg on the bench and lowering your head to your knee.

Standing Leg Curls: Some gyms provide a standing leg curl machine as shown in the photos. The difference here is that you are standing rather than lying and you're working one leg at a time. You just need to adjust the pad until it rests on the back of your ankle. Simply curl the pad to your buttocks. Squeeze and slowly lower the weight back down until your leg is fully extended. When curling the weight, you can lean slightly forward for leverage while holding on to the handle provided. Be sure to start with a very light weight.

I don't consider stiff-leg deadlift as a basic exercise. It is difficult to perform and taxing on the lower back. Unless you plan to compete in a bodybuilding contest, stick with leg curls to develop your hamstrings.

Calves _____

There seems to be some confusion about the two muscles of the
calves, **gastrocnemius** and the
soleus.

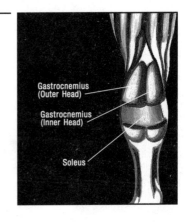

Gastrocnemius
(Outer Head)

Gastrocnemius
(Inner Head)

Soleus

The gastrocnemius is a two-
headed muscle that can be seen
and felt. The medial head is the
inside part of the gastrocnemius
located on the same side as your
big toe. The lateral head is the outside part of the gastrocnemius located on the same side as your pinky toe.

Most people think that the soleus is the lower part of the calf
that lies "underneath the gastrocnemius." The soleus does lie
beneath the gastrocnemius, but *deep* beneath it. The confusion
is a matter of semantics. You can not see the soleus. The lower
part of the calf is the tendon of the gastrocnemius. The diagram above helps explain the confusion by showing an excellent view of the soleus lying deep beneath the gastrocnemius.

Calf Exercises

There are two basic ways to train calves. One way is with the
knees locked and the other is with the knees bent. Exercises
with the knees locked, such as standing calf raises, work the
gastrocnemius. Exercises with the knees bent, such as seated
calf raises, work the soleus. When the knees are bent, the
stress is relieved from the gastrocnemius and put on the
soleus. Donkey calf raises *(which will be explained later)*,
performed with a slight bend in the knees, tie in the gastrocnemius and soleus.

Standing Calf Raise: Most gyms provide a standing calf raise machine such as the one shown in the photos. Although there are only two photos, it's actually a three-step process. First, position the balls of your feet only on the platform provided. This will allow for step two, which is to fully lower your heels. Once your calves are fully stretched in step two, rise up on your toes for step three. You can vary your feet position with all calf raise exercises. You can point your toes straight, out, or in. You should feel more of the inside part of your calves when you point your toes out and the outside part of your calves when you point your toes in.

Standing Calf Raise using a dumbbell: If you don't have access to a calf machine, or if you want to work your calves at home, you can use a dumbbell and perform calf raises on a step or anything that will allow you to lower and raise your heels. You will also need to hold on to something sturdy. If you are performing these at home on a staircase, you can simply hold on to the banister. Remember, since your legs are locked, you are working your gastrocnemius. So don't bend your knees.

You can work one leg at a time if you want to use a dumbbell for extra resistance. If you start with the left leg first, hold a dumbbell in your left hand and hold on to something with your right hand as shown in the photo. Position the ball of your left foot on the step or platform. Your right leg can just hang nearby. From here, slowly lower the ball of your left foot, pause, and then rise up on your toes squeezing at the top.

Seated Calf Raise: This exercise works the soleus part of the calf. The main difference between this exercise and the standing calf raise is that your knees are bent at 90 degree angles. Jeannine demonstrates using a seated calf raise machine provided by most gyms. The form is the same with standing calf raises. Just be sure to position only the ball of your feet on the platform and lower your heels all the way down. On the way up, I like to lean in rather than lean back. This puts more pressure on the calves.

Important Tips for Calf Training:

- Use a full range of motion. Your heels should come down as far as possible.
- Do not bounce. You will be using momentum to raise and lower the weight rather than your calf muscles.
- Pause at the bottom and at the top of each rep for one second. This will ensure a good stretch and will avoid any bouncing and momentum.

Donkey Calf Raise: As explained earlier, donkey calf raises tie in the gastrocnemius and the soleus because now your knees are only slightly bent. I'm shown below, performing them on a donkey calf raise machine that only some gyms provide. If you don't have access to this machine, you will need to go back to the old fashion donkey calf raise. That is with someone sitting on your lower back as Jeannine and I demonstrate. In that case, you will need a step and something sturdy to lean against. The important thing to remember during this exercise is to maintain the slight bend in your knees throughout the entire range of motion.

Abdominals

Major Muscles:

- Rectus Abdominis
- External Oblique
- Internal Oblique
- Serratus Anterior

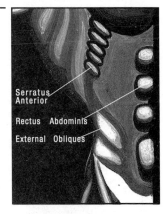

Serratus Anterior

Rectus Abdominis

External Obliques

The **rectus abdominis** is a long wall of muscle that stretches across the midsection of the body. Although it appears to be a cross section of eight individual muscles, four on each side, it is instead one mass of muscle.

The **external obliques** lie adjacent to the rectus abdominis and directly above the **internal obliques**. The internal obliques can not be seen because they lie beneath the external obliques.

The **serratus anterior** lies above the external obliques and below the pectoralis major.

In the first edition of this book, I started this section with abdominal exercises and routines. This time I'm going to start with the most important part of having great abs, *eating right!* I'm also going to be tougher this time around, so I'm warning you, you may not like what you are about to read, but it's the truth.

I don't care if you work your abs every day. Buy all the ab rollers and ab machines advertised on TV. If you don't eat right, *it aint gunna happen!* You would have a better chance of showing your abs by improving your eating habits only without working your abs than if you worked your abs every day and didn't improve your eating habits.

Have you ever noticed the well-defined abs on lean, young kids? You can see everything from abs, ribcage, to veins. Most of these kids of course will grow older and cease to look as lean and may no longer show their abs. The point is, these young kids have abs because they are lean, not because they work their abs. They have probably never performed an ab exercise in their short lives. They show abs because no layers of fat cover their abdominal wall.

When I competed in bodybuilding contests, I showed great abs as well as most of the other competitors. I could tell you that about one month following my contest, and about 15 to 20 pounds later, my abs didn't look nearly as good as they did during contest. Does that mean that in order to get my abs back that I needed to work them harder or more frequently? Or better yet, should I have bought an ab roller and used that every day? WRONG! I had to shed some of the weight that I put on. My abs didn't go anywhere. They were just covered with some fat. Not to say I didn't show my abs at all. You could still see them, but not as well as when I was 15 pounds lighter.

Of course the optimal thing to do is eat right and perform the right exercises with the right routines discussed and shown in this book. Notice I haven't used the word *diet,* but rather *eat.* That's because diet to most people means short term. Eating on the other hand means something you do every day, for a very long time. You can't decide to diet hard for one or two weeks and then go back to your normal eating habits. You need to change the way you eat for ever, that is if you always want to show your abs.

I don't want to monopolize this chapter about eating right and losing fat. I have other chapters dedicated to that. But I do want to say this:

Some people tell me they started walking to fulfill their aerobics part of their fitness plan to shed fat. Let me tell you something, taking a stroll through the park isn't going to do much in regard to shedding fat. You got to work hard. If you power walk, increasing your heart rate to at least 120 beats per minute, then your doing something. Don't get me wrong, walking is good to increase your overall health and activity. It's also better than sitting home in front of the TV. But I'm talking about SHOWING ABS! I'm talking decreasing your bodyfat! I'm talking about working hard!

People tell me that I'm blessed with good genes. Bull! I work hard! I'm in the gym five to six days per week. And more importantly, I struggle to eat right. Yes, struggle. People think I don't like to eat sweets and fatty foods. I bet I like eating more than most people, but I like looking better than most people too. So I do whatever it takes!

Even though I don't compete anymore, I still like to show my abs. I got to admit, my abs don't look as good as they did when I competed, but I still make a conscious effort to improve my own eating habits. In my case I need something to motivate me, since I don't compete anymore. Posing for this book was one motivating factor. You need to find your motivating factor such as getting ready for the summer, spring break, vaca-tion..... Or, take some before and after photos of yourself. That would be a great start to help you focus on your goals. The first thing you need to do is take a photograph of yourself right now. Then go to the supermarket and buy some healthy, low-fat, foods, and use this book and go to the gym. Now, let's get to work!

Although young kids show abs, they don't show well-developed abs. The only way to get well-developed abs is to train them hard.

The only way to train abs is to move quickly from one exercise to the other. There are a few ways you can do this: supersets, circuit training and with staggered sets. The following photographs show **my favorite** and most effective abdominal exercises utilizing the following routines (See Chapter 12, Training Techniques for more details).

1. **Supersets:** Choose two exercises, preferably one for the upper abs and one for the lower abs and superset them. A superset is when you perform an exercise for one bodypart and then immediately perform another exercise for the same body part.

For example, perform a set of curlups, for the lower abs and then immediately perform a set of cable crunches for the upper abs as shown in the following pages. Repeat this process two or three more times. Then select another two exercises, hanging knee raises and crunches. Superset them by performing a set up hanging knee raises first for the lower abs and then immediately perform a set of crunches for the lower abs. Repeat this process another two or three times. Then finally select two more ab exercises and superset them.

Your fitness level determines the number of sets and exercises to perform. If you are just starting out, select two exercises, superset them and repeat only once. Then select another two exercise and repeat them only once.

2. **Circuit Training**: Another way to work you abs is by circuit training. Select three exercises: crunches, curl ups and knee raises. First perform a set of crunches, then immediately perform a set of curlups and then perform a set of knee raises. That's one circuit, with no rest. From here you can repeat the circuit two or three more times. Once again, your fitness level

will determine how many times to repeat the circuit. I usually perform the circuit three times and that's it. The entire abdominal workout usually takes me no more than 10 minutes.

3. **Staggered sets:** A staggered set is when you perform an exercise for one bodypart and then immediately perform another exercise for a different bodypart. For example, perform a set of benchpresses for chest and then immediately perform a set of curlups for your abs.

I usually perform staggered sets using ab exercises when I'm training chest, shoulders, or back. If I'm working my chest, I perform a set of bench presses and then immediately perform a set of abs, such as curlups. The concept here is, rather than waste time and rest between chest exercises, use your time efficiently by working ab exercises between chest exercises.

I like using curlups with benchpresses because I use the same bench to perform my curlups. When I'm finished with a set of bench presses, I immediately grab the bench and start my

Curlup 1

Curlup 2

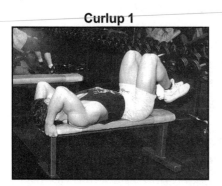 

curlups. From here, repeat the process two or three more times, assuming you perform three or four sets of benchpresses. My favorite, three, ab exercises that I use religiously are curlups, knee raises, and rope crunches.

Curlups: This is my favorite abdominal exercise. Curlups are easy, accessible and very effective for working your abdominals. Although considered a lower abdominal exercise, curlups work the entire abdominal wall. Since you are raising your lower body up towards your upper body, you should feel more stress on the lower part of your abdominal muscles.

Curlups can be performed on a bench. Simply grab the end of the bench as shown in the photos on the previous page and raise your buttocks off the bench. In the photo, I'm exaggerating step two. You really don't need to raise your buttocks that high. You do want to lower your buttock all the way down to the bench and then repeat. Notice the bend in my knees. Extending your legs will make this exercise extremely difficult, but will put unneeded stress on your lower back. Try to keep your knees as close to your body as possible.

Curlups can be performed at home. They're probably just as effective or in my opinion, more effective than using any ab roller. I usually perform them during commercial breaks during my favorite TV shows. All you need to do is grab the bottom of your couch with your hands over head and follow the same procedures above. I usually perform about 15 to 20 repetitions, rest for about 30 seconds and then repeat two or three more times. It really depends on the duration and frequency of the commercial breaks!

If curlups hurt your lower back, then try them with your hands underneath your buttocks rather than over your head. This will help support your lower back. If you can only perform a few curlups at a time, then gradually increase your reps. As your abdominal muscles strengthen, you will be able to perform more reps every time you try.

Curlups on a decline bench: If curlups get too easy, then try performing them on a decline bench. The decline makes it more difficult because it increases the range of motion. Your buttocks travels a longer distance and against the center of gravity.

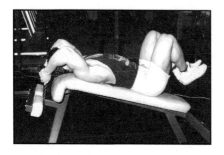

With this exercise, I use a rope to wrap around the leg part of the bench for my grip. From here, just simply raise your buttocks up just as before.

Knee Raises:
This is another lower abdominal exercise because you are raising your lower body towards your upper body. Once again, this works your entire abdominal wall, but targets the lower portion of the abdominals. The easy way to perform this exercise is by using an apparatus that Jeannine uses in the

photos. Although they look easy, they're really not. It takes some upper body strength to hold yourself up. I mean *easy* in respect to positioning yourself and simply raising your knees up to your chest. It's not a complex exercise. Just be sure to fully lower your legs before repeating.

Hanging Knee Raises: If your gym doesn't provide the apparatus shown on the previous page, hang anywhere and perform knee raises. These are a lot more difficult than regular knee raises. Here you need a lot of upper body strength to hold yourself up. It's more difficult because you're hanging freely without any back support to push yourself up. I actually call these *torso raises*. Because, what you want to do is raise your torso rather than your knees only. This will increase your range of motion, forcing your abdominals to work harder.

I sometimes use wrist wraps to help keep my grip. You may want to consider investing in a pair. Be sure to perform these slowly. Actually, you won't have much of a choice. If you go to fast, your body will start swinging uncontrollably. You want to pause once you completely lower your legs and squeeze at the top.

Hanging Knee-Raise To The Side

As with most abdominal exercises, you can simply twist your torso to one side and target the sides of your abs. Here I'm shown twisting my body to the right. You can perform a set raising your knees straight up. You can perform another set alternating sides. Or you can mix them all in one set. It's up to you. To start, try completing a set with your knees straight up and then mix it up after you got the *hang* of it.

Rope Crunches: These are performed from a cable machine using a rope. If a rope is not available, try using a towel or anything you can secure to the hook. I got to admit that this is not a basic exercise like a regular crunch. However, because they are so effective, I really want you to learn how to properly perform them.

Start by holding the rope with your hands towards the top of your head from a kneeling position. Your body position when starting, when performing, and when finishing a rep is so important. Some things should remain the same during the entire exercise and some things need to change.

Things that stay the same:
- Your hands and the bend in your elbows when holding the rope should remain the same from beginning to end. Don't let the rope up on the way up; keep it near your head. Don't pull it either. You want your abs to pull the rope, not your arms.

- Your buttocks should be up all the time. Do not sit on your legs. You want to keep constant stress on your abs. Sitting on your legs will take stress away from your abs.

Things that change:
When you start, arch your lower back as shown in step one. In step two, when you are crunching, round your back. This will ensure that you are contracting your abs. After you crunch and begin to raise your torso to the original position, slowly and gradually arch your back again.

Once you get the hang of that, then you can experiment by crunching to the side as shown here.

Rope Crunches To The Side

Other abdominal exercises:

Crunches: This is probably the most basic abdominal exercise the can be performed. Jeannine demonstrates using a flat bench. With your hands behind your head and feet flat on the bench, raise your torso just enough until your shoulders clear the bench. Squeeze your abs at the top and slowly lower yourself back down. Be sure not to jerk your head forward. Your hands are behind your head solely to support your head and neck. Your arms should remain open behind your head. If you clamp them around your head, then you are probably jerking your neck.

Side Crunches: You can perform crunches to the side to target more of your internal and external obliques. Rather than have both feet flat on the bench, simply cross one leg over the other as Jeannine shows in the photos. If you cross your left leg over your right leg, then place your right behind your head. Use your left hand to hold on to the bench. From here, crunch up and over to your right trying to touch your right elbow to your left leg. It's not necessary to touch your knee with your elbow; just aim for your knee. Once you perform a set on the right side, then immediately switch your arms and legs and perform them to the left side.

Clams: This exercise ties in your upper and lower abs. All you're doing here is performing a crunch and a curlup in one movement by driving your knees towards your head while raising your torso to towards your knees. Start with your knees bent and feet off the bench and act like a *clam* by opening and closing your body without letting your feet touch the bench. This will keep constant stress on your abs.

Knee Extensions on a bench: This is a lower abdominal exercise since you are bringing your lower body to your upper body. Sit on the very edge of a bench holding the bench on both sides near your buttocks. Simply extend your legs forward. You don't need to fully extend your legs, instead, maintain a slight bend in your knees. Fully extending your legs may hurt your lower back. Once your legs are out in front of you, simply bend them back to your chest

Side Knee Extensions: As you can see, knee extensions can also be performed to target your sides by simply adjusting your buttocks to one side as Jeannine demonstrates.

Example Abdominal Routines

Example 1: Supersets

Exercise	Reps	Repeat Sets
Knee Raises	10	2 or 3 times
Crunches	15	
Curlups	10	1 or 2 times
Cable Crunch	15	

In this example, superset knee raises and crunches. Perform a set of knee raises and immediately perform a set of crunches. Repeat this process at least once or maybe twice depending on your fitness level. Once you have repeated supersetting knee raises and crunches, perform a set of curlups and then immediately perform a set of cable crunches. Repeat this process once or twice more. If you really want to work hard, select two more exercises and superset them a total of two or three times. Or you can stick with four exercises and just repeat more than two or three times. It's up to you.

Example 2: Circuit Training

Exercise	Reps	Sets	Repeat
Hanging Knee Raise	10	1	1 to 3 times
Cable Crunch	10	1	
Clams	15	1	

Here, you are setting up a circuit of exercises using hanging knee raises, cable crunches, and clams. Start with a set of hanging knee raises and try to get 10 reps. Immediately perform a set of cable crunches and immediately finish with clams. Repeat this circuit anywhere from one to three times, once again depending on your fitness level. If you feel that you can continue, then do it. If you feel like you're going to pass out then take a rest or call it quits. As long as you work hard!

Example 3: Staggered Sets

Exercise	Reps	Sets	Repeat
Bench Press	10	1	2 or 3 times
Curlups	15	1	
Incline Dumbbell Press	10	1	2 or 3 times
Cable Crunches	10	1	
Flyes	10	1	2 or 3 times
Knee extensions off bench	15	1	

Here, I'm working my chest and supersetting abs. I perform a set of bench press and then immediately perform a set of curlups on the same bench. I repeat this process at least three times performing four sets of bench press and four sets of curlups. Then I go to my next chest exercise, the incline dumbbell press. I perform a set up dumbbell presses and immediately go to the cable machine and perform a set of cable crunches. I repeat this two or more times. Then I finish chest with dumbbell flyes and superset them with knee extensions off a bench. Repeat this process two or three times. That's it; you're done!

CHAPTER 4

Building Muscle Using
Basic Exercises

Building Muscle Using Basic Exercises

"As soon as I had pushed against pieces of iron, the world made sense. I only had to squeeze to find it. Every time the pain came, I washed it away with cold iron and surging blood. Doing that day after day made me stronger, harder, more immune."
Bob Paris, <u>Gorilla Suit</u>, St. Martin's Press

Next time you ask how long it will take to build muscle, remember this quote by Bob Paris. Building muscle is very difficult to accomplish. It takes a lot of planning, discipline, hard work, proper nutrition, and the right exercises. This book provides the right plan and exercises; the rest is up to you (*see Eat to Build in the Nutrition chapter*). Below are the most commonly asked questions specific to building muscle. I already answered the results and time oriented question. *(Also in this chapter are several examples of training programs.)*

What exercises should I perform?

To build muscle, using basic exercises such as presses, rows, squats, and deadlifts are extremely important. As I mentioned in Chapter 1, basic exercises target the major muscle groups and help you establish a foundation to build on. These exercises will put muscle on your frame. They will allow you to use maximum weight for each body part because they require maximum effort from other major muscle groups as well. For example, exercises such as bench presses and dips require a tremendous amount of work from the shoulders. Cable crossovers on the other hand will not do much for building muscle. Let others waste their time performing cable crossovers while you add mass to your chest by performing weighted dips. I have used cable crossovers, not to build muscle, but to define and shape my chest.

This is what I mean by building a strong foundation. Use "defining" exercises once you have added some muscle to your frame. You can't define what's not there! Don't get me wrong; I perform cable crossovers, occasionally to add some variety to my chest workouts. But you want to build muscle.

If you plan to compete in a bodybuilding contest, then save these defining exercises for the remaining few months before a contest. The Precontest section of this book discusses *cutting up* or defining exercises.

Using proper form when performing your exercises can make a big difference when trying to build muscle. Lifting heavy weights does not guarantee the best physique. You want to use a full range of motion when performing all of your exercises. A full range of motion means using lighter weights assuring the use of more muscle fibers. For example, I see too many people use too much weight when performing a bench press. As a result, they bounce the bar off their chest using momentum to lift the weight. Lifting this way limits range of motion and greatly increases risk of injury.

How many sets and reps per body part?

When building size is your goal, perform multiple sets and fewer reps, and take longer rests between sets. As a rule of thumb, perform a realistic range of 10 to 12 sets for large body parts, (chest, back, shoulders, legs) and six to eight sets for smaller body parts, (biceps, triceps, calves, forearms). You should gradually pyramid your weights allowing a range of four to ten reps. Pyramiding your weights simply means gradually increasing your weights every set. This means as you increase your weights, you will naturally perform fewer reps.

Performing three to four sets of three to four different exercises for each large body part and two to three sets of three different exercises for each small body part is ideal. For example, perform four sets of pullups for your back, three sets of one-arm rows, and three sets of seated rows. For triceps, you can perform three sets of close-grip bench, three sets of french curls and three sets of pushdowns.

Your current level of muscle development, size, and endurance, will also determine the range of sets and reps to use. I sometimes perform 15 to 18 sets of chest, back, and legs and 12 sets of biceps and triceps without overtraining. This is not realistic or recommended for a beginner. The example above included, a total of nine sets for triceps. This contradicts my recommendation of performing six to eight sets for small bodyparts such as triceps. But my recommendations are just that, recommendations. For the most part, my recommendations include ranges of sets. If I say a range of six to eight sets, that could also mean five sets or nine sets. Nothing is set in stone! The important thing to remember is that you don't want to overtrain a muscle group. Your arms are easy to overtrain because they are an attractive muscle group and you want them to get big by training them harder than the rest of your body.

If you train large body parts hard and intensely, using a full range of motion, then 10 to 12 sets is all you really need. Same goes with small bodyparts. Six to eight hard and intense sets will do the job. You can consider performing more that 12 sets for large body parts and more than eight sets for small body parts once you have reached an advanced level of bodybuilding, where you have competed at least once or have been lifting weights for a long time.

How much rest between sets?

The muscles require longer rests to recover from previous sets to allow you to lift heavy weights repeatedly. However, that does not mean talking to your buddy for three minutes or taking five minute water breaks either. Rests between sets should be no longer than a minute and a half. Try performing abs or calves between your sets rather than standing around doing nothing*(see staggered sets)*.

How many days?

Your fitness level, goal, and the number of days you can devote to training will determine the number of days to train. If building muscle is your goal, and you are just getting started, try to train three days per week consistently. The key word here is *consistently*. That means train three days, week in and week out. Narrowing your training to two days per week obviously won't be as beneficial as three consistent days. I currently try to train at the very least three days, but usually get a fourth day during the weekend. I'm not looking to get any bigger, but want to maintain my size and shape. When I was competing, I would always get four to five days of heavy training during my building stage of contest preparation. When I was a few months away from a contest, I was in the gym almost every day. If your goal doesn't include competing, then three to four days is more than enough to build size.

I will be discussing different split routines, but the important thing to remember is try to train on the same days every week. This will ensure consistency because training on the same days means a less chance of interruptions during the week. On the other hand, if you don't plan your days and just decide to wing it, there will be less consistency in your training. That means missed workouts.

If you decide on three days, you can split it up in different ways. You can train every other day. For example: Monday, Wednesday and Friday, training chest, bies, and abs on Monday, back and tries on Wednesday, and shoulders and legs on Friday.

If you are just starting out, I would suggest at least one day rest between workouts. More than likely, you will be very sore and will need to recuperate between workouts even if you train different muscle groups. For example suppose you train chest and biceps and Monday. On Tuesday, not only will your chest and biceps be sore, but there's a good chance that your shoulders and triceps will also be sore. Also, trying to train any muscle group with sore shoulders is difficult and not recommended.

Split Routine

Three Days Per Week, One Day Rest Between Workouts

Mon	Wed	Fri
chest	back	shoulders
biceps	triceps	legs
abs		

You can also use a two day split where you train two days in a row take the third day off and resume on the next day. For example, train chest and biceps on Monday and back and triceps on Tuesday. Take Wednesday off and train shoulders and legs on Thursday.

Three Days Per Week, Two Days On, One Day Off

Mon	Tue	Wed	Thurs
chest	back	off	shoulders
biceps	triceps		legs

If you had to, you can train three days in a row, making sure you break up your body parts as I have shown throughout these examples.

Three Days In A Row

Mon	Tue	Wed
chest	back	shoulders
biceps	triceps	legs

If you decide to train four days per week, you can train three days in a row; rest one day and start again on day five. As a rule of thumb, never train the same body parts two days in a row; your muscles need a chance to recover. I usually wait one full week before training the same body part again. If you use this spit routine, you can train one body part twice in one week. For example, you can train chest and biceps on Monday and again on Friday, if you are not still sore from Monday's workout. From here, you can start the next week with back and triceps on Monday and repeat that workout on Friday. This way you rotate training different body parts twice per week rather than just training chest and biceps twice per week. Besides, if you train chest and biceps on Monday and then again on Friday, Saturday and Sunday will probably not be enough time to train them again the following Monday. Here's a good, three week example of rotating your body parts.

**Four Days per week, Split Routine,
Three Days On One Off (3 week rotation)**

Mon	Tues	Wed	Thurs	Fri
chest	back	shoulders	off	chest
biceps	triceps	legs		biceps

Mon	Tues	Wed	Thurs	Frid
back	shoulders	chest	off	back
tries	legs	biceps		tries

Mon	Tues	Wed	Thurs	Frid
shoulders	chest	back	off	shoulders
legs	biceps	triceps		legs

The great thing about using the examples above is that you don't get stuck having to train chest every Monday. I know you probably like to start the week off with a good chest workout, but it's so difficult finding an open bench to get started. That's because everyone else is training chest on Mondays. Try to be different! Train back and triceps on Monday instead, or shoulder and legs.

You can split your four day routine however you want it to fit your schedule. You can train two days in a row, take the third day off and train two more days in a row. It really doesn't matter. Be sure not to overtrain by training sore muscle groups. Try to be consistent and plan. Use your calendar as a tool *(see Planning Is Everything)*. Be prepared for changes in your schedule.

Grouping Bodyparts

The grouping of bodyparts shown in this chapter is my personal preference that I discuss fully in Chapter 2. But I do change it around once in a while for variety. Here are other examples:

Mon	Tue	Wed	Thurs	Friday
chest	aerobics	shoulders	aerobics	biceps
back		legs	abs	triceps

In this example, I train chest and back on the same day. I know I suggested earlier not to train two large body parts in the same workout. If you are just starting out and want to build muscle, I wouldn't suggest it. But I have been doing this for a long time. I have the muscle endurance to sustain an intense workout that includes two large muscle groups. I usually use staggered sets for chest and back *(see Staggered Sets)*.

I never train chest and shoulders in the same workout because the shoulders work hard during bench presses, especially during incline bench presses. Training shoulders with heavy weights would be difficult after a chest workout. My shoulders would be totally fatigued from my chest workout, resulting in a nonproductive workout. Working chest and shoulders together can also increase your risk of a serious shoulder injury because of all the stress put on them.

Mon	Tue	Wed	Thurs	Fri	Sat
chest	quads	back	shoulders	off	hamstrings
bies		tries	abs		calves
					abs

In this example, if you decide that you want to concentrate on building your thighs, you can train them alone. You can train hamstrings and calves on a separate day. If you train your thighs with great intensity, you want to save all your energy to train them alone.

If you decide to train five days, you can train four days in a row with one or two days to rest before resuming your workouts. If you train four days on and one off, try to train legs on the fourth day to give your upper body a two day rest. Taking at least a one day rest when trying to build muscle is very important. Two days per week is even better. This results to a five-day training week. Remember, your muscles grow when they rest, not while you work them. They need ample time to rest and rebuild in order to grow.

Building a Huge Chest

If you want to build a huge chest, forget cable crossovers, forget using machines to substitute bench presses. When adding mass to your chest is a goal, the basic bench press on a flat bench is a key exercise. When not over used, the bench press will prove to be a major component to building a huge chest. It can be performed using a barbell or with dumbbells. You will be able to use more weight with a barbell versus using dumbbells. I usually start my chest workout with barbell flat bench press and then go incline dumbbell presses.

Performing bench presses on different angles will target different areas of the chest and will add more shape to it.

When performing bench presses on an incline, be sure that the incline does not surpass a 45 to 50 degree angle. Anything higher than 45 to 50 degrees will take stress away from the chest and put it to the shoulders. Think about it, if you continued to raise the incline, you would eventually be performing a shoulder press. At a proper incline, you will be stressing more of the upper chest.

Like the incline, don't exaggerate the angle on the decline. You only need a slight decline for this exercise to be effective. I prefer to perform this exercise with dumbbells because I get a fuller range of motion versus using a barbell. Also, it's safer and you really don't need a spotter. I definitely feel the upper part of my chest when performing incline presses, but I'm not totally convinced that decline presses target the lower part of the chest. However, I do like the variety and the different feel of using different angles.

Another effective exercise for adding mass to the chest is the weighted dip. I have performed dips with over 200 pounds hanging from my waist. Remember to keep your elbows out and get a good stretch when performing dips.

The standard flye adds both mass and shape to the chest. I usually finish my chest workouts with flyes. You can perform flyes on a flat, incline, or decline bench. I prefer and incline position because I get a better range of motion. See the previous chapter on how I perform flyes off the end of a bench. I also call them pullover flyes.

My favorite finishing chest exercise has always been the pullover with a heavy weight. Pullovers are great for the muscles surrounding the rib cage and for the inside part of the chest. If done properly, you should feel a stretch throughout the entire abdominal wall.

Chest Building Workout 1

Chest		
Bench press	**Sets**	**Reps**
	warm-up	10
	set 1	10
	set 2	8
	set 3	6
	set 4	4
DB incline press	**Sets**	**Reps**
	set 1	10
	set 2	8
	set 3	6
Weighted dips	**Sets**	**Reps**
	set 1	10
	set 2	8
	set 3	6
DB flyes	**Sets**	**Reps**
	set 1	10
	set 2	10
	set 3	10
	12 total sets	

Chest Building Workout 2

Chest		
Weighted Dips	**Sets**	**Reps**
No Weight	set 1	12
25 pound plate or dumbbell	set 2	10
45 pound plate or dumbbell	set 3	8
45 plus 25 pounds	set 4	6
Barbell Incline Press	Sets	Reps
	set 1	10
	set 2	8
	set 3	6
	set 4	4
Pullovers	Sets	Reps
	set 1	10
	set 2	10
	set 3	10
	11 total Sets	

Biceps

The biceps are very small compared to your chest, back, and shoulders and don't require as many sets. Six to eight sets is more than enough to build your biceps. Use the basic exercises such as barbell curls, preacher curls, and dumbbell curls described in the previous chapter to build your biceps. Barbell curls target the entire biceps. You will be able to use more weight with the standing barbell curl than with any other exercise.

Not only do barbell bicep curls tie in the entire biceps, but they also require a lot of work from the shoulders. I found that when I have excluded standing barbell curls from my workouts, my shoulder/biceps tie-in wasn't as shaped as it once was. For a long time I excluded this exercise from my biceps workout because I had hurt my back and minimized any standing exercises. So I relied mainly on preacher curls and dumbbell curls to build my biceps. The preacher curl is my favorite biceps exercise, but it doesn't tie-in the shoulders. That's the whole idea with preacher curls; isolate the biceps. I noticed after almost two years of not performing standing barbell curls, that the part of my arm where my shoulder ties in with the biceps was lacking in shape. So once I was able to perform heavy standing barbell curls again, initially, my shoulders felt incredibly sore. Once I consistently included them back to my biceps regime, I noticed the shoulder/biceps tie-in reshape again and that my shoulders didn't feel sore anymore.

As I mentioned above, the preacher curl tries to isolate the biceps. More specifically it works more of the bottom part of the biceps. With this exercise, there is no doubt that I feel more stress on the bottom part of the biceps. That's because of the position of the arms on the preacher bench. Dumbbell biceps curls on the other hand work the biceps through an entire range of motion tying in the entire biceps, especially when gradually turning the wrists during the exercise.

Biceps Building Workout 1

Biceps

Barbell curls	Sets	Reps
	set 1	10
	set 2	8
	set 3	6
Preacher curls	**Sets**	**Reps**
	set 1	10
	set 2	8
	set 3	6
Standing DB curls	**Sets**	**Reps**
	set 1	10
	set 2	10
	set 3	10

9 total sets

Building Biceps Workout 2

Biceps		
Preacher Curls	Sets	Reps
	set 1	10
	set 2	8
	set 3	6
Seated Dumbbell Curls	Sets	Reps
	set 1	10 each side
	set 2	8 each side
	set 3	6 each side
Standing E-Z bar curls	Sets	Reps
	set 1	12
	set 2	10
	set 3	10
	Total Sets 9	

Summary

In example 2, I start my biceps workout with preacher curls. This allows me to use heavier weight during this exercise by performing them first. I like to alternate standing barbell curls and preacher curls as my first exercise because they are my primary, power biceps building exercises. I sometimes like to finish off my biceps with a light set of standing E-Z bar curls. Notice the reps remain high from 10 to 12. Sometimes after performing heavy sets of the first two exercises, I like to finish a little lighter than usual. I get a great pump by ending my biceps workout by *repping* out lighter sets of standing curls with either a straight bar or curl bar.

Back

The first thing about adding size and width to your back is to stop waiting for the lat machine and perform pullups instead. Notice the before and after photos. The before photo shows my lack of back development before I started performing pullups. The after photo shows the increased width and thickness of my back after performing pullups for one year.

Once you are able to perform about 10 pullups on your own with good form, increase the intensity by adding weight. You can either use a special weight belt to tie weight around your waist or position a dumbbell between your regular weight-lifting belt. If you have trouble maintaining a good grip on the bar, use wrist straps. (*See back cover of this book to order wrist*

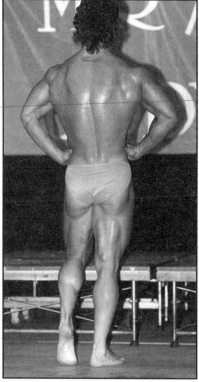 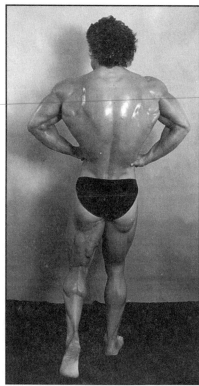

Before   *After (one year later)*

The before and after photographs above show the difference in my back development that performing pullups can make.

straps.) Try training back with a partner so he or she can spot you. When you have a spot available, perform negatives with weight around your waist. Have your partner push you up. Once your chest is up to the bar, squeeze your back, then come down as slowly as possible. *(See chapter 12 for Negatives.)*

Back Building Workout 1

Back		
Weighted pullups	**Sets**	**Reps**
	warm-up *(no weight)*	12
	set 1	10
	set 2	8
	set 3	6
	set 4	6
T-Bar rows	**Sets**	**Reps**
	set 1	10
	set 2	8
	set 3	6
Seated rows	**Sets**	**Reps**
	set 1	10
	set 2	8
	set 3	6
	10 total sets	

Back Building Workout 2

Back		
Weighted Pullup	Sets	Reps
	warm-up (*no weight*)	12
	set 1	10
	set 2	8
	set 3	6
Deadlifts	Sets	Reps
	set 1	10
	set 2	8
	set 3	6
	set 4	4
DB One-Arm Row	**Sets**	**Reps**
	set 1	10
	set 2	8
	set 3	6
	10 total sets	

Shoulders

Basic exercises such as overhead presses, upright rows, and lateral raises are best for building the shoulders. Although the reverse flye is not used frequently, it is considered an essential exercise to build and balance the shoulders. It is responsible for building the rear part of the shoulders, an area in which most people lack muscle development. When performing heavy upright rows, use wrist straps to ensure a good grip on the bar.

Shoulder Building Workout 1

Shoulders		
Behind-the-neck military press	**Sets**	**Reps**
	warm-up	12
	set 1	10
	set 2	8
	set 3	6
Upright rows	**Sets**	**Reps**
	set 1	10
	set 2	8
	set 3	6
DB lateral raise	**Sets**	**Reps**
	set 1	10
	set 2	10
	set 3	10
Shoulder shrugs	**Sets**	**Reps**
	set 1	10
	set 2	10
	set 3	10
	total sets 12 *(including shoulder shrugs)*	

Shoulder Building Workout 2

Shoulders

Arnold Presses	Sets	Reps
	set 1	10
	set 2	8
	set 3	6
	set 4	4
Barbell Upright Rows	**Sets**	**Reps**
	set 1	10
	set 2	8
	set 3	6
DB Reverse Flye	**Sets**	**Reps**
	set 1	10
	set 2	10
	set 3	10

Total sets 10

Shoulder Summary

- In workout 1, I included shoulder shrugs. You can work them with either shoulders or back. Since they are not directly targeting the deltoids, you won't be overtraining your shoulders with a total of 13 to 14 sets.
- If behind-the-neck military presses hurt your shoulders, then do them in front.
- When performing heavy upright rows, use wrist straps to get a good grip on the bar. The same goes for shoulder shrugs.

Be sure to see reverse flyes in Chapter 3 for proper form. Notice I left the reps consistent at 10. That means you don't need to increase the weight. The rear delt is a small section of your shoulders. It doesn't require heavy weight for development. It does require light weight and proper form to develop the right muscle balance.

Triceps

Exercises where you can use heavy weight are great for building big triceps. The close grip bench is a good example. For best results, be sure to lower the bar to the top of your chest. Most people lower the bar to their stomach, taking the stress off the triceps.

French Curls never fail to get my triceps sore. They're great because you work through a full range of motion by lowering the bar far behind your head. Pressing it back up from this position is difficult, but effective. I love performing French curls with a heavy dumbbell. I sometimes grab a 100 pound dumbbell, lower it behind my head and press it back up. I really feel the triceps working hard!

I usually finish my triceps routine with pushdowns. This is one of the most basic, but improperly performed triceps exercises. When performed properly, it can prove to be a very effective mass builder. I prefer to use a short, straight bar rather than the inverted "V" bar. I feel my triceps working more with a straight bar.

Triceps Building Workout 1

Triceps		
Close-grip bench	**Sets**	**Reps**
	set 1	10
	set 2	8
	set 3	6
French curls	**Sets**	**Reps**
	set 1	10
	set 2	8
	set 3	8
Pushdowns	**Sets**	**Reps**
	set 1	10
	set 2	10
	set 3	10
	9 total sets	

Triceps Building Workout 2

Triceps		

French Curl with a dumbbell	Sets	Reps
	set 1	10
	set 2	8
	set 3	6
Lying Triceps Extensions	Sets	Reps
	set 1	10
	set 2	8
	set 3	6
Pushdowns	Sets	Reps
	set 1	10
	set 2	10
	set 3	10

9 total sets

Quadriceps

You want big legs? Then squat using good form! It's funny; I see just about every leg machine being used in the gym. I see the squat rack used for just about every exercise except squats. When I do see people squatting, it's with improper form. It's no wonder why I rarely see well-developed legs in the gym. So, get under that squat rack and perform three or four quality sets of squats!

Leg presses are also very effective for adding mass to the thighs. Although lunges are not as effective as squats and leg presses for adding size to your thighs, they are great for shaping them. I also enjoy performing hack squats. They really isolate the thighs because of the angle of the machine and as a result, I feel an incredible burn throughout my thighs.

Quadriceps Building Workout 1

Quadriceps		
Squats	**Sets**	**Reps**
	warm-up	15
	set 1	12
	set 2	10
	set 3	8
	set 4	6
Leg press	**Sets**	**Reps**
	set 1	10
	set 2	8
	set 3	6
Walking lunges	sets (3)	
	10 total sets	

Quadriceps Building Workout 2

Quadriceps		
Squats	**Sets**	**Reps**
	set 1	12
	set 2	10
	set 3	8
	set 4	6
Hack Squats	**Sets**	**Reps**
	set 1	10
	set 2	8
	set 3	6
	set 4	6
Stationary Lunges	**Sets**	**Reps**
	set 1	10 each side
	set 2	10 each side
	set 3	10 each side
	set 4	10 each side
	Total Sets 12	

Summary
- The most important thing about adding size to your legs is to stick with the basic exercises using good form. Performing the basic exercises is not enough. You really need to work your legs through a full range of motion. So lighten up the weight and do it right.

- I like keeping my reps high when training legs. Legs will still grow by performing high repetitions with good form.

- When performing walking lunges, be sure to allow enough room to travel across the gym floor. You want to take at least 12 steps across the floor and then immediately return.

- When performing stationary lunges, be sure to alternate legs. Keep the reps high. This is not a mass builder, but will add shape and definition to your legs when performed consistently.

- I rarely trained hamstrings and calves during my quadriceps training because quadriceps drained all my energy. If you are serious about adding mass to your thighs, and plan on training them with high intensity, then train them alone. Train hamstrings and calves on a separate day. If your days are limited, then it's OK to train hamstrings and calves with quadriceps, as I do now, since I don't compete anymore.

Hamstrings

Building the hamstrings is very important to balance leg strength and size. Leg curls are the most basic to perform. Some gyms provide a standing leg curl that allows you to use one leg at a time. This ensures for an even greater balance of strength and size for the legs. If one leg is stronger than the other, the imbalance of strength can be detected and corrected by using this piece of equipment. I used stiff-leg dead lifts religiously to build and shape my hamstrings during contest training. If you don't plan to compete, then they are really not necessary. The risk of hurting your back permanently is not worth it. If you experience lower back pain when performing these, try using light weights or don't perform this exercise at all.

Hamstrings Building Workout 1

Hamstrings		
Stiff-leg deadlifts	**Sets**	**Reps**
	set 1	10
	set 2	10
	set 3	10
Leg curls	**Sets**	**Reps**
	set 1	10
	set 2	8
	set 3	8
	set 4	6
Single leg curls	**Sets**	**Reps**
	set 1	12
	set 2	10
	set 3	10
	10 total sets	

Hamstrings Building Workout 2

Hamstrings

Leg Curls	Sets	Reps
	set 1	12
	set 2	10
	set 3	10
	set 4	10
Single Leg Curls	**Sets**	**Reps**
	set 1	10 each side
	set 2	10 each side
	set 3	10 each side
	set 4	10 each side

Total Sets 8

Calves

Nothing looks worse than having big thighs and small calves. Working the calves consistently with the basic exercises below will ensure a proper balance between the thighs and calves. Working both parts of the calves, the gastrocnemius and the soleus, is essential for building them. Be sure to work your calves through a full range of motion by lowering your heels as far down as possible.

Calves Building Workout 1

Calves		
Donkey calf raises	**Sets**	**Reps**
	set 1	15
	set 2	12
	set 3	10
	set 4	10
Seated calf raises	**Sets**	**Reps**
	set 1	15
	set 2	12
	set 3	12
	set 4	12
	8 total sets	

Calves Workout 2

Calves		
Standing Calf Raise	**Sets**	**Reps**
	set 1	12
	set 2	10
	set 3	10
	set 4	10
Seated Calf Raise	**Sets**	**Reps**
	set 1	12
	set 2	10
	set 3	10
	set 4	10
	Total sets 8	

Summary:
To build and shape the calves, I think it's essential to keep your reps high because calves respond better to high reps. This is what I have noticed and this is what I have heard and read throughout my years of bodybuilding. Notice, in the examples, the reps are no fewer than 10. Not to say you can't occasionally perform less than 10 reps. For the most part, keep your reps high. This means that you won't be significantly increasing your weights.

Overview

I do not count warm-up sets as full sets. I only count sets that exert energy where a good, hard, and an intense effort is made. For example, my warm-up set with weighted pullups is performed without weight, so I don't count it. Also, my warm-up set with squats is performed with only 135 pounds, so I don't count that either. Both of these warm-up sets I perform with ease, so I do not count them.

Notice that the last two exercises for chest and biceps (flyes and dumbbell curls) the reps remain constant at 10. Flyes and dumbbell curls should be performed with moderate weight for at least 10 repetitions. They are exercises mainly responsible for shaping and defining. Other exercises such as bench presses and standing barbell curls are the mass builders.

I do not train hamstrings or calves on my quadriceps day because training quadriceps drains all my energy. Add a day to train solely hamstrings, calves and maybe even abs. This was usually my *easy* day of training during contest time.

For hamstrings, you can perform single leg curls on a machine that a good bodybuilding gym provides.

For quadriceps, leg extensions are optional. Squats, leg presses, and lunges, are sufficient. You can vary your workouts using leg extensions with supersets. *(See Training Techniques)*. I sometimes use leg extensions as a warm-up for my quadriceps training.

For calves, a total of six to eight sets is sufficient. You can alternate other exercises that target both parts of the calf: the gastrocnemius and the soleus. Also notice that the repetitions remain high for calves. They seem to respond with lighter weights and more repetitions.

CHAPTER 5

Dorm Room & Dungeon Training

Dorm Room Training ─────────────────

Unless you plan to compete, it's not totally necessary to use machines and weights to tone your body. You can perform exercises in your dorm room or at home with the help of a few items:

- two books of equal weight
- light dumbbells
- Dynabands®
- broom stick
- exercise mat
- chair

Remember, try to work all body parts to avoid imbalances of muscle strength and shape.

Chest

MODEL: AMY GINSBERG

Modified pushups: Start with your knees on the floor and your hands shoulder-width apart out in front of you. Lower your chest to the floor keeping your elbows out and push yourself back up and repeat.

Regular pushups: If modified push ups are not challenging enough, then try performing regular push ups. Start on your toes rather than on your knees with your hands in the same position. Lower your chest to the floor without allowing your hips to touch the floor, then push yourself up.

Flyes: You can perform flyes with a pair of light dumbbells or with two objects of equal weight such as books. Position your upper back on the seat of a chair with the dumbbells or books straight up over your chest. Lower the weight in a circular motion over your chest keeping a slight bend in the elbows. On the way up, use the same circular motion as on the way down. Think about hugging a tree as you squeeze the chest.

Back

One-Arm Row: This exercise can be performed with a Dynaband, book or with a dumbbell. Position one foot forward on one end of a dynaband and the other foot  back bending both knees. Grab and pull the other end of the dynaband up past your body squeezing the upper back. Be sure to keep a slight arch in your lower back, chest out, and head up.

 ***Dynaband Low Row:*** Sit on the floor with your legs out in front of you with your knees slightly bent. Wrap the Dynaband across the bottom of both feet. Holding both ends of the dynaband, pull back squeezing the muscles of the upper back. Be sure to get your shoulders back and your chest out. This will assure pulling with your back and not your biceps.

Shoulders

Upright Rows: With two dumbbells: Hold two dumbbells in front of you with your arms fully extended. Raise the dumbbells under your chin keeping your elbows out. With Dynabands, stand on the ends of two dynabands and get a good grip on the other ends. With the knees slightly bent, pull the dynabands up keeping your elbows out and squeeze the shoulders.

Lateral Raises: Hold either two dumbbells or books at your sides, and raise them to your sides and parallel to the floor. Be sure to keep your elbows slightly bent. With dynabands, step on one end of each of the two dynabands and grab the other ends. Pull the Dynabands away and to the sides of your body.

Triceps

Dynaband Triceps Extensions: Sit on a chair holding one end of a Dynaband behind your head. Hold the other end with the other hand behind your back. Extend the Dynaband over your head squeezing the triceps. A dumbbell or book can also be used.

Triceps Kickback: Start with your elbow positioned up holding a book, dumbbell, or a Dynaband in the one hand bracing yourself on a chair with the other hand. Extend the arm back squeezing the triceps.

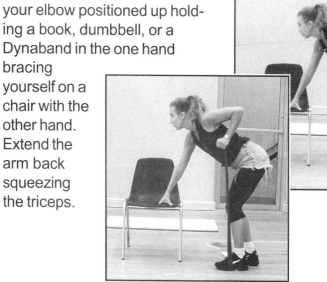

Dips on a chair:
With your back facing a chair, position your hands on the seat of the chair with your legs extended in front of you. Lower your body bending the elbows until your buttocks almost touches the floor. From here, push yourself back to your original position. For more resistance, try placing your heels on another chair performing the same movement.

Biceps

Biceps Curl: You can perform biceps curls with either books or dumbbells. Simply curl the weight up turning the wrist at the top of the motion. Alternate arms and be sure to complete one arm before starting the other.

Legs

In the first of edition of this book, this chapter included floor exercises to help tone your lower body. I have excluded those floor exercises because I really think they are a waist of time. All you need to perform are squats and lunges to tone your lower body.

Squat with a broomstick.   *Squat with books.*

Lunges: Hold two dumb-bells or books at your sides for additional resistance or rest a broom stick on your shoulders for balance. Starting with your feet together, take a step in front keeping the rear foot planted and the stepping knee at a 90 degree angle with the floor. Push off the front foot back to your original position keeping the rear foot planted. Pause and repeat alternating legs. For your inner and outer thighs, perform **side lunges**. *(See Women & Bodybuilding in Chapter One, for proper form.)* Side lunges are performed by stepping to the side rather than in front.

Calf Raises: Use either a chair or wall to lean against. From the ball of your foot, raise your heel off the ground and squeeze the calf. Position the other foot on the working foot for extra resistance as shown in the photo.

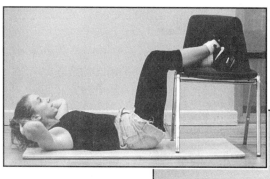

Abdominals

Crunches: Your legs over a chair will ensure that your

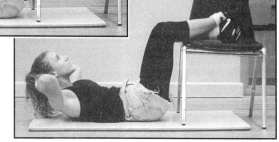

lower back is flat on the floor. Raise your torso just enough until your shoulders clear the floor. Squeeze your stomach muscles and then slowly lower yourself back down and repeat _(see Chapter 3 for additional abdominal exercises)_.

Since you will be experiencing light resistance with light weights and Dynabands, you can train the entire body in one workout, three to four times per week _(see Chapter 2 for more on sets and reps)_. Perform at least one set of each of the exercises shown in this chapter for a range of 15 to 20 repetitions. This should take you no more than 20 to 30 minutes. For best results, try to move through your workouts quickly with minimum rest in between sets.

Although the resistance is light, you still may experience some soreness, especially from squats and lunges. If so, allow one day to rest between workouts to let your muscles to recuperate. If only your legs are sore, train your upper body only. On the days where you are too sore to perform resistance exercises, perform aerobic exercises instead.

To increase the intensity in your workouts, perform either more sets and repetitions for each exercise, or see Staggered and Supersets for different training techniques.

Dungeon Workouts

Welcome To The Dungeon!

Not too often, but occasionally, I get in the mood for a dungeon workout. With jeans, work boots, and T-shirt *(until I start sweating, then I take my T-shirt off)* I go down to the dungeon and often, get a great workout. I first crank my favorite music. Since it's a dungeon workout, I find the heaviest metal music I could find. It's usually Metallica or Rage Against the Machine, or even some old KISS. I make sure there's always a mirror nearby so I could really get into it! For some reason, I get a better pump with dungeon workouts. Sorry, that's something I can't explain. And no doubt, I sweat profusely, obviously because I'm in the dungeon. I mean look at this place! This is actually my basement, a great atmosphere for a hard, heavy metal, old fashion workout. I'm surrounded by grey brick walls. It even has the string and light bulb above me. No treadmills, no stairmasters, no machines, just my bench, barbell, dumbbells, chairs, and my door gym. That means no waiting for equipment, no attitudes, no air conditioning, no fans. No doubt, this is going to be a great workout!!!

I got to admit, my dungeon workouts were usually chest and biceps workouts, until I recently purchased a *door gym* that allows me to perform pullups, my favorite and most effective back exercise. So now I include back workouts as well as chest and biceps.

Chest:

In addition to using my bench and weights for the standard bench press, I do need to get a little creative. I first warm up with some pushups.

Pushups 1

Pushups 2

I then start my chest workout with my favorite chest exercise, the dip. Without them, my chest workout is not complete. I don't have a dip station to perform my dips, so here's where I get a little creative. I position two chairs back to back as shown in the photos and I dip away. Chair dips are just as effective as using a regular dip station. From here, I can add weight by positioning a dumbbell in my belt.

Chair Dips 1

Chair Dips 2

Another creative chair, chest exercise is what I call, the chair flye. I could always just use my bench to perform my flyes, but if you don't have a bench at home and do have dumbbells, you can perform flyes. I prefer to use a chair or the end of a bench with my feet on the floor to perform my flyes as apposed to lying on the bench all together. Using a chair or the end of a bench allows a fuller range of motion. Try it; you will feel a much better stretch in your chest.

Chair Flyes 1

Chair Flyes 2

I usually start my chest workout with four sets of chair dips. Then I perform three to four sets of bench presses and then finish with three sets of dumbbell flyes or pullovers or both for a total of about twelve sets of chest. If I'm feeling real *dungeon-like,* I'll superset light sets of pullovers with my flyes. A superset is when you perform an exercise for a bodypart and then immediately perform a different exercise for the same bodypart. In this workout, after completing a set of flyes, I immediately perform a set of pullovers. I love finishing chest with pullovers. I get a great stretch throughout my entire upper body.

Pullover 1

Pullover 2

Biceps:

No dungeon workout is complete without working biceps. So I perform about three or four sets of standing barbell curls and finish with three sets of dumbbell curls. I prefer to do my dumbbell curls seated on the bench. This leaves little room for cheating. Be sure to sit straight up with your chest out and work through a full range of motion. I usually perform an abdominal exercise between my biceps curls using staggered sets. A staggered set is when you perform an exercise for a body part and then immediately perform another exercise for a different body part. This differs from supersets. A superset as I explained above is when you perform a different exercise for the same body part. In this example, after completing a set of biceps curls, I immediately perform a set of an abs exercise. The curlup is my favorite ab exercise because I simply lie on a bench and do a quick set. The idea here is rather than wasting time between sets of biceps, I perform a set of abs. I get done faster and get a better workout.

Dumbbell Curl

Curl up

Back:

Now that I have a door gym, I get great back workouts as well as chest workouts. I perform four sets of pullups, mixing up my grips as shown below.

| **Wide Grip Pullup** | **Close Grip Pullup** | **Reverse Grip Pullup** |

(See order form at the end of this book to order your own door gym. Or visit my website: www.bodybuildingbyfrank.com.) It's easy to use and fits in most doorways.

I then perform four sets of dumbbell one-arm rows and finish with four sets of T-Bar rows. I also stagger triceps into my back workout. Between my sets of pullups I perform close grip bench presses. For example, I perform a set of pullups, then immediately perform a set of close grip bench presses. I repeat this process three more times and then move to one-arm row. Then I stagger over-head dumbbell press using only one dumbbell *(see Chapter 3 for form).* Then I finish back with T-Bar rows and choose another exercise I can stagger for triceps such as a French Curl.

Dumbbell One-Arm Row 1

Dumbbell One-Arm Row 2

T-Bar Row 1

T-Bar Row 2

Shoulders:

For shoulders, you can perform mostly any exercise at home with a barbell and dumbbells as you do in the gym such as, overhead press, upright rows, dumbbell lateral raises, front raises, reverse flyes (see Chapter 3).

So if you have some weights in your basement, clear the dust off the bench, play your favorite music and prepare to sweat!

Nutrition

Nutrition

Whether your goal is to build muscle, lose weight, decrease fat, or tone-up, you have to eat the right foods, at the right time, in the right quantity.

Nutrients are the major chemical constituents that make up the calories in your food. They include carbohydrates, proteins, vitamins and fat.

What is a calorie?

By definition, a calorie is a unit of energy expressing heat-producing or energy-producing value in food when oxidized in the body. Simply, calories make up the value in food.

One gram of carbohydrate or protein is equal to about four calories compared to about 10 calories for every gram of fat.

The general consensus among the government, *(The U.S. Department of Agriculture)* nutritionists, and bodybuilders is that carbohydrates should make up about 60% to 70% of your calories. That leaves only 30% to 40% to allocate for protein and fat. The allocation of protein and fat is controversial. To maintain my physique, I currently consume about 65% carbohydrates, 25% protein, and 10% fat. The government recommends a breakdown of 60% carbohydrates, 10% protein, and 30% fat. As you can see, we are close with carbohydrates, but not with protein and fat. We'll get to that later.

To figure out your percentage of carbohydrates, protein, and fat, as a percentage of your total caloric intake, is easy:

For carbohydrates and protein:
- Count the number of grams of carbohydrates and protein you have consumed in one day.
- Multiply each gram of carbohydrate or protein by four.
- Divide the product by the total number of calories consumed.
- Multiply by 100

For example:
I usually consume about, 2000 calories a day, 325 grams of carbohydrates, 125 grams of protein, and 20 grams of fat.

For carbohydrates: 325 grams X 4 calories = 1300 calories
1300÷2000 = .65
.65 X 100 = 65%

For protein: 125 grams X 4 calories = 500 calories
500÷2000 = .25
.25 X 100 = 25%

For Fat:
- Multiply each gram of fat by 10.
- Divide the product by the total number of calories consumed.
- Multiply by 100

For example:
20 grams X 10 = 200 calories
200÷2000 = .10
.10 X 100 = 10%

Carbohydrates

There are two types of carbohydrates, complex and simple. Complex carbohydrates are starchy foods that get stored in your muscles as glucose for long-lasting energy expenditure. Simple carbohydrates are used immediately and stored for a very short period of time. Complex carbohydrates are stored longer because they must be broken down before being used. For optimum health and performance, most of your carbohydrate intake should be complex, like the ones listed below. They contain important minerals and vitamins that simple carbohydrates don't and are excellent sources of dietary fiber. Simple carbohydrates are also higher in calories and shoot up your blood sugar levels. This can make you feel tired after your blood sugar comes crashing down.

Complex Carbohydrates	Simple Carbohydrates
breads	sugar
hot cereals	candy
grains	fruit
legumes (beans, lentils, peas)	
potatoes	
rice	
barley	
vegetables	
pasta	

Although legumes, such as beans, are sources of complex carbohydrates, consuming too much of them can cause severe gas and discomfort.

Lately, new diets have been limiting the amount of carbohydrates and increasing protein in order to lose weight. Personally, I have no problem with this. My theory is that the weightloss comes from the decrease in total calories, not from the switch from carbs to protein. That's because most people consume significantly more carbohydrates than protein. When carbohydrates are limited, so are calories. It's difficult to substitute protein for carbohydrates. It's time consuming to prepare protein. Carbs are so easy: open the refrigerator, pull out a piece of bread and eat. Protein on the other hand isn't as accessible because it usually needs to be cooked.

Protein & Amino Acids

Aside from water, protein makes up about 99% of the skeletal muscles. Common sense will tell you that if you want muscle in any way shape or form, you need to consume protein. Proteins are made from amino acids. Amino Acids are the building blocks of proteins categorized as essential amino acids and nonessential amino acids.

Nonessential amino acids are naturally synthesized by the body. These include:

Alananine	Glumatic Acid	Hydroxyproline
Aspartic Acid	Glutamine	Proline
Cysteine	Glycine	Serine
Tyrosine		

Essential amino acids are not synthesized by the body in quantities sufficient to meet the basic needs of muscle growth, repair, and maintenance of the body. Therefore, since the body alone cannot produce essential amino acids, you need to eat foods that contain them.
The nine essential amino acids:

Histidine	Lysine	Threonine
Isoleucine	Methionine	Tryptophan
Leucine	Phenylalanine	Valine

Foods, primarily from animal sources are complete proteins, providing the nine essential amino acids. These foods include, fish, beef, poultry (chicken, eggs, turkey) and dairy products where milk is present. Soybean products such as tofu and soybean milk are known to be complete proteins. As with legumes, soybean products are difficult to digest and can cause gas and stomach discomfort.

For vegetarians, it's difficult to consume complete proteins, but not impossible. Combining beans with rice, cheese, corn, nuts, sesame seeds and wheat can be considered an alternative for meat and poultry.

How Much Protein Do You Need?

Alas! As I mentioned above, the answer has been a topic of controversy among the government, nutritionists, and body-builders. As far as I'm concerned, it basically comes down to your goals. Originally, when I was competing, my protein intake was much higher than it is today. My goals have changed. I'm not looking to be huge anymore, but I do want to maintain my current musculature. I'm currently about 170 pounds. My bodyfat is very low, at about 5 or 6%. Enough about me, let's hear what *they* have to say about protein.

We already know that the U.S. Department of Agriculture recommends that 10% of your calories should be protein. Let's say that the average person consumes 2000 calories. So 10% of 2000 equal 200 calories. 200 calories divided by 4 calories is 50 grams of protein. So that's one recommendation. Let's summarize:

- **U.S. Department of Agriculture's protein recommendation for a 2000 calorie diet: 50 grams or 10%**

The problem with this recommendation is that if you are looking to build, tone, or shape your muscles by lifting weights intensely, you are no longer an average person. Do you think your protein intake should be the same as a couch potato. Why would it be so important for a couch potato to need extra protein?

The *PDR® Family Guide to Nutrition and Health,* a reputable resource for health information, takes this into consideration. It suggests to include 1.5 grams of protein for each kilogram of body weight to build a more powerful physique. To figure this out, the first thing you need to know is that 1 kilogram equals

2.2 pounds. So if you weigh 170 pounds, divide 2.2 into 170 and multiply by 1.5. This gives you 116 grams of protein. If you consume 2000 calories a day, this is about 23% protein compared to the government's 10%. Lets summarize:

- **PDR® Family Guide to Nutrition and Health protein recommendation: 116 grams or 23% of total calories for a 170 pound person.**

Prescription for Nutritional Healing, a widely read nutrition book recommends that a 170 pound man, doing light work, should consume 25 to 30 grams of protein. If this person consumed 2000 calories, then that is only 5 to 6% of total calories. Let's summarize:

- **Prescription for Nutritional Healing recommends 25 to 30 grams or 5 to 6% of total calories for a 170 pound person.**

Let's try another source: Fitness for Dummies™ recommends .4 grams of protein per 1 pound of body weight. This is easy to figure out. If you are 170 pounds, just multiply 170 by .4. This gives you 68 grams of protein. Let's summarize:

- **Fitness for Dummies recommends 68 grams of protein for a 170 pound person.**

And finally, one of my favorite bodybuilding books, Beyond Built, written by my favorite bodybuilder, Bob Paris, recommends that an average weight-trained athlete should consume 20% protein. For a 170 pound person consuming 2000 calories, that would be 100 grams of protein. A competitive bodybuilder should take in 30% protein. For a bodybuilder consuming 2000 calories, that would be 150 grams of protein, which is almost one gram of protein for each pound of body weight. Let's summarize:

- *Bob Paris, Beyond Built recommends 20 to 30% of total calories for an average weight trainer and competitive bodybuilder respectively. For a 2000 calorie diet, that would be 100 to 150 grams of protein.*

So there you have it, five different protein recommendations. I think a happy medium between the *PDR Family Guide to Nutrition and Health* and Bob Paris's *Beyond* Built would be the best recommendation. That is, 20 to 30% of your total calories, depending on your fitness goals or 1.5 to 2.0 grams of protein per 1 kilogram of body weight. For a 170 pound person, that would be a range of 116 to 155 grams of protein. That's a good range. I would say that I am currently at the lower end of that range. When I competed, I was at the higher end.

Experts say protein foods such as meats allow your body to use amino acids to make new proteins that build muscle tissue. There's no argument there. But most experts also say that more protein doesn't necessarily mean bigger muscles. It's like saying that if one aspirin gets rid of your headache, why take two. With drugs, an increase in dose doesn't necessarily mean an increase in efficacy. However an increase in dose does mean an increase in side effects. Excess amounts of protein on the other hand shouldn't harm you, but if you are taking in excess protein, that also means you are taking in excess calories. If your body can't use the protein, it will store it as fat. Remember, you want to build or tone muscle, not get fat. Just keep it simple; try to **consistently** consume two to three *small* protein meals a day. That means four egg whites and one whole egg in the morning, some tuna for lunch and one or two chicken breasts for dinner. It doesn't mean a 12 ounce steak three to four times per week!

Fat

Would you believe that fat in its pure state is tasteless, color-less, and odorless? How can something that tastes so good be tasteless, colorless, and odorless? I guess a little sugar and other tasty substances can really spice up any food.

Fats are broken down into two main categories, saturated and unsaturated. When chemical bonds between the carbon atoms of the fat molecule contain all the hydrogen atoms that they are capable of holding, then the fat is saturated. If the fat molecules have capacity for additional hydrogen atoms, they are considered unsaturated.

Saturated fats are mainly animal fats solid at room tempera-ture. They are related to heart disease because they stick to the walls of the arteries constricting the flow of blood to the heart. They also increase the amount of cholesterol in the blood. Unsaturated fats are extracted from vegetable and fat seeds in liquid form.

We can get into the break down of how much fat to consume, but let's not kid ourselves. We can all stand to decrease the amount of fatty foods we consume. The less fat you consume, the healthier you will be and the better you will look.

Lose Fat and Keep the Muscle in 5 easy steps

1. Restricts fat intake.
2. Eat small frequent meals throughout the day
3. Avoid meals after 8:00 p.m.
4. Exercise with weights.
5. Incorporate aerobic activity such as biking, jogging, or stair climbing.

Restrict Fat Intake: To lose fat, you need to first restrict your fat intake. Remember, one gram of fat is about 9-11 calories compared to four calories for every gram of carbohydrate or protein. Also, if you are consuming excess calories from protein and carbohydrates, then they too will be stored as fat.

Below is a list of foods high in fat and low fat substitutes. Many fattening foods are now replaceable with non-fat or low-fat alternatives. They may not taste quiet as good, but are good enough to satisfy your palate. Once you make the change, your taste buds will not recognize the difference. For example, when you substitute skim milk for whole milk, you will not even remember how whole milk tastes. More importantly, you will be restricting your fat intake substantially by making a few changes. For example, by substituting skim milk, fat-free margarine, and fat-free salad dressing, you already cut out about 20 grams of fat! That is 200 calories by three simple and realistic substitutes. The following shows other examples of foods high in fat with good substitues.

Foods high in fat	Substitute
potato chips, nuts	pretzels
butter	jam or all fruit jelly
margarine	fat-free margarine
peanut butter	low fat peanut butter
mayonnaise	low fat or non fat
whole milk	skim milk or 1% milk
cheese	cheese made with skim milk
salad dressing	fat-free dressings
bacon or sausage	lean red meat
french fries	baked potatoes
rich sauces	canned tomatoes
pizza	pizza with no cheese

Eating small, frequent meals will help speed up your metabolism *(Metabolism is how fast and frequent your body burns calories),* but more importantly, you will be eating less. Your body uses small portions of food more efficiently, preventing most of it to be stored as fat.

Consume your calories during the most active times of your day. If you are a nine-to-five person, avoid meals after 8:00 p.m. Most people skip breakfast, eat a quick lunch, eat a huge dinner, and end with late night snack. Eating breakfast immediately jump starts your metabolism in the morning. The lack of eating during the day causes your body's metabolism to shut down, preserving energy and fat rather than burning it. By dinner, you are probably starving and ready to eat a horse. The huge dinner and late night snacking overload your digestive system with food that your body cannot possibly break down and use. Even low-fat foods in large quantities will eventually get stored as fat.

Lifting weights will help increase your muscle density. People with more muscle have an easier time losing fat. Muscle requires more energy than fat for the body to sustain. Fat just lies there getting fatter while muscles use energy and burn calories. A pound of fat contains 3500 calories and burns 2 calories a day to sustain itself. A pound of muscle contains 700 calories and burns 75 calories to sustain itself. There's no guarantee that lifting weights will make you lose fat. You still need to eat right. You do not need to lift heavy weights; use light to moderate weights.

Aerobic exercise is an important catalyst to losing fat, but once again, without the right eating plan it will be difficult regardless of the amount of exercise you do. Exercises such as stair climbing, biking, jogging, and rowing, combined with a good eating and weight lifting plan can prove to be an effective strategy to losing fat. Twenty to thirty minutes of aerobic exercise three times per week is more than enough.

Losing Weight

The formula for losing weight is pretty simple. Calories-in minus calories-out equals weight loss (CI - CO = WL). Eating controls calories-in and exercise controls calories-out. Some people think that working only the second part of the equation, calories out, by exercising, will help them lose weight. WRONG! I don't care if you exercise every day, if you don't control what and how much you put in your body, seeing results will be difficult.

Losing weight doesn't have to mean starving yourself. It requires choosing a reasonable diet that includes eating at least three times per day. It may require decreasing and counting your calories, a similar concept for gaining weight, except you will be decreasing your caloric intake rather than increasing it. Follow the same recommendations discussed early in this chapter for allocating your carbohydrates, protein, and fats to assure proper nutrition.

The most important thing to remember when losing weight is to lose fat and not muscle. Keeping your muscle means eating enough food to develop a shapely body rather than a flimsy one. How much fat you need to lose will determine your plan. If you need to lose 50 pounds, then you will definitely need to decrease your calories. If you are not overweight, but have some excess fat, then you may want to take a different approach. Your goal here is to decrease your body fat, not necessarily lose weight. So before you start depriving yourself of food by decreasing your calories, try the five easy steps to losing fat discussed in this chapter. If you are obese and need to lose a lot of weight, implement both the decrease in calories and the five easy steps to losing fat.

Eat To Build

If you want to build quality muscle, then you have to eat quality food. It is very difficult to build muscle. Gaining weight and building muscle are not the same. You can gain weight and build a minimal amount of muscle, gain very little weight and build a respectable amount of muscle, or you can gain a lot of weight and build a lot of muscle. Eating everything and anything at any time results in weight gain primarily of fat. Eating the right foods at the right time in the right amounts helps build muscle.

In order to gain a lot of weight and a lot of muscle, the same formula mentioned for losing weight applies, but it changes slightly. Calories-in need to be greater than calories out. That means you need to eat more than you are eating now. It doesn't mean to exercise less! You need to eat more of the right foods. You must consume foods rich in complex carbohydrates and restrict simple carbohydrates such as simple sugars and candy. Complex carbohydrates help build muscle; they should make up at least 60% of your caloric intake. My favorite muscle building carbohydrates include, baked potatoes, pasta, and rice. These foods are great to fuel your muscles for hard workouts and are very low in fat and sodium.

Follow my recommendation for protein intake discussed earlier to build muscle. That is to consume 20 to 30% of your calories from protein. My favorite muscle building proteins include chicken, fish, turkey, and small portions of lean, red meat. Red meat has received a bad reputation over the years because of its high fat content. Lean cuts of red meat eaten in small portions can prove to be a crucial nutritional component to building muscle.

The best way to include red meat to your diet is to first go to the supermarket or local butcher. Ask them for the leanest cuts available and to trim off any additional fat. Then have them grind it for you. Season the meat with onion powder, oregano, and other spices. Make patties from the seasoned meat; cook one on the grill and freeze the rest for easy preparation later. Try to limit red meat to once per day and no more than three days per week.

As I mentioned above, to build a lot of muscle you need to increase your calories. That means you need to keep track of your calories. You can't just decide that you are going to eat more and wing it. You need to know how many calories you are taking in now to maintain you current body weight and then need to increase your calories appropriately.

In order to keep track of your caloric intake, you must use a food diary (*see Keeping A Food Diary in this chapter for sample diets to build muscle using a food diary*). Start increasing your calories by 500 for the first week, and see how your body reacts. Depending on how much muscle you want to add to your frame will determine the increase in your calories.

For example, from using your food diary, you know that your average caloric food intake is 2000 calories. If you experience no weight gain after increasing your calories to 2,500, then increase to 3000. If you find that you gained one pound after a week of 3000 thousand calories, then you know you will need 10 weeks to gain 10 pounds.

We have answered the questions of what to eat, total daily calories, and the distribution of those calories. Eating them in the right portions and at the right time are also important when trying to build muscle. For example, if you consume 3000 calories per day, you want to evenly distribute those calories, preferably eating six, 500 calorie meals per day rather than three 1000 calorie meals per day. Eating smaller portions will assure efficient use of those calories. It is very difficult for your body to use 1000 calories of food in one meal. Most of it no matter what the distribution of carbohydrates, protein, and fat, will be stored as fat.

I sometimes ate six or seven times a day. I started with a good size breakfast before my workout that usually included oatmeal or cream of rice with three or four egg whites and one whole egg. After my workout, I usually ate a baked potato or a protein shake. I ate a good size lunch that always included protein and carbohydrates. I included a snack between lunch and dinner, maybe some rice cakes or a can of tuna. Dinner included broiled fish or chicken and sometimes lean, red meat along with a *clean* carbohydrate, usually plain pasta. *(Be sure to see examples at the end of this chapter.)*

Most of the foods I ate were easy to prepare. I didn't like wasting a lot of time preparing food. I frequently used my microwave oven. For example, rather than boil rice and having to wait almost an hour, I used Success® Rice, which is available in microwavable bags. They cook in 10 minutes! I also drank protein shakes, either before or after a workout. I have to admit, the only protein shake that doesn't upset my stomach and tastes great is Met-Rx®. I still love to drink them. I usually mix them with skim milk, a banana, and ice.

Toning

You may not need to lose weight or want to build muscle, but simply tone your muscles. Toning requires decreasing your body fat and lifting light weights. As with losing weight and building muscle, you need to know how many calories you consume daily. This will let you know how many calories you consume to maintain your body weight. If you want to maintain your body weight and tone, you may need to redistribute those calories.

For example, you know that 2000 calories per day maintains your body weight. You calculated that 35% of those calories is from fat and only five percent is from protein and the remainder is from carbohydrates. To tone, you want to decrease your fat intake to 20 to 25% of your total calories and increase your protein to 10 to 15%.

In the end, it all comes down to eating right and working hard in the gym.

Keeping A Food Diary

Whether your goal is to build quality muscle or lose weight, keeping a food diary is essential to helping you attain your goals. I had printed my own version of a food diary. It's actually called the *Exercise Log & Food Diary With Calorie Counter (See back cover of this book for ordering).* In addition to a food diary and calorie counter, it also includes an exercise log for recording your exercise. This can help monitor your progress and plan your workouts. Using this tool serves as a constant reminder of your goals. It will help you make a lifestyle change by being consistent with your eating plan and exercise.

Your food diary should contain the name and the amount of food, the time of consumption, total calories, carbohydrates, protein, and fat of each meal.

In order to gain weight, you need to increase your caloric intake. If you want to lose weight, you either need to decrease your caloric intake, decrease your fat intake, or both.

Before you do any of this, first you need to know how many calories you consume per day and the value of those calories. You also need to know the ratio of carbohydrates, protein, and fat in relation to your total caloric intake. In order to know this, you must write down what you eat.

Using a food diary is part of the planning process discussed in the contest preparation part of this book. A similar plan should be used regardless of your goals.

If you don't plan, then don't plan on reaching your goals. Keeping a log of your daily food intake in a well-organized fashion will prove to be a crucial component to achieving your goals.

By logging your food, you can determine your caloric intake and the distribution of those calories that maintain your current body shape. You then need to modify those calories by redistributing your carbohydrates, protein, and fat. Remember the distribution recommendation discussed in this chapter: 60 to 65% of your calories should come from carbohydrates, 20-25% from protein, and 10 to 15% from fat.

Decrease or increase your calories depending on your goal. For example, if you weigh 140 pounds and your average caloric intake is 2000 calories per day, try decreasing your calories to about 1800 to lose weight. How do you know how much to decrease or increase your calories? Answer: By trial and error. Decrease or increase your calories by 200 per day and see how your body reacts. Everyone is different. Everyone burns calories at a different rate. This is called your metabolic rate, how fast your body burns calories. That is why keeping a food diary is so important. It will chart your calories, carbohydrates, protein, and fat You will know the quantity and quality of food you are consuming. You can then use this information to make the necessary changes to reach your goal. If you find that after a week of decreasing your calories by 200 per day that you lost too much weight, then only decrease by 150. You want to lose about one pound a week. If you are trying to gain weight and find that after two weeks of increasing your calories by 200 per day you haven't gained weight, then increase to 300 calories per day.

Example for Building Muscle:

Using the food diary part of my *Exercise Log & Food Diary*.

Date: 9/15/90
Food Diary

Food	Cal	Carb	Prot	Fat
6:30 Breakfast				
OATmeaL 2serv	210	45	6	4
3 eggwhites 1 whole	160	0	16	6
2 small muffins	250	50	4	4
9:00 AM Snack				
① LaRGE Baked Potato	300	60	6	0
12:00 Lunch				
1 CAN TUNA 6oz	210	0	45	2
1 cup Pasta 2oz	240	48	7	1
w/Broccoli	50	12	0	0
3:00 SNACK				
Oatmeal 2serv	210	45	6	4
Raisins 1 cup	220	50	0	1
5:30 Dinner				
Baked Fish/halibut 6oz	300	0	40	4
Baked Potato	200	50	2	0
7:00 Snack				
Protein Shake	500	34	45	2
6 eggwhites/3 rice cakes	210	50	21	0
TOTAL	3060	444	198	28
Distribution		58%	26%	40%

©1994 Power Writings   Printed in U.S.A.

Summary of Example 1

■ First, notice the distribution of my calories: 58% carbohydrates, 26% protein, and less than 10% fat.

■ This distribution is consistent with what I recommend in this chapter.

- In this example, I consumed 3060 calories, 444 grams of carbohydrates, 198 grams of protein, and only 28 grams of fat.

- The distribution of carbohydrate, protein, and fat as a percentage of total calories is shown below:

1.) Add up total calories: **3060**
(*use a calorie counter and measuring cup*)

2.) Add up total grams of carbohydrates: **444**
Multiply total grams of carbohydrates by 4:
(444 X 4 = 1,776)
Divide the product by total calories:
(1,776 ÷ 3060 = 58%)

3.) Add up total grams of protein: **198**
Multiply total grams of protein by 4: **(198 X 4 = 792)**
Divide product by total calories: **(792 ÷ 3060 = 26%)**

4.) Add up total grams of fat: **28**
Multiply total grams of fat by 10: **(28 X 10 = 280)**
Divide product by total calories: **(280 ÷ 3060 <than 10%)**

- What I simply did was multiply every gram of carbohydrate or protein by four and divide that number by total calories. Multiply every gram of fat by 10 and divide that number by total calories.

- The sum of the percentages should add up to about 100%. It's not exactly 100%, but close enough.

- Note: The proteins from rice, oatmeal and other cereals, hot or cold, are not complete proteins. They don't include the essential amino acids discussed in this chapter.

Example 2 For Building Muscle:

Date: 9/16/90

Food Diary

Food 6:30 AM	Cal	Carb	Prot	Fat
Cream of Rice 3serv	300	69	6	0
6 egg whites	60	—	18	0
9:00 AM SNACK				
3 Ricecakes w/Jelly	150	50	3	0
12:00 Lunch				
2 Chicken Breasts	300	0	45	8
1 Cup of Rice	300	66	8	2
3:00 Snack				
① Baked Potato	200	50	2	0
Protein shake	500	34	45	2
5:00 Dinner				
4oz lean red meaT	300	0	30	10
① Baked Potato	200	50	2	0
① Cup veggies	50	12	0	0
7:00 pm				
PosT Workout				
1 CAN Tuna 6oz	210	0	45	3
1 Cup Pasta plain 2oz	240	48	7	1
TOTAL	2810	379	211	26
Distribution		54%	30%	40%

Example 1 of my food diary during my weight loss goals:

Date: 2/10/90
Food Diary

Food	Cal	Carb	Prot	Fat
5:30 am				
Cream of Rice 2oz	200	50	6	0
1 Banana	100	25	0	0
8:00 am				
6 egg whites	60	0	18	0
3 Ricecakes w/Jelly	150	50	3	0
10:00 am Snack				
3 Carrots	30	7	0	0
12:00 lunch				
Tuna 6oz	210	0	45	3
Oatmeal 2oz	210	45	6	4
2:30 snack				
1oz Rice/veggies	150	32	3	0
4:30 pm				
2 Chicken Breasts	300	0	45	8
Baked Potato	200	50	3	0
7:00				
Baked Fish halibut 6oz	300	0	40	4
1 cup Pasta	240	48	7	1
Total	2150	307	176	20
		57%	33%	10%

Summary of weight loss example 1:

The major difference between my building diet and my weight loss diet is about 1000 calories. I would gradually start decreasing my calories in January for an April contest. In the building stage, I consumed about 4000 calories, gradually decreasing my calories to 3000, and then to 2000 by February. Finally, by March and April, I cut to about 1500 calories a day, losing about one pound per week. You might be wondering why I'm using these examples from my competition days if your goal is not to compete. The answer is that you should be eating and planning similarly as if you were competing. And because it works! You just got to make it work!!

Another difference between this weight loss diet and my building diet is that I'm up earlier. Notice in the diary that my first meal is at 5:30 am rather than 6:30 am. That's because I couldn't wait to get up and eat. I would wake up pretty dam hungry! I was hungrier because of the decrease in calories. Also, as my contest came closer, I was training twice per day, once in the early morning after my first meal and again at night.

My second meal at 8:00 a.m. was after my morning workout. Here I took some time to prepare egg whites. Since I was cutting calories and fat, I excluded one whole egg.

Also, I increased the number of meals from about five or six to about seven or sometimes eight. This really helped jump-start my metabolism. Eating small frequent meals means your body is constantly burning calories and using every calorie efficiently. Also, since I was eating less and was hungrier, adding small meals helped hold me over until lunch or dinner.

Weight Loss Example 2:

Date: 4/1/90

Food Diary

Food	Cal	Carb	Prot	Fat
5:30 AM				
Cream of wheat 3oz	200	50	6	0
8:00 am				
6 egg whites	60	0	18	0
3 Rice cakes	105	21	3	0
10:00 AM SNACK				
1 chicken Breast 3oz	100	0	20	2
1:00 Lunch				
Rice (brown) 1 cup	150	33	4	1
Tuna 6oz in water	210	0	45	3
Fat Free Salad Dressing	50	12	0	0
3:30 snack				
2 Rice cakes	70	14	1	0
5:30pm Dinner				
2 chicken Breasts	300	0	45	8
1 Cup. veggies	100	25	0	0
1 baked Potato	200	50	3	0
7:00 pm Fruit Salad	100	25	0	0
TOTAL	1645	230	145	14
Distribution		56%	35%	7%

©1994 Power Writings Printed in U.S.A.

189

Other tips:

- Be sure to eat tuna in water. This was constant regardless of my stage of training.

- Squeeze as much fat out of chicken as possible after cooking it. I would wrap the cooked chicken in paper towels and squeeze until it was bone dry.

CHAPTER 7

Supplements

Supplements_____

The United States Government has estimated that health supplements make up 10 billion dollars a year in business. Every one is looking for the quick fix. Walk into a health food store to purchase amino acids and vitamins and see 1000 different brands make false claims. There is no significant, scientific evidence that proves vitamin supplements enhance energy, strength, or athletic performance.

Do not get ripped off buying vitamin supplements. Supplements are big business today and companies will charge a premium for them. Do not rely on supplements to build or shape your physique. Remember the basics: train hard, eat right, and get plenty of rest. Trust me, no over-the-counter vitamin or supplement will increase muscle mass or burn fat. Forget about the quick fix and get to work!

If you are consuming quality foods in the right amounts from the four basic food groups, you will not need to spend your money on supplements.

The four basic food groups:

- **Milk group**
- **Meat group:** beef, veal pork, lamb, poultry, fish, and eggs
- **Vegetables and Fruit group:** dark green or deep yellow vegetables, citrus fruit or other vitamin C-rich fruits or vegetables
- **Bread/Cereal group:** whole-grain

The four basic food groups supply all the essential nutrients and vitamins. Vitamins are responsible for general growth and health of the body. They cannot be produced by the body alone. Without them, certain diseases can occur. Research does indicate that the lack of certain vitamins such as the B vitamins, can result in lagging athletic performance.

Vitamins are classified by their water and fat soluble capacities. Water soluble vitamins are not easily retained by the body and must be provided by a well-balanced diet. Fat soluble vitamins are more easily stored in body tissues. Vitamins A, D, E, and K are fat soluble while vitamin C and the B complex vitamins are water soluble.

- Vitamin A
- Vitamin B Complex
- Vitamin C

- Vitamin D
- Vitamin E
- Vitamin K

Vitamin A is mainly responsible for eyesight and healthy skin. It also contributes to healthy teeth and bones.

Vitamin B Complex consists of Vitamins B1, B2, B3, B5, B6, B9, and B12. These are important in the breakdown, absorption, and utilization of complex carbohydrates. They play an important role in growth and normal development. Vegetarians should supplement with B complex vitamins since they are abundant in meats.

B1 *(Thiamin)* is important in the metabolism of carbohydrates. Few foods supply thiamin in concentrated amounts such as pork, organ meats, lean meats, eggs, green leafy vegetables, whole enriched cereals, berries, nuts, and legumes.

B2 *(Riboflavin)* is important in the metabolism of carbohydrates. Sources of riboflavin are organ meats, milk, eggs, green leafy vegetables, whole grains, and legumes.

B3 *(Niacin)* has shown to lower fat and cholesterol in the blood. It's even available by prescription as a cholesterol lowering agent.

B5 *(Pantothenic Acid)* helps the body release energy from carbohydrates, proteins, and fat and helps the body grow.

B6 *(Pyridoxal phosphate)* A recent *(February, 1998)* study published by the *American Heart Association*, showed evidence that vitamin B6 and B9 *(Folic Acid)* play a role in preventing heart disease and strokes. The vitamins showed up at lower levels in people with heart disease and stroke than in healthy people. Those with vitamin B6 deficiencies were nearly twice as likely to develop heart disease and stroke. B6 involves the metabolism of fat and is essential to the synthesis of amino acids. It also helps with the body's immune system. Daily sources of vitamin B6 include meats, fish, bran, whole wheat flour, wheat germ, rice, bananas, carrots, lentils, soybeans, and sunflower seeds.

B9 *(Folic Acid)* is available in leafy green vegetables and liver. It helps form *DNA (gene makers)* and RNA *(follows DNA instructions).* It also helps produce red blood cells. This is a particularly important vitamin for women because it's involved in making babies.

B12 *(Cobalamin)* is a complex cobalt, nitrogen, and phosphorus compound that plays an important role in the synthesis of nucleic acids such as RNA *(see RNA's role in steroids).* Daily sources of B12 are liver, kidney, meats, eggs, fish, milk, and cheese.

Vitamin C *(Ascorbic Acid)* Like Vitamin B, Vitamin C is water-soluble, and is more easily destroyed than any other vitamin. It is responsible for the formation of collagen, the protein that supports many body structures. It also plays an important role in the development of teeth and bones as well as supporting the immune system and muscle recovery. Since the human body cannot store Vitamin C, it is important to consume foods such as: citrus fruits, strawberries, cantaloupe, pineapple, and a variety of green vegetables.

Vitamin D plays a classic role in the development of teeth and bones. Natural sources include: milk, eggs, fish, and liver oil.

Vitamin E: There is no conclusive evidence of what Vitamin E really does in the human body. A deficiency showed changes in blood-making, muscle development, circulation, and in the central nervous system in rats. Food sources include: green leaves, embryos of the seeds of barley, corn, cottonseed, peanuts, rice, soybeans, and wheat. Any claim that Vitamin E enhances your sex life is merely a claim. Read the chapter on Sex and Bodybuilding for more viable information on sex enhancement.

Vitamin K is responsible for blood clotting. The richest sources of Vitamin K are alfalfa and fish livers.

Vitamin Supplements

During the last six weeks of precontest dieting, most bodybuilders eliminate fruit, dairy products, egg wholes, red meat, and cold cereals. These foods are rich in the essential vitamins discussed above, especially vitamin C and B complex. During this time, it is recommended to supplement with a one-a-day vitamin, Vitamin C, and B Complex vitamins.

If you are a vegetarian, you should consult a nutritionist for the right amount of supplementation. The B Complex vitamins mainly found in meats contain nutrients that are essential for normal growth and development.

Chromium Picolinate: Here is a product that you have heard a lot about. It gained national attention from *one* study conducted on young athletes in 1989. The young athletes participated in a weight lifting program, but maintained their normal eating habits. They received 200 micrograms daily of chromium picolinate or a placebo. The chromium picolinate group showed greater gains in muscle and total body weight than the placebo group. The size of the biceps and calves of the chromium group showed a slightly greater increase than the placebo group. And the average body weight increase was about four to five pounds compared to two to three pounds of the placebo group. A greater decrease in body fat was also reported in the chromium group.

First of all, this is one study compared to many other studies that showed no benefits at all! Second, this study was conducted on athletes participating in a vigorous weight lifting program. Of course you will see an increase in muscle mass. The argument of the study is that the athletes given chromium picolinate showed more benefits that the control group. Even still, other factors such as diet, heredity, gender, exercise frequency and intensity, need to be considered. Also, many bodybuilders that have tried this agent have reported no additional muscle building or fat reducing benefits.

On a more positive note, chromium picolinate has shown to improve blood sugar tolerance and reduce blood cholesterol levels.

Creatine: This is yet another product promising unrealistic results. Before we get into that let me explain what creatine is. It's a *naturally* occurring amino acid found in raw meat and fish. Once digested, it gets stored in the skeletal muscles. The first thing I'll say about creatine: If you really think it will help you build muscle, then eat plenty of fish and meat. The only problem is creatine gets reduced by cooking. We can't really say how much of it gets reduced by cooking, but it will depend on how long you cook your food. It's like saying protein from fish and meat gets reduced by cooking, but it doesn't mean you are not getting protein from your cooked food. But companies that sell creatine claim that it is **destroyed** in food when cooked. Obviously they want you to think you can't get creatine from food so that you buy it.

Creatine is known to increase short term, high intensity, exercise performance by delaying muscle fatigue, which can increase the ability to work harder. This can result to better workouts and potentially some muscle gain. But there is no known mechanism of action in creatine that builds muscle. It's not to say that people taking creatine haven't built muscle either, because some studies and athletes working with weights have claimed muscle gains.

In a June 4, 1998 USA TODAY article titled *"1 in 3 sports teams say 'no' to creatine,"* trainers and conditioners for 21 professional sports teams surveyed disapproved the use of creatine for their players. They say that creatine causes muscle cramps, tears, and gastrointestinal problems. However, some athletes and teams say that creatine is safe and helps increase strength and size. A trainer from the Los Angeles Lakers says that it works. He tried it himself during a summer of weightlifting and found that creatine increased his capacity to lift weights. Utah Jazz center, Greg Foster says that creatine helped him increase his strength and size and experiences better energy levels. Other pro athletes using creatine include Mark McGwire of the St. Louis Cardinals, Shannon Sharpe of the Denver Bronco, Mike Piazza of the New York Mets, and others. However, some of these athletes mentioned in the article promote creatine for the marketers of creatine. So we really don't know if they truly experienced gains or just talking up the product for endorsements.

Other evidence suggests that creatine may be advantageous to a bodybuilder interested in "ornamental" muscle development; however, disadvantageous for football players interested in "functional" muscular development. As a result, some professional football teams don't allow its players to use it.

Studies conducted on runners and swimmers to measure exercise performance showed no performance benefits. *(Medical Science Sports Exercise. 1997, Volume 29, No. 2, pp 216-219.)* In the study on swimmers, 20 highly trained national competitors were given either creatine or a placebo. The research did show a weight gain in the creatine group compared to the placebo group, but no performance benefits. Keep in mind, even though the creatine group showed and increase in body weight, it doesn't mean it was necessarily muscle. And also, using only 20 subjects in the study is hardly considered a significant finding either way. When pharmaceutical companies conduct studies on drugs to show whether or not they work, they use thousands of subjects where the findings have to be significantly better than the placebo.

The Food and Drug Administration is reviewing whether creatine was responsible for two people who suffered seizures. The FDA says that much is unknown about creatine and recommend that people use it under a doctor's care.

Even if creatine helps increase your intensity and energy that results to better workouts, you have to continue using it to potentially experience and maintain any benefits. So if you want to spend your money for something that might work, go ahead, because it's not cheap. It costs anywhere between $35 to $50 for a 300 gram package. Companies recommend taking 5 grams four times per day. That's 20 grams per day. So that's enough for 15 days if you take it seven days per week. For a month, it will cost you anywhere from $70 to $80. U.S. Sales of creatine were about $100 million in 1997 and are expected to grow.

My recommendation is to try creatine if you are really curious and have the money to spend. But I still believe that consistently eating right and working hard are the key components to building the best physique possible. Everything else is trivial.

Amino Acids: Do You Really Need Them?

During my years of contest preparation, I did include amino acids after every meal during the last six weeks before my contests. I worried that my decreased caloric intake reduced the amount of protein I was consuming. Although I increased my protein meals to three per day, they were of smaller portions. If I had to do it all over again, I would rely on hard boiled egg whites and chicken slices for supplements.

One ounce of chicken which is equivalent to a small slice, has about seven grams of protein. Why not keep small slices of chicken in your refrigerator and use them for additional supplements? It's much less expensive and more nutritious than any amino acid supplement. You can also keep hard boiled eggs in your refrigerator and use the egg whites as supplements. One egg white has about three grams of protein. You can consume 12 egg whites, which is about 36 grams of protein for less than one dollar. On the other hand, a bottle of 100 tablets of amino acids costs about $30, with each tablet containing about one gram of protein. That same 36 grams of protein will cost you about $11! The irony is that these supplements are made from food, especially eggs.

Read the nutritional information on any bottle of amino acids and notice the recommended consumption: five to seven tablets after every meal. There are usually about 100 cap-sules per bottle that sells anywhere from $25 to $35. You will also notice that five to seven capsules equals about 10 grams of protein. You will eventually consume the entire bottle in less than a week to supplement 100 grams of protein.

Protein Powders

The first question you have to ask yourself is why do you want to include a protein drink in your diet? Is it to supplement protein that you think is lacking in your diet? Is it to gain weight for muscle building goals? Or, is it just a post workout treat? Personally, I just love the way some of them taste. These are all fairly legitimate reasons to want to consume protein drinks, but once again, this can get very expensive. You would have to be consistent in consuming these drinks to gain the benefit. That means spending a lot of money for something that can be easily and very inexpensively accomplished with food.

If you are trying to build muscle and want to consume additional calories and protein, consuming a protein drink with skim milk, and one banana, could add about 500 good calories to your diet. Suppose you are 150 pounds and want to gain 10 pounds. And let's suppose you figured you are currently consuming about 2000 calories a day. So you know that 2000 calories a day maintains your current body weight, but you find it difficult eating more food. Drinking a protein shake can help add 500 calories a day. If you are consistent in drinking these extra 500 calories every day, in addition to your 2000 regular calories, you would possibly gain about one pound per week. Because 3500 calories equals one pound. The math is easy, 500 calories times 7 days equals 3500. So it would take you about 10 weeks to gain ten pounds by simply increasing your calories by 500 per day, assuming everything else remains constant: your food intake and calorie expenditure.

I enjoy drinking MET-Rx, not because of its claims of decreased body fat and increase muscle, I don't believe that part at all, but because it tastes great and doesn't upset my stomach. I love drinking a cold MET-Rx mixed with skim milk, a banana, with crushed ice after a hard workout. Other than

MET-Rx, the only other protein powder I recommend is one that contains 100% egg albumen. Egg albumen is the protein in egg whites. I do not recommend carbohydrate drinks or powders. Besides the fact that they can upset your stomach and cost a fortune, carbohydrates are not usually lacking in the average diet. We usually consume too many carbohydrate meals and not enough protein meals.

CHAPTER 8

Steroids

Steroids

This chapter is to educate you about steroids and their potential effects on your body. I have used venerable sources to compile the best information possible. I have presented the information so that it could be easily understand and to help you make a more educated decision about using steroids rather than playing a game of Russian Roulette.

Before we get into how steroids work, let's define *Anabolic* steroids. The word anabolic simply means building up as apposed to catabolic that means breaking down. Anabolic steroids are manufactured or synthesized derivatives of the male hormone, testosterone. Testosterone has two main functions on the body, the anabolic effect and the androgenic effect.

1. The anabolic effect is responsible for growth, muscular development, and the masculine body contour of the adult male.

2. The androgenic effect stimulates the development of the male secondary characteristics after puberty, causing growth of the beard, pubic hair, development of the penis, and change of voice.

In order to understand how steroids work, you first need a brief lesson in pharmacology. Pharmacology is the study of drugs in your body. It is important for you to know exactly what happens when a drug enters your system to understand the *effects* that drugs have on your body, more specifically, the effects of anabolic steroids.

There are basically two types of effects drugs have on your body, *therapeutic effects* and *nontherapeutic effects*. Therapeutic effects are the intended effects of a drug. Nontherapeutic effects are simply the side effects or the adverse effects. In the case of steroids, the therapeutic effect would be the increase muscle size. The side effects are all the undesirable things that can occur. We will get into all the potential side effects of steroids later. For now, I want to educate you on how they work.

All drugs have their own way of working, or what is called, a *mechanism of action.* Most drugs' mechanisms of action involve drug receptors. Drug receptors are located on cells in your body. To understand this concept, all you need to do is first picture one of your cells and then picture an outlet, like the one on your wall. Now picture several of these outlets, better known as receptor sites, on the cells. These receptor sites or outlets located on or in your cells either trigger or block *biological* activity when stimulated or occupied. Drugs occupy, bind or plug into the outlets to either stimulate or block biological activity.

Biological activity means all the biochemical and physiological activities that normally occur in the body such as your heart rate. It is important to note that drugs do not create effects of their own, they change the biological processes already occurring in the body. For example, you have always had a heart rate, *hopefully*. Some drugs can change your heart rate by either speeding it up or slowing down.

Anabolic steroids work by stimulating the anabolic effect discussed earlier by binding or plugging into protein receptors in or on the cells that help create new proteins in the cells. This increased biological activity is called an increase in Ribonucleic Acid Activity *(RNA Activity).* The construction of new proteins helps increase muscle size and strength. Remember, this normally happens in the body. The steroids stimulate or increase this biological process by binding to the receptor sites on the protein cells.

Just to give you an idea of how other drugs work similarly: Aspirin works or relieves pain by binding to receptors on cells that are responsible for transmitting pain and inflammation. By binding on the pain receptors, aspirin blocks pain and inflammation. On the other hand, aspirin causes stomach upset by also blocking the production of a protective enzyme in the stomach.

A betablocker is a type of blood pressure medication that works by binding to beta receptors on your heart cells that have a direct effect on blood pressure. By binding to the beta receptors on the cells, betablockers prevent the heart from working harder, which helps decrease blood pressure. On the other hand, betablockers sometimes cause fatigue and even impotence by blocking or stimulating other biological activities.

So remember, there is always a tradeoff!

Steroids are also known to increase nitrogen retention, another biological activity. Nitrogen is found in proteins where it plays an important role in the building of tissues. Those who use steroids have been known to have a positive nitrogen balance, a preferred state where intake of nitrogen from proteins is greater than excretion of nitrogen.

Once a drug enters the body, the body begins to process the drug that includes four processes:

1. absorption
2. distribution
3. metabolism
4. excretion

Absorption

Drugs are usually administered either orally or intravenously.

When drugs are administered orally, absorption is much more complex than when administered intravenously. The drug has to bypass a number of barriers before it can get into the blood stream and do its thing. First, it must get past the acid in the stomach. Second, it must over come bacteria in the small intestines. Third, it must survive changes in the small intestines. Finally, it must survive the *metabolism* process in the *liver* known as the **first pass effect**.

During the first pass effect, blood travels to the liver as part of a filtering system where enzymes in the liver metabolize or change part of a drug before it enters the bloodstream. Enzymes are proteins that change drugs in the body and also help biochemical reactions occur as discussed above.

Drugs are absorbed faster when administered intravenously. They enter the blood stream immediately, and aren't *absorbed* like when taken orally. They bypass metabolism in the liver, skipping the first pass effect.

Distribution

The distribution process simply involves the transportation of drug throughout the blood stream.

Metabolism

Metabolism is the chemical change a drug goes through in the body. The major place where this takes place is in the liver. This is where most people run into problems with steroid usage which I will get into shortly.

Excretion

Excretion is simply the removal of drug from the body. The kidneys are responsible for most drug excretion through the urine. Some drugs such as steroids are excreted by the liver. Drugs are also excreted through the breast, skin and lungs. You will see how drug excretion directly relates to the adverse effects of steroids.

Side Effects

The amount of drug that enters the body will determine the two effects we discussed early, the therapeutic effect and the side effect, also called *toxic* effect. Therapeutic effects, the desirable effects, are not always dose related. This means that 400 milligrams of aspirin may work as well as 800 milligrams to cure a headache. A doctor's goal is to administer the lowest effective dose because side effects are dose related: The higher the dose, the greater the side effects. If 400 milligrams of a drug will cure your headache, why take 800 milligrams?

Anabolic steroids are very toxic to the liver where they are metabolized and excreted. You better believe that the side effects from steroids are dose related. There are many bodybuilders who take more steroids than they need to see the desired results. There is no need to take five tablets when one is just as effective.

The biggest risk you take with steroids is damage to the liver. The liver is the most versatile and amazing organ in the body. Every minute, about three pints of blood pass through the liver. At any time, the liver contains about 10% of all the blood in the body. It helps the blood digest food substances and excrete waste materials, toxins, steroids, estrogen, and other hormones. It also stores sugar and glycogen, iron, copper, vitamin A, several of the B vitamins, and Vitamin D and also produces proteins. Without a properly working liver, you are in big trouble!

When steroids, such as Anadrol 50, are taken orally, they need to be detoxified by the liver through the metabolism process discussed above. The liver works harder to eliminate poisonous substances and toxins produced by steroids. As a result, hepatitis or inflammation of the liver can occur. Hepatitis can easily lead to cirrhosis of the liver, a condition of progressive scarring. Cirrhosis is a disease so severe, that it kills all the liver cells, causing liver failure.

Steroids can also disease the heart. The blood carries basically two types of cholesterol, HDL *(high density lipoproteins)* the good cholesterol and LDL *(low density lipoproteins)* the bad cholesterol. The good cholesterol helps get rid of the bad cholesterol. The bad cholesterol is responsible for clogging arteries. Lower levels of HDL and higher levels of LDL directly correlate to heart attacks. Steroids increase the levels of LDL and decrease the levels of HDL. Studies have shown that steroid users have lower levels of HDL and higher levels of LDL.

Another very common side effect related to steroids is gynecomastia, better known as "bitch tits." Gynecomastia is a condition where small tumors develop near the nipple area of the chest, giving a female breast-like appearance. This condition occurs when steroids change to estrogen, the female hormone, during the metabolism process. The higher levels of estrogen enlarge the mammary glands in the male chest. The development of mammary glands in the nipples is regulated by estrogen. Estrogen is secreted in the form of milk by the pituitary gland *(located in the brain)* and is *excreted* via the breast. This condition in steroid users usually requires surgery to correct. It is very painful and can disfigure your chest permanently. Gynecomastia is an indication that steroids are being abused.

Women who take anabolic steroids suffer more from the side effects than men. That's because steroids mimic the male hormone, testosterone, which naturally exists in the male body. It doesn't exist in women. The female hormone is estrogen. If estrogen was injected in men, we would see more changes than if injected in women. Women who abuse steroids experience what is called *virilization.* This means taking on male characteristics such as deepening of the voice, hair growth on the arms, legs, back, and other unusual places.

On the other hand, women experience male pattern baldness. To prevent irreversible changes in women, drug use must be stopped immediately once these changes are first detected. Some of these changes are irreversible even after prompt discontinuance of steroids. Women also experience menstrual irregularities.

Acne is also a very common side effect of steroids and once again more prevalent in women than in men. Since steroids are also excreted through the skin, the result is a high level of bacteria on the skin. This leads to severe acne mainly found on the chest and back. In some cases, the acne results in heavy scar tissue that can leave the skin distorted for life.

Since drugs are also excreted through the lungs, bad breath can also be a side effect. It may not be as serious a side effect as the others, but can prove to be very embarrassing.

Some steroid users justify the use of injectable steroids because they bypass the metabolism process in the liver or the first pass effect discussed earlier. However, even injectable drugs are excreted by the liver where serious damage can occur.

Infections are very common among steroid users who choose to inject. The area of penetration is very susceptible to infection when skin surrounding the point of injection is not clean. Infection occurs when the syringe is not sterile or is reused.

Sterile abscess is yet another common occurrence from injecting. An abscess develops from injecting the syringe in the same spot repeatedly causing a build-up of scar tissue and pus. These abscesses, if not treated properly, grow, get infected, and need to be surgically removed.

Speaking of infections, cases of AIDS have been reported among steroid users who share the same syringes!

Black market steroids pose yet another risk. Many individuals have been arrested for making fake steroids in their basement. The risk here is that you don't know what you are administering in your body. Hopefully it could be only cooking oil, but there have been reported cases of rat poisoning.

Severe muscle tears are very common among steroid users. Steroids quickly enhance muscle mass and strength allowing for individuals to use much heavier weights than before. Tendons and ligaments, tissues that hold muscle to bone, do not strengthen in relation to the muscles, causing them to tear, sometimes off the bone! They just cannot withstand the added pressure from the heavier weights. It is not unusual to hear that someone using steroids increased their bench press by 100 pounds in a matter of two months. This drastic change in strength is too much for the tendons and ligaments to handle. So they tear, sometimes requiring surgery to repair the damage.

A recent study of 284 steroid users showed that over 80% of all side effects were caused by two powerful and highly used steroids, Anadrol and injectable testosterone.

Anadrol-50 (oxymetholone) CIII 50 mg tablets: In the first edition of my book, I wrote that Anadrol was no longer available. That might have been a mistake, because it is available from a company called Unimed Pharmaceuticals. One thing I wasn't mistaken about was its potency and side effects. Anadrol is known as the most powerful oral steroid in the bodybuilding community, but its toxicity is ignored.

Anadrol is an anabolic steroid derived from testosterone. It has both anabolic and androgenic effects. It is indicated for patients with anemia due to deficient red blood cell production. Anemia is not a disease, but rather a symptom of various diseases. Anadrol helps restore red blood cells. It works like most other anabolic steroids by binding to andro-genic receptors on protein cells *(see beginning of this chapter for full explanation of how this leads increase muscle size).* Anadrol like other anabolic agents also improves nitrogen bal-ance which may help with the utilization of protein-building.

The *CIII* after the name means that it is a schedule three drug. The Food and Drug Administration (FDA) schedules drugs based on its abuse or addiction potential. The sched-ule is between I and IV. The lower the number, the higher the potential for abuse. The higher the number the lower the abuse potential. Narcotic drugs such as heroin and hallucino-gens are schedule I drugs. Drugs like antidiarrheals are schedule V.

The warnings, precautions, and adverse reactions fill up most of the package insert. Hepatis, blood-filled cysts on the liver, liver failure, intra-abdominal hemorrhage, liver cell tumors, malignant tumors, blood lipid changes which includes an increase in the low density lipoprotein (bad cholesterol) and a decrease in the high density lipoproteins (good cholesterol).

Some of the precautions include signs of virilization (deepen-ing of the voice, excessive hair growth, acne, enlargement of the clitoris). Its own package insert even states that some of these side effects can be irreversible. The list goes on and on.

The recommended daily dose for children and adults with anemia is 1-5 mg/kg/ body weight per day. The package insert also states that the usual effective dose is 1-2 mg/kg/ day. That means you have to figure out your weight in kilo-grams by converting from pounds to kilograms and then multiplying that number by 1-5 milligrams or 1-2 kilograms. For example, if you weight 150 pounds, you have to divide 150 by 2.2 kg because 1 kilogram equals 2.2 pounds. 150 divided by 2.2 equals 68 kg. Now you have to multiply 68 kg by 1 to 5 mg. Let's use two milligrams as an example. 68 times 2 equals 136 milligrams per day or 3 tablets a day.

The only problem with this example is that there is no usual effective dose for people who decide that they want to use Anadrol for muscle building purposes. I remember people telling me that they saw results with 1 tablet a day. So you are taking a big risk with side effects and the black market. There's always that chance of getting fake drugs. Anadrol is supplied in bottles of 100 white-scored tablets imprinted with 8633 and UNIMED (NDC0051-8633-33).

Testosterone Cypionate is still manufactured by Upjohn and Starr Pharmaceuticals. It's an oil based injectable form of testosterone that is highly androgenic and anabolic and a very effective muscle builder. One common quality among the testosterone drugs is that they retain a lot of water in the body. Those who overuse testosterone have that puffy look especially in the face. A bodybuilder's common dosage is about four ccs per week, two ccs twice per week.

Testosterone Enanthate: The difference between Enanthate and Cypionate is that Enanthate has a longer life and only has to be injected once every 10 to 12 days. Both Cypinonate and Enanthate come in 200 mg/ml 10 cc vials.

Testosterone Propionate is very similar to Cypionate, but does not stay in your system as long as Cypionate.

Testosterone Suspension is a water soluble, powdery-white, injectable. It resembles the drug Winstrol V. Like Winstrol, it is said to be very painful when injected. Because it is water soluble, it is fast acting and does not stay in the body for more than one day leading to more frequent injections.

Below is a description of other common steroids used by bodybuilders and other athletes:

Anavar (oxandrolone): This drug is no longer available. This was once a favorite among steroid users manufactured by Searle. Anavar was popular because of its strength building qualities with minimal side effects. It was very low in androgen levels and known not to promote water retention.

Durabolin (nandrolone phenpropionate) This product is still listed in the *Physician Desk Reference Guide,* but with no information accept that it's supplied in 25 mg/ml-5mL vials and 50mg/ml-2 mL vials. *Deca* was known to be the most commonly used injectable and also the most popular counterfeit steroid in the black market. Deca is known to have low levels of androgen qualities and is considered *safe* among steroid users. It is known as a *cutting up* drug rather than a bulking drug among steroid users. It is also responsible for faster recuperation time between workouts because of its high nitrogen retention qualities.

Dianabol (methandrostenolone) This oral drug was one of the first and most popular muscle building steroid used by bodybuilders and other athletes. It was discontinued years ago. So if you know anyone that claims to have it; it's fake.

Equipoise (boldenone undecylenate) If you remember what the prefix Equi means from your SAT's, then you will know that this injectable steroid is made for horses and ironically used by bodybuilders and other athletes. It is an oil based steroid derived from testosterone with high anabolic and moderate androgen levels. Equipoise is very popular with bodybuilders because of its *cutting up* abilities and low risk of side effects.

Finajet (trembolone) Another oil based veterinarian steroid from Europe. It has very high levels of androgen that can be toxic to the liver and kidneys. Frequent injections of about 1 cc of Finajet are taken by bodybuilders every other day because it is said to be used by the body quickly.

Parabolan (trenbolone) Usually pronounced "power bone" is a French steroid that is popular because it does not convert to estrogen and is known for its cutting and building qualities. Parabolan is an injectable that comes in 76 mg per 1.5 cc ampules.

Winstrol V (stanozolol) is a very popular steroid among bodybuilders known for it's *cutting up* capabilities. Winstrol is still available in tablets and injectable forms by Sanofi Winthrop Pharmaceuticals. It is a synthetic derivative of testosterone.

Winstrol is indicated to decrease the frequency and severity of *angioedema.* This is an attack where skin breaks out in an itchy rash or hives. The package insert includes a black box warning about peliosis hepatis, liver tumors, liver failure and blood lipid changes. The black box warning means patients have experienced these side effects. Peliosis hepatis is a condition when the liver tissue is replaced with blood-filled cysts that has lead to liver failure. The blood lipid changes mean that Winstrol has been found to increase low-density lipoproteins *(the bad cholesterol)* and decrease high-density lipoproteins *(the good cholesterol).*

Growth Hormone

Growth Hormone or *GH* has been another more recent muscle building enhancer with few known side effects used by bodybuilders and other athletes today. Human growth hormone is produced by the pituitary gland. The pituitary gland is located at the base of the brain and is responsible for promoting growth and the functioning of all endocrine glands.

Currently, Eli Lilly, Genetech, and Serono pharmaceuticals, manufacture injectable forms of growth hormone that are therapeutically equivalent to human growth hormone of the pituitary gland. Eli Lilly makes Humatrope (Somatropin). Genetech makes Nutropin (Somatropin) and Protropin (Somatrem). Serono makes another version of (Somatropin) called Serostim. They are all indicated for long-term treatment for children who have growth failure due to an inadequate secretion of normal growth hormone. It stimulates linear and skeletal growth. It is an anabolic and anti-catabolic agent. It also results in an increase in both the number and size of muscle cells. Serostim, is the only one that is indicated for AIDS wasting. That is, patients with AIDS who are wasting away. Their lean body mass burns away, including muscle and organ tissue, instead of fat.

The most common side effects are musculoskeletal discomfort that includes pain, swelling, and or stiffness and swelling of the hands and feet. These side effects are usually mild to moderate, and usually subside when treatment is discontinued.

CHAPTER 9

Alcohol and Bodybuilding

Alcohol and Bodybuilding _____

How many times have you planned to work out a particular morning and couldn't because of a hangover? I'll be honest with you; I've done it several times myself. I enjoyed drinking beer just as much as the regular college student, but when I started competing, it all came to an end.

You are probably wondering how you can go to college and not drink. If you are striving to build the ultimate physique and want to look the best you can, you must then cut down on drinking. I am not saying stop altogether, but try drinking moderately.

If you are looking to compete, then there is no excuse to stop drinking altogether. I would bet most successful bodybuilders do not drink alcohol when preparing for contests. I'm pretty sure most of the college bodybuilders at Rutgers University, stopped drinking to compete in the largest college bodybuilding contest in the country, The Mr. & Ms. Rutgers Bodybuilding Contest *(see Chapter 20)*. Even the ones in fraternities and sororities took a back seat to drinking. You can say we probably had the best incentive to stop drinking: getting on stage in front of thousands of people and a panel of judges critiquing our almost naked physiques. This was our motivating factor. If that won't encourage you to stop drinking, little else I can think of will.

Why should you stop drinking when trying to build muscle or getting in shape?

Drinking alcohol in any form can,

1. increase body fat.
2. wipe out a week of hard training.
3. deplete energy stores.
4. decrease muscular performance.
5. impair temperature regulation

An average drink contains about 15 grams of alcohol that contains about seven calories per gram. A can of beer contains anywhere from 110-160 calories depending on the type. All those calories are empty and stored as fat. A commonly asked question regarding beer is,

"If beer contains no fat how can it get you fat?"

The calories are considered empty because they have little nutritional value. When your body has no use for empty calories, it stores them as fat. You don't necessarily need to consume fat to get fat. If you consume 5000 calories of low fat food a day, you will still get fat because your body has no use for that many calories and stores them as fat.

The other question most commonly asked:

"What about the carbohydrates in beer?"

True, beer contains carbohydrates, but only about seven grams. That makes up only 28 of the approximate 160 calories in a 12 ounce beer. Compare that to a 12 ounce glass of orange juice that contains about 25 grams of carbo-hydrates that makes up all 100 calories.

After a good night of drinking, you can feel the effects the entire week. You feel tired and your stomach hurts. By the time you recover, the weekend has arrived and you are ready to drink again.   Building muscle or getting into shape can prove to be difficult with this type of lifestyle.

Lifting weights requires a tremendous amount of energy. To see any results, you need the proper nutrition *(see Nutrition)*. Not only does alcohol drain your energy stores, but it also inhibits muscle growth and performance.

Alcohol is a sports-inhibiting drug. It is easily absorbed by the stomach and can damage the stomach lining and other surrounding organs. The irritation to the stomach interferes with the absorption of minerals and vitamins. Basically all the healthy food you prepared and ate that particular day went to waste.

The liver works overtime to break down the intoxication agent, ethanol. The extra energy generated by the liver to rid the body of ethanol produces toxic substances that cause tissue damage. This process causes fatty deposits on the liver that can lead to cirrhosis, a deadly liver disease. Ethanol also causes an excess of lactates that lower glucose levels and glycogen stores in the muscles causing extreme fatigue.

Beer As A Sports Drink?

Hardly! Some bodybuilders have taken up drinking beer during and following training sessions for energy and carbo-hydrate stores.

When you finish exercising, the average person needs about 100 grams of carbohydrates to restore glycogen in the muscles within 15 to 30 minutes following the workout. As noted before, the average beer only contains about seven grams of carbohydrates, you would need about 14 beers to restore glycogen stores.

There have been several articles and books written on the importance of replacing water and other nutrients lost during perspiration during an intense workout. Alcohol has the reverse effect. It dehydrates you even more and has a diuretic effect on the kidneys.

CHAPTER 10

Measuring Body Fat

Measuring Body Fat _____

Your body composition is basically made up of lean mass and fat mass. Lean body mass includes your muscles, bones, and internal organs. Fat mass is well, fat.

Although I think using a scale is a common sense approach to measuring weight loss or weight gain, it doesn't measure fat loss or body composition. Even so, I'm willing to bet that if you are overweight, and a scale later shows that you lost 20 pounds, I can guarantee you lost fat.

The most commonsense approach to measuring fat loss is to just look at yourself in the mirror. If you notice that you lost your love handles after working out consistently and eating right then who cares what the scale reads. The optimum thing you want to do is maximize your fat loss and minimize your muscle loss.

Why do we need to measure our body composition if you can simply look in the mirror?

I guess the answer to that question depends on your goals. If you are an athlete or bodybuilder, I still think that the commonsense approach is best. Most likely, you will have so little fat on your body, that you will be able to see if you are losing fat rather than muscle. When I competed in bodybuilding contests, the mirror told me the entire story. But if you just want to fulfill your curiosity and find out approximately how much of your body is fat, then you need a body composition test. To tell you the truth, I was very curious myself and had one performed before I started losing weight for a contest and one when I lost the weight. But I'll tell you more about that later.

If you are obese and losing weight then you want to be sure that most of your weight loss is fat and not muscle. This is a good reason to want a body composition test.

Before we get into the most accurate methods of measuring body fat or body composition, I would first like to define the terms, *overweight* and *obesity*.

Although overweight and obesity are related terms they do differ in meaning. *The Metropolitan Life Insurance Company* tables *(universally used)* define overweight as an excess amount of total body weight whereas obesity refers only to excess body fat. This helps us explain why a muscular person with very little body fat can be overweight, but not obese. For example, during the off season of my bodybuilding career, I consistently weighed well over 200 pounds at only five feet eight inches tall, but I only carried about 12% body fat.

Even though I wasn't obese, I was overweight. Studies show that overweight and obese people die sooner than people who are not. Even though my body fat was only 12%, I still ran a long term health risk. My heart worked much harder at 215 pounds than at my current body weight of 170 pounds.

Obesity has been further defined by the Metropolitan Life Insurance Company based on mortality risk data compiled in the 1950's. People who lived the longest were considered to be in the ideal weight range for a particular height and weight. Based on this data, a new definition defines obesity as *weighing approximately 20% above your ideal body weight.*

There is now a newer calculation to further determine obesity, **body mass index (BMI).** This calculation correlates more closely with total body fat using a person's height and weight. It divides your height in meters squared into your weight in kilograms:

$$BMI = kg/m2$$

If you are like me and hate math and don't want to calculate this formula, then use the following BMI chart that does it for you. A BMI between 20 and 25 is desirable whereas values between 27 and 31 correspond to approximately 20 to 30% above ideal weight respectively.

For simplicity, this BMI chart uses weight in pounds and height in feet and inches.

Body Mass Index (BMI), kg/m²

Table for determining Body Mass Index						
	Height (feet, inches)					
Weight (pounds)	5'0"	5'3"	5'6"	5'9"	6'0"	6'3"
140	27	25	23	21	19	17
150	29	27	24	22	20	19
160	31	28	26	24	22	20
170	33	30	27	25	23	21
180	35	32	29	27	24	22
190	37	34	31	28	26	24
200	39	35	32	30	27	25
210	41	37	34	31	28	26
220	43	39	36	32	30	27
230	45	41	37	34	31	29
240	47	43	39	35	33	30
250	49	44	40	37	34	31

BMI $\geq$ 30kg/m²
Approximately 30%
above ideal weight

BMI $\geq$ 27kg/m²
Approximately 20%
above ideal weight

Let's use me as an example. I currently weigh about 170 pounds and stand about 5'9" tall. *(The chart doesn't include 5'8", my real height, so I just rounded off my height to 5'9".)* If I run my finger down to 170 pounds and across to 5'9" I find my BMI: **25**. This shows that my body weight is in the ideal range. If I was 215 pounds, my BMI would be between 31 and 33. I would then be considered obese, even though I had low body fat.

The BMI method doesn't calculate body fat. It just estimates whether or not you are obese. There are three common methods for calculating body fat or body composition:

- underwater weighing or hydrostatic weighing
- bioelectrical impedance
- skinfolds calipers

As I indicated before, your body composition is made up of lean body mass (muscles, bones, organs) and fat mass. The results of these tests provide you with a number that represents a percentage of your body fat in relation to your body composition. For example, a result that reads 19% body fat, means that 19% of your body consists of fat. The remaining 81% is lean body mass.

Underwater weighing is the most accurate way to measure body fat. You are lowered from a swing into a special water filled tank. Before entering the water, the air in your lungs needs to be exhaled. Your body weight under water is compared to your regular body weight.

The concept here is that because lean body mass is heavier than fat, it sinks while fat floats. With the use of scientific formulas, your body composition is determined. This method is not only expensive, up to $150, but is not easily accessible.

Bioelectrical impedance can also be very accurate if performed properly and it is more accessible. Electrodes are attached to the ankles and wrists for an electrical current to run through your body. The concept here is that electricity runs through lean body mass easier than through fat. Thus, the easier the current runs through the body, the less body fat you have. The machine itself works like a computer and provides you with a printed copy of the results. This method is available at most health clubs for a small fee ranging from $10 to $20 dollars.

I used this method to calculate my body fat before I started dieting for my contest and again a few days prior. On January 8, 1990 I weighed 205 pounds. My body fat was 13% or 26 pounds of fat. I was 87% lean or 179 pounds of lean body mass. On April 11, 1990 I weighed 172 pounds. My body fat was 2% with only 4 pounds of fat. I was 98% lean with 168 pounds of lean body mass. I can't say this is healthy, but necessary for bodybuilding.

The most common method for measuring body fat is with skinfolds calipers. I also used this method to confirm the results of the bioelectrical impedance. This method is performed by pinching and measuring the fat from certain areas on the body. The sum of these pinched sites determines your body fat by scaling them according to sex and age.

The most common sites pinched:
- Back of the triceps
- Below the scapula
- Abdomen, near the naval
- The suprailliac, located above the hip bone
- Chest, between the nipple and shoulder
- The middle of the thigh

The accuracy of this method depends on the person who conducts it, and the calipers. The pinched sites need to be accurately measured. If you use this method, try to have the same evaluator perform the procedure for consistency and accuracy. The calibration of the skinfolds calipers can also determine accuracy as well. If the needle is not set exactly on "0" it will affect the accuracy of the results, similarly as if a scale is not calibrated properly.

A good caliper could cost well over $100. You can buy a pair inexpensively for about $20 with a respectable amount of accuracy. One home testing kit is called, **Accu-Measure**™.

Accu-Measure™ is a simple, inexpensive, and convenient way to measure your body fat. It comes equipped with a durable skinfold caliper, easy to follow instructions, and a body fat interpretation chart. It is simple and accurate because you only need to measure one area of your body, the

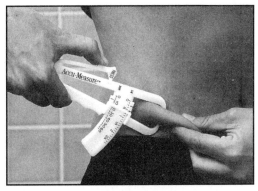

To use the Accu-Measure™*, just grab midpoint of the skinfold right above the hipbone in the gauge.*

suprailliac. Your suprailliac, an area where most of us carry fat, is located about one inch above your hip bone. Other sites measured such as the biceps or the pectorals, do not carry as much fat.

The Accu-Measure™ can be ordered by sending a check or money order for $19.95, plus $3.00 for shipping and handling to:

Power Writings
PO Box 11320
New Brunswick, NJ 08906-11320
Or by visiting my website: www.bodybuildingbyfrank.com (see order form in back of book for more ordering details)

Recommended Body Fat Levels

The following is a list of acceptable body-fat percentages according to National Institute of Health and the American College of Sports Medicine.

General	
Men	*Women*
11-15%	18-25%

Mean Values for Athletes	
Men	*Women*
5-11%	9-18%

Women naturally carry more fat than men primarily for child bearing reasons. They tend to hold most of their fat in their hips and triceps.   Men hold most of their fat right around the waist, like a tube or tire.

Diet is the main determinant of fat. Research has shown that less than two percent of obesity in the United States is linked to dysfunctional glands. Fat is decreased through proper dieting and exercise *(see Nutrition in Chapter 6).*

You can not spot reduce fat on the body. Some people think that exercising a certain area of the body will rid the fat from that area. Unfortunately, that is not possible.   Sit ups and other abdominal exercises will not produce a leaner stomach. It will help firm the muscles, but not the fat.   Fat is not capable of being firmed.   Unless you get rid of the fat around the abdomen, you will not see a wash board stomach.

CHAPTER 11

Aerobics and Bodybuilding

Aerobics and Bodybuilding _____

Not until the last eight to ten years has aerobic exercise been recommended for bodybuilders. The fallacy was aerobic exercise burned muscle away. Of course we now know better. Aerobic exercise can help enhance a bodybuilder's physique by burning fat, not muscle.

Bodybuilders aiming for competition should incorporate some type of aerobic activity year round to help reduce fat during the off season. Thirty minutes, two to three times per week is plenty.

If you need to lose weight before a competition, include aerobics to your training at least three months before the contest. Getting into contest shape can be less of a nightmare by including some type of aerobic exercise as well as eating right during the off season.

The word *aerobic* means with oxygen. Aerobic activity includes rhythmic and continuous exercises using large muscle groups that require the use oxygen. Examples of aerobic activities are, biking, running, brisk walking, rowing, rope jumping, stepping, and others. My favorite aerobic exercise is the stairmaster. I use manual control rather than a variable speed, course. I prefer a steady heart rate between 120 and 150 beats per minute rather than an erratic heart rate.

Warm Up

Every aerobic activity should begin with a warm-up that includes any aerobic activity performed at a low intensity for about five minutes. This allows the body temperature to rise, reducing the risk of injury and permitting your heart rate to increase gradually.

Duration and Frequency

Perform at least 20 to 30 minutes of aerobic activity two to three times per week. Some studies have shown that the body starts to burn fat after 20 minutes. For faster and better results, work up to at least 30 minutes. I think that anything over an hour is too much. If you are not losing fat, then start evaluating your diet. Don't rely on exercise alone to lose fat.

Intensity

Intensity answers the question: *How hard, how fast, or at what level should you be working.* Your heart rate helps measure intensity during aerobic exercise.

Target Heart Rate Zone

Your age and fitness level determine the rate at which your heart should beat during aerobic activity. There are several ways to calculate target heart rate ranges. The Karoven Method is easiest.

Karoven Method for Determining Your Maximum Heart Rate

1. To get the lower end of your range, subtract your age from 220.

$$220 - 26 = 194$$

194 is the maximum heart rate for a 26-year old person, meaning that the heart should never exceed 194 beats per minute.

2. Multiply your maximum heart rate by 65% or .65.

194 x .65 = 126 rounded off

126 beats per minute is the lower end of the range for a 26 year old.

3. Multiply your maximum heart rate by 80% or .80 to get the higher end of your range.

194 x .80 = 155

155 is the higher end of the range for a 26 year old.

The target heart rate range is 126 to 155.

Note: The Karoven Method uses a range of 65% to 85% of a maximum heart rate. A heart rate lower than 65% of your maximum heart rate is not very effective. 85% may be too high, especially if your goal is to burn fat.

In this example, the target heart rate range for a 26 year-old is 126 to 155 *(126 is the lower end of the range and 155 is the higher end of the range).* To find your range, see the conversion chart below.

Your goal determines your target heart rate range. A heart rate at the lower end of your range for a longer duration will help you burn fat. A faster heart rate at the higher end of your range, for a shorter duration will help improve cardiovascular endurance, burning more carbohydrates than fat.

To burn fat, a 26 year-old should train between 130 to 140 beats per minute for at least 30 minutes and a range of a range of 140 to 155 beats per minute to improve cardiovascular endurance. Your target heart rate is also dependent on your current physical condition. Start gradually and be consistent!

Target Heart Rate Zones

Age	65% Low	80% High
20	130	160
25	127	156
30	124	152
35	120	148
40	117	144
45	114	140
50	111	136
55	107	132
60	104	128

Taking Your heart Rate

Heart Rate Conversion *(10 seconds = 1 minute)*

8 = 48	12 = 72	16 = 96	20 = 120	24 = 144
9 = 54	13 = 78	17 = 102	21 = 126	25 = 150
10 = 60	14 = 84	18 = 108	22 = 132	26 = 156
11 = 66	15 = 90	19 = 114	23 = 138	27 = 162

During aerobic activity, find your pulse on either your wrist *(radial pulse)* or on the side of your neck *(carotid pulse)*. If you use your wrist, be sure to use your index and middle finger rather than your thumb. Your thumb has its own pulse and will make your count inaccurate. To take your carotid pulse, find your carotid artery located on each side of your neck, just above the Adam's apple.

Once you have located your pulse, count it for ten seconds and multiply the number of beats by six. This is easier than counting beats for one full minute. For example, suppose you counted 22 beats in 10 seconds. Your heart rate would be about 132 beats per minute. Since you are not counting for the full minute, 132 is only an estimate of your heart rate, but enough to determine where you fall in your range.

Remember, you want to exercise at the lower end of your range to help burn fat. If you work at the higher end of your range, your body will use your immediate sources of energy. Carbohydrates will be used before fat.

If your goal is to build and define your muscles using high intensity weight training, lift weights first and leave aerobics for last. Most of your energy will be needed to get you through high intensity weight workouts.

CHAPTER 12

Training Techniques

Training Techniques_____

Staggered Sets

Staggered sets are my favorite! In addition to adding variety and intensity to your workouts, you also experience cardiovascular benefits as well as you getting through your workouts faster.

What is a staggered set?

Before we answer that question, let's re-define some common gym terminology. A *rep* is how many times you perform an exercise consecutively. For example, let's say you perform 10 pushups consecutively. That is one set of 10 repetitions, or one set of pushups. A set could be anywhere from one repetition, to two, three, four, five.... As long as they are done consecutively. If you perform 10 consecutive pushups, rest, and then perform another 10 reps, that's two sets of ten repetitions. The number of repetitions and sets you perform depends on your goals and fitness level (*see Chapter 1 for more on goals*).

A staggered set is when you perform a set of an exercise for one body part and immediately perform another set of an exercise for another body part. For example, perform a set of 10 repetitions of bench presses for chest and immediately perform a set of ten pullups for the back. That is one staggered set for chest and back respectively.

The essence of a staggered set is that while one body part is working, the other is resting. In the example above, while the chest is working during the set of bench presses, the back is resting and vice versa. This allows you to use maximum weights for each body part. Since the chest is resting while you are performing your pullups, it will be recuperated enough to perform a quality set of bench presses immediately following your set of pullups.

From here, you can perform another two to three bench press/pullup staggered sets. For example, after performing your first staggered set of bench presses and pullups without resting, repeat the process two or three more times. That would be three to four staggered sets of bench presses and pullups.

After completing those three to four staggered sets, go to your next chest/back staggered set. Choose another exercise for chest such as dumbbell incline presses and another exercise for back such as dumbbell one-arm rows.

Perform a set of dumbbell incline presses and immediately perform a set of one-arm rows. Repeat this combination another two or three times.

Let's finish off chest and back with one more combination: Let's choose flat bench flyes for chest and seated rows for back.

At this point of your workout, you should be getting tired, your heart will be racing, sweat should be flowing off your body, and your muscles will be pumped to the max.. KEEP GOING! Only one more round to go. Perform a set of flat bench flyes and immediately perform a set of seated rows. Finish by repeating this process another two or three more times.

In this example, nine to twelve sets are performed for both the chest and back for a total of 18 to 24 grueling sets. Now this may be an ideal workout for me because I have been doing this for many years. It may not be realistic for you.

Once again, the number of sets you perform depends on your goals and fitness level. If you are just starting out, I suggest performing only two staggered sets for each combination. This equals six sets for chest and six sets for back for a total of 12 sets.

For example, perform a set of bench presses and pullups and repeat only one more time. Then perform a set of incline dumbbell presses and immediately perform a set of pullups and repeat only one more time. Then finally perform a set of flat bench flyes and immediately perform a set of seated rows and repeat only once more. Here, you're performing a total of six sets for chest and six sets for back, for a total of 12 sets.

If you move quickly from one exercise to the other, your heart will be racing for the entire workout. So not only do you experience the muscle toning and building benefits, you also experience the aerobic benefits as well. Also, you train two body parts in one workout in a shorter period of time!

Other good staggered set combinations,

- Shoulders and legs (either thighs or hamstrings)
- Back and triceps
- Chest and biceps
- Shoulders and back

Or you can choose a major body part and stagger your sets with abs or calves. For example, perform a set of shoulder presses and then immediately perform a set of crunches for abs.

For best results, prepare a list of exercises to choose from for each body part like the one I prepared on the next page. This will save time during your workouts. Rather than think about what exercise to use during your workout, move quickly from one piece of equipment to the next.

Most importantly, have a contingency plan ready! If you planned to perform bench presses and all the benches are being used, choose an alternate exercise from your list. Do not wait for equipment. Waiting for equipment wastes time and interrupts your intensity. If all the flat benches are being used, then use an incline or decline bench. Better yet, perform dips.

Dips are perfect for staggered sets not to mention their effectiveness for toning and building your chest. You'll never find yourself waiting for the dip station because it's rarely ever used. You don't have to waste time adding or changing weight or looking for clamps or clips to secure the weights. You just walk over to the dip station and do it! Similarly with pullups, a fantastic exercise to develop your back, but yet, most would rather wait to use the lat machine. The pullup station is usually accessible and often includes a variety of grips to choose from.

Prepared List of My Favorite Staggered Set Exercises

Chest
- dips
- flat bench presses
- incline bench presses
- decline bench presses
- flyes (flat, incline, decline)
- cable cross overs
- cable flyes
- pullovers

Back
- pullups
- pull downs
- dumbbell one-arm rows
- bent-over rows
- T-bar rows
- seated rows

Shoulders

- barbell overhead press
- dumbbell overhead press
- barbell upright rows
- front raises
- dumbbell upright rows
- side raises
- reverse flyes (for back of the shoulders)

Triceps

- close grip bench
- french curls
- lying triceps extensions
- pushdowns
- single arm pushdowns
- kick backs

Biceps

- standing barbell curls
- preacher curls
- standing dumbbell curls
- seated dumbbell curls
- concentration curls
- cable curls
- machine curls

Thighs

- squats
- leg presses
- leg extensions
- hack squat
- lunges

Hamstrings

- leg curls
- single leg curls
- stiff leg dead lifts

Calves
- seated calf raises
- standing calf raises
- donkey calf raises

Abdominals
- crunches
- rope crunches
- knee raises
- side crunches
- curlups

Be creative, choose different exercises for each body part and stagger away!

Supersets

A superset is when you complete an exercise for a body part and immediately perform another exercise for the same body part. For example, after completing a set of bench presses for chest, immediately perform a set of dumbbell flyes. This is one superset; two exercises performed for the same body part without a rest.

Supersets differ from staggered sets. A staggered set is when you perform an exercise for one body part and then immediately perform another exercise for a different body part.

I recommend supersetting large muscle groups such as chest, back, shoulders, and legs. I don't recommend supersetting small muscle groups such as biceps, triceps, forearms, and calves. The larger muscle groups can sustain the extra intensity without overtraining them. On the other hand, smaller body parts cannot sustain the intensity and are susceptible to overtraining.

Overtraining simply means that you are doing too much and are not benefiting from the exercises. The biceps and triceps are probably the most overtrained muscles. Not only do most people perform too many sets, but the arms get a lot of work when performing chest, shoulders and back exercises. Six to eight sets is recommended for a good biceps or triceps workout.

Calves are extremely difficult to superset. After performing a set of calf raises, at least a one minute rest is needed before performing another set. They just do not have the endurance to sustain the intensity of supersetting. My experience with trying to superset calves has been severe cramps.

When supersetting, it is important not to perform the same type of movement. For example, dumbbell bench presses and barbell bench presses do not make a good combination. These are considered two "power" movements that tremendously stress the shoulders as well as the chest. Here you can easily overtrain your shoulders preventing good quality sets for chest. Try varying your movements as shown below.

Good chest supersets:

- Dumbbell incline presses with pec-dec flyes
- Dips and barbell decline presses
- Barbell presses and pullovers
- Barbell incline presses and flat bench flyes

In the first example, after performing a set of dumbbell incline presses, immediately perform a set of pec-dec flyes. Same thing with the next example, after performing a set of dips, immediately perform a set of barbell decline presses.

Why superset at all?

Benefits of supersetting include:

- Increased muscle endurance
- Shaping and toning your muscles
- A great aerobic workout as well as muscle tone and strength
- Intensity and variety to your workouts
- Efficient use of time

Performing two exercises consecutively for the same body part will help increase muscle endurance. If you have a problem with muscle fatigue where your muscles give out during a set or early in your workout, supersets can definitely help.

You basically have two types of muscle fibers, fast twitch and slow switch. The fast twitch muscle fibers are more responsible for short duration, bursting and power movements. For example, a sprinter has more fast twitch fibers than slow twitch. Conversely, a marathon runner has more slow twitch than fast twitch muscle fibers. Supersets can help increase your muscle endurance by building your slow switch fibers as well as your fast twitch muscle fibers.

Supersets can also help with shaping and toning your muscles. Pounding a body part with supersets almost shocks the muscle into shape. Bodybuilders like using supersets about one to two months prior to their contests to add more shape their muscles.

Moving from one exercise to the other without a rest is grueling! This will increase your heart rate and add intensity and variety to your workouts. If you continue to perform the exercises without a rest, you will benefit from a great aerobic workout as well as gaining the benefits of toning and shaping.

Your heart rate should be anywhere from 120-150 beats per minute for most of your workout. This will answers the question, HOW HARD ARE YOU WORKING?

Supersets are also a great way to break out of that same old routine. You can look forward to trying something new with your workouts. Pick a body part, select some exercises and superset!

If you are in a rush and want to get a quick workout for a body part, then supersets are the way to go. You can realistically train any body part in 20 minutes with supersets by performing six to nine supersets.

Let's take an example using the following leg supersets:

Leg Supersets

- Squats with leg extensions
- Leg press with lunges
- Lying Leg curls with standing single leg curl

Perform a set of squats and immediately perform a set of leg extensions. That is one superset. Repeat this combination two more times for a total of three supersets. Then go to leg presses and superset them with lunges. Repeat this two more times. Then finish with three more supersets of lying leg curls with standing single leg curls for a total of nine supersets.

If you ever want to physically challenge yourself, then try supersetting legs! Leg exercises such as squats alone require a tremendous amount of energy. Supersetting squats with leg extensions can prove to be quite an experience.

Once again, choose good combinations such as the ones I provided. Supersetting squats with leg presses would not be considered a good combination. These are two "power" exercises that require a lot of energy and also stress the lower back.

Below are good supersets combinations for the rest of the body:

Back Supersets:

- Pulldowns with dumbbell one-arm rows
- T-bar rows with cable one-arms rows
- Pullups with seated rows

When supersetting back, try to use combinations that will not stress the lower back. For example, you would not want to superset bent-over rows with seated rows. Both exercises put a tremendous amount of stress on the lower back. This could easily lead to injury.

Shoulder Supersets

- Upright rows with dumbbell lateral raises
- Barbell overhead press with reverse flyes
- Dumbbell overhead press with cable upright rows

How many sets and reps with supersets?

When supersetting, you really don't have a choice of how many reps to complete. Since you are performing continuous exercises for the same body part without a rest, your muscles will fatigue much faster than performing a regular set with a rest. In that case, you should perform repetitions to failure, until you can't do anymore.

Perform a range of six to twelve supersets for any large body part. As we discuss earlier, the total number of sets you perform will depend on your goals and fitness level. If you decide to perform a total of nine supersets for a body part, then the leg workout explained on the previous page is a perfect example.

You can reasonably perform a total of 12 supersets in the leg workout by performing one extra superset for each combination:

- Superset squats and leg extensions four times rather than three.
- Superset leg presses and lunges four times.
- Superset leg curls and standing single leg curls four times for a total of 12 supersets.

Or you can add another two leg exercises and perform that combination three times. For example, you can superset hack squats with leg extensions with your toes pointed out.

You do not need to use supersets for your entire workout. You may decide that you will only superset the first two exercises for a body part and then perform regular sets for the remaining exercises. For example perform a set of overhead press and then superset lateral raises for shoulders. After repeating this combination three times or for three supersets, perform three regular sets of upright rows and then three regular sets of reverse flyes.

Before you start your workout, you should know what exercises to perform for your supersets. This will avoid delays between exercises. You shouldn't have to think about what your next exercise will be. If you need to log the exercises you plan to perform, then write a plan prior to your workout and bring it with you.

Also, have a contingency plan ready as well. If you planned to superset lat pulldowns with one- arm rows and the lat pulldown machine is being used, have an alternate exercise in mind. Don't wait for equipment. Keep moving through your workout without delays.

Strip Sets

A strip set is when you perform a set of repetitions with a heavy weight and then immediately decrease to a moderate weight performing additional repetitions. You can continue stripping weights and performing additional repetitions to failure

For example, perform a set of bench press with a heavy weight, then immediately lower the weight and perform additional repetitions, then immediately lower the weight again and perform one more "mini-set" of repetitions. A "mini-set" is one of the small sets you perform during strip sets. In the example above, there are three mini-sets performed, one with the heavy weight, one with the moderate weight, and one with the light weight.

The concept is to perform continuous repetitions by *stripping* or lowering the weight. Since the muscles fatigue when performing each "mini-set," you need to strip the weight to allow you to continue performing repetitions. The time it takes to strip the weight is the only time you get to rest. Stripping the weight should only take about one or two seconds.

The last "mini-set" should be performed to failure, where you can't do anymore. The second "mini-set" should be performed almost to failure. You don't want to perform the first and second "mini-sets" to failure because you still need enough energy to perform the last "mini-set."

How many repetitions?

When performing strip sets, I usually perform at least four to six repetitions each time I strip the weight. For example, perform six repetitions of bench presses, lower the weight, then perform six more, lower the weight and perform a final six repetitions or to failure, which ever comes first.

How Much Weight Should You Use?

In the definition of a strip set, I state to start with a heavy weight, however, not too heavy where you can't perform at least four to six repetitions. Choose a weight that you could regularly perform 8-10 repetitions. For example, I can perform a set of bench presses with 225 pounds 10 times. The tenth repetition is usually a struggle. For me, this would be a good weight to start my first six repetitions, or mini-set.

Why not perform all 10 repetitions?

Because I don't want to burn myself out. I still have two more mini-sets to perform. If you can't perform at least four repetitions, then the weight you are starting with is too heavy. If you can barely perform four repetitions, the weight is still too heavy.

After performing my set of six repetitions with 225 pounds, I usually strip down to 185 and perform another six, and then strip the weight down to about 155 pounds and complete my last "mini-set."

How much weight should you drop each time you strip the weight?

This will be a matter of trial and error. Remember, you want to perform at least four to six repetitions each time you strip the weight. I found that stripping from 225 pounds to 185 pounds to 155 pounds works for me. You need to find out what works for you. Very important, although you would be able to perform more than six repetitions during your first "mini-set" you should not be able to perform more than six repetitions during your second and last "mini-set." Actually, the last "mini-set" should be done to failure. For example, after I strip from 185 pounds to 155 pounds, I should continue performing repetitions with 155 pounds until I can't do anymore. Remember, I stated at least four to six repetitions.

That's the whole idea, to burn the muscle to failure! If you find that you can perform a lot more than six repetitions, then you stripped too much weight off.

Tips when performing strip sets

I usually strip set during the last set of an exercise. For example, if I planned to perform a total of four sets of bench presses, I would perform the strip sets on the forth set. For example, let's assume I use 225 pounds for my last set of bench presses. After performing six repetitions with this weight, I would then strip the weight to 185 pounds and then to 155 pounds as explained above.

Why wait until the last set?

Because if I strip set during my first set of bench presses, my chest would be too fatigued to finish my last three sets. I like to perform my first three sets with fairly heavy weight. Trying to perform heavy bench presses after strip sets would be almost impossible.

Use a spotter to strip the weight for you.

You want to perform strip sets immediately. If you have to get up and switch the weight yourself, too much time may elapse, allowing your muscles time to recuperate. This defeats the whole purpose. Also, it's easier if someone else does it for you.

For example, let's assume you want to perform strip sets with leg presses. In this case, you would have to get up off the leg press, take the weight off each side, sit back down, perform a second *mini-set*, get up again, take the weight off each side again, sit back down and perform your last set. This kind of takes the fun out of it. It's too much work. It's great to have someone standing over you waiting for your instructions to strip.

Allow about two to three inches between the plates on the bar.

Stripping the weight should be done quickly and easily. Leave a couple of inches between the plates to make it easier to take the weights off as shown above.

Use weights that will easily allow you to strip immediately.

In my bench press example above, I would not use two 45 pound plates on each side to equal 225 pounds. *(Most bars weigh 45 pounds. Two 45 pounds plates on each side plus the bar equals 225 pounds.)* Think about it. I would need to take one 45 pound plate off each side and still add a 25 pound plate to each side to equal 185 pounds. Instead, I use four 25 pound plates on each side. This adds up to a little more than 225 pounds, but as long as I could still perform at least four to six repetitions, the weight is OK.

Six repetitions is my personal preference. If I could only perform four or five repetitions during my last mini-set, then no big deal. It's still an intense set! Remember, you can bend the rules; nothing is written in stone.

For extra intensity, strip for more than three mini-sets.

Stripping the weight twice and performing three mini-sets is the example used throughout this chapter. I sometimes strip the weights performing anywhere from four to five mini-sets. For example, the leg press is my favorite piece of equipment to strip set with. For my last set of leg presses I will have about seven 45 pound plates on each side. I usually strip one plate off each side after each mini-set.

- I start with seven plates on each side.
- Perform four to six repetitions.
- Strip until there are six plates on each side.
- Perform another four to six repetitions.
- Strip until five plates remain on each side.
- Perform another four to six reps.
- Finally strip another plate off each side and perform my last four to six repetitions.

This is a total of four mini-sets.

My favorite exercises for strip sets:

- Leg Presses
- Squats
- Bench Presses
- Flyes
- Dips with weight
- Upright Rows
- Seated Rows
- Preacher Curls
- Pushdowns

Forced Reps

Forced reps are performed using very heavy weights that require the use of a competent spotter. Your goal is to perform about four to six reps using a weight close to your maximum for that particular exercise. For example, suppose your bench press maximum is 225 pounds, where you can perform 225 one time only. Load the bar with about 250 pounds and have a spotter help you to perform four to six repetitions. The spotter should be competent because you will be using heavier weights than usual. You want to be sure your spotter is experienced and strong enough to assist you to perform the forced reps.

Forced reps are great for breaking out of your strength slump. Every one reaches a plateau, where you find that your strength has not increased in months. Forced reps can help you break out of that slump by shocking the muscles by introducing them to a foreign weight. The only way your muscles will ever be able to lift a heavier weight is for them to experience it. Your muscles, joints, tendons, and ligaments have to adapt to the heavier weight; they adapt by growing and getting stronger.

How Often Should You Perform Forced Reps?

Forced Reps should be seldomly performed *(a maximum of once per month)*. Using extraordinary heavy weights can increase your risk of injury. You do not want to expose your body to that type of stress too often.

Recommended Exercises For Forced Reps

- Barbell Bench Press
- Weighted Chins *(pullups)*
- Overhead Press
- Barbell Curls
- Lat Pulldowns

With Barbell Curls, be sure to maintain good form. You can cheat slightly, but not where you break your form completely over arching the lower back and risking injury.

When performing Forced Reps, you want to slowly lower the weight and gain the benefits of negative movements. The negative movement I feel is just as important as the positive when trying to build muscle.

Negatives

Negatives are similar to forced reps because heavy weights are used and a spotter is needed. Negatives differ from forced reps because little effort is used when performing the positive movement and most of your effort is focused on the negative or eccentric movement. For example, when performing negatives on the bench press, lower the weight slowly to your chest taking about four to six seconds to lower the weight. Once you reach your chest, have your spotter pull the weight off your chest with minimal effort from you. Once again, be sure to use an experienced and competent spotter because he or she will be lifting most of the weight during the positive movement.

You want to use a weight that allows you and your spotter to perform sets of about four to six repetitions. The last repetition should be performed where you cannot prevent the weight from coming down slowly.

Most negative movements will involve lowering the weight. There are few exercises where the negative movement will be elevating the weight slowly. One is the lat pulldown. The positive movement is pulling the weight to your chest while the negative is lowering it slowly. The major difference between negative and positive movements is that the muscle elongates during the eccentric movement and contracts during the positive movement. For example, during a biceps curl, the biceps contract when curling the bar and elongate when lowering it.

Negatives are equally important as positives for muscle strength and size. Experiments on negative training have shown tremendous strength increases. The theory is based on mass and friction. Anything that has mass produces friction including muscle mass. During muscle contraction, friction is produced on the positive motion, against external force, gravity and weight, increasing strength in the muscles. During the negative movement when the muscles elongate, internal friction is produced within the muscles producing more strength.

Negatives can be performed for any weightlifting exercises. The following are my favorites:

Chest
bench presses
flyes

Back
pullups
lat pulldowns

Shoulders
behind-the-neck military press
lateral raises

Biceps
barbell curls
preacher curls

Quadriceps
leg extensions
leg press

Hamstrings
leg curls

Calves
standing calf raises

Note:
Negatives are not effective for triceps exercises because they involve short range of motions.

Antagonistic Training

Antagonistic Training is when you perform an exercise for a particular body part and then perform another exercise with the same movement, but with the opposite resistance.   For example, a lat pulldown can be performed by PULLING the bar behind your head.   An antagonistic movement is behind-the-neck military press by PUSHING the weight from behind your head.   You can be creative by performing any exercise and performing an antagonistic movement for it.   Below are some examples listed by body part.

Antagonist Exercises by Body Part

Chest/Back
bench press/bent-over row

Chest /Rear Deltoids
flyes/ reverse flyes

Back/Shoulders
pulldown behind neck/ behind-the-neck military press
pulldown in front/ dumbbell Arnold presses
stiff-arm pulldown/ front raises

Stiff-arm pulldown is exactly what is says it is: pulling a bar down from a lat machine or cable machine with your arms completely locked or stiff utilizing the back muscles (see Chapter 16, Precontest Training for photo and form).

Biceps/Triceps
barbell biceps curls/ triceps pushdowns
dumbbell biceps curls/ single arm pushdowns

Quadriceps/Hamstrings
leg extensions/ leg curls

Abs/Lower back
situps/ back raises or hyperextension

A total body workout can be performed using this training technique. Be sure to include the entire body by using the examples above. For example, start with a chest exercise, *flyes*, when finished with flyes, perform an antagonistic movement, *reverse flyes* for shoulders. For back, perform a *lat pulldown*. An antagonist movement is *behind-the-neck military press*. For triceps, perform a triceps pushdown and then a biceps curl for the antagonist movement. For abs, perform a *crunch* and then a *back raise* for the lower back.

You can be creative. For example, what can be an antagonistic exercise for a seated row? Think about it, *seated pushing*, if your gym has a seated bench press, then that would be the antagonistic movement. You may find that there isn't always an antagonistic movement for every exercise. But anything close will work.

CHAPTER 13

High Intensity Workouts for Advanced Bodybuilders

High Intensity Workouts for
Advanced Bodybuilders _____

This chapter includes examples of my high intensity workouts. When using these workouts, try to train one body part a day. Since the workouts are so intense, you want to focus all your energy on one body part.

Quadriceps Training

I usually train quads on a different day than hamstrings and calves because the quads require a tremendous amount of energy.

On the following pages you will find some of my intense leg workouts that I used religiously during contest preparation.

High Intensity Quad Workout #1

Exercise	Weight	Reps	Sets
Front squat	135	20	1
	185	20	1
	225	15	1
	275	10	1
(superset)			
Leg extension	100	12	4
(strip set)			
Front squat	275	6	1
	225	6	1
	185	6	1
	136	6	1
(strip set)			
Leg extension	150	6	1
	100	6	1
	75	6	1
Leg press	5 plates	15	1
	6 plates	15	1
	7 plates	10	1
	8 plates	10	1
(strip set)	8 plates	6	1
	7 plates	6	1
	6 plates	6	1
	5 plates	6	1
Hack squats	2 plates	12	1
	3 plates	12	1
	4 plates	8	1
	5 plates	6	1
(strip set)	5 plates	6	1
	4 plates	6	1
	3 plates	6	1
	2 plates	6	1
Lunges	95	20	1
	105	16	1
	125	12	1

Recap High Intensity Quad Workout #1

This is an extremely intense workout that not many people can withstand. Notice the high reps in both of the workouts. When trying to build and define the legs, you have to train them with an almost frightful intensity. You can add intensity by adding weight, increasing reps and sets, using various training techniques, or moving through the workout quickly. This particular workout includes all of the above. You may think that I perform too many sets, but judging from my leg development, I would say not. Some of you may need to build up to this intensity level. Remember, you do not want to injure yourself.

- I started with four sets of front squats supersetted with leg extensions.

- The last grueling set of front squats was stripped.

- Leg extensions were completed with three strip sets immediately following the front squat strip set.

- Immediately after leg extensions, four sets of leg presses are performed with about one minute and a half rest between sets. The last set is also stripped.

- Four sets of Hack Squats have my Quads burning beyond belief. I then finish Hack Squats with the last grueling strip set of my leg workout.

- Lunges are a great way to finish a leg workout. Here I perform three sets of light stationary squats.

High Intensity Quad Workout #2

Exercise	Weight	Reps	Sets
Squats	135	20	1
	225	20	1
	275	20	1
	315	15	1
	225	15	1
Leg presses	5 plates	15	1
	6 plates	15	1
	7 plates	10	1
	8 plates	8	1
Hack squats	2 plates	15	1
	3 plates	15	1
	4 plates	12	1
	5 plates	6	1
Travel lunges	135	1	
	155	1	
	185	1	
	225	1	

Recap High Intensity Quad Workout #2

Start with five sets of regular squats with the bar behind your neck. If you are working with a partner, immediately begin your sets upon completion of your partner's. Complete four sets of leg presses and hack squats, and finish with four sets of travel lunges across the gym floor. Be sure to make room for the travel lunges so that you do not bump into equipment. Both of these workouts can be performed for building or defining purposes.

Hamstring Training

High Intensity Hamstring Workout

Exercise	Weight	Reps	Sets
Leg curl	70	15	1
	100	10	1
	110	8	1
	90	10	1
(superset with stiff-leg deadlifts)			
Stiff-leg deadlifts	95	15	1
	135	12	3
Single leg curls	40	15	1
	50	12	1
	55	10	1
	40	15	1

■ For Hamstrings, you can perform standing single hamstring curls on a machine that a good bodybuilding gym provides.

■ After supersetting four sets of leg curls with four sets of stiff-leg dead lifts, go straight to leg curls. Try using a spotter to squeeze out those last few reps of leg curls.

Calf Training

High Intensity Calf Workout #1

Exercise	Weight	Reps	Sets
Donkey calf raises	people	20	4
Standing calf raises	200	15	1
	220	15	1
	250	10	1
Seated calf raises	2 plates	20	1
	3 plates	15	1
	4 plates	12	1

High Intensity Calf Workout #2

Exercise	Weight	Reps	Sets
Standing calf raises	150	20	1
	200	15	1 *(toes in)*
	250	12	1 *(toes out)*
	280	10	1 *(toes straight)*
Single leg calf raises	40	15	1 *(holding a DB)*
	50	12	1
	55	10	1
Seated calf raises	2 plates	20	1 *(toes in)*
	3 plates	15	1 *(toes out)*
	4 plates	12	1 *(toes straight)*

Chest Training

High Intensity Chest Workout #1

Exercise	Weight	Reps	Sets
Bench press	135	10	1
	225	10	1
	275	8	1
	315	8	1
	365	6	1
DB incline press	100	10	1
	110	10	1
	120	8	1
	130	4	1
Weighted dips	45	10	1
	90	8	1
	135	6	1
	90	8	1
DB flyes	45	10	
	50	10	
	55	10	

High Intensity Chest Workout #2

Exercise	Weight	Reps	Sets
Barbell incline	135	10	1
press	225	10	1
	275	6	1
	315	4	1
Weighted dips	1 plate	10	1
	2 plates	10	1
	3 plates	8	1
	4 plates	4	1
	3 plates	6	1
	2 plates	8	1
	1 plates	6	1
Flyes superset with pullovers	45	10	3
DB flyes	75	10	3

Biceps Training

High Intensity Biceps Workout #1

Exercise	Weight	Reps	Sets
Straight bar curls	95	10	1
	105	10	1
	115	8	1
	125	6	1
	135	6	1
Preacher curls	65	10	1
	85	10	1
	105	8	1
DB curls	35	10	1
	45	10	1

High Intensity Biceps Workout #2

Exercise	Weight	Reps	Sets
Standing DB curls	50	10 each	1
	60	8 each	1
	45	12 each	1
Preacher curls	65	10	1
	85	10	1
	105	8	1
Barbell curls (light bars)	85	15	1*
	65	15	1*
	55	15	1*

* Little rest between sets

Back Training for Upper Back and Lats

High Intensity Back Workout #1			
Exercise	*Weight*	*Reps*	*Sets*
Weighted	no wt.	12	1
pullups	25	10	1
	45	10	1
	55	10	1
	25	10	1
	no wt.	10	1
Bentover rows	135	10	1
	185	10	1
	225	10	1
	185	10	1
Seated rows	170	10	1
	190	10	1
	200	10	1
	210	10	1

Weighted pullups can be performed with either dumbbells or plates suspended from a weight belt.

Back Training for Traps and Lower Back

High Intensity Back Workout #2			
Exercise	*Weight*	*Reps*	*Sets*
Deadlifts	135	10	1
	225	10	1
	275	8	1
	315	6	1
	365	4	1
Barbell shrugs	135	10	1
	225	10	1
	275	10	1
	315	10	1
	365	10	1
DB shrugs	75	10	1
	100	10	1
	110	10	1
	120	10	1
Back raises with weight	20	15	1
	25	15	1
	45	12	2
	no wt.	20	1

Note:

Back has always been a weakness for me, so I tried to get both of these workouts in the same week spread out as far as possible.

Shoulder Training

High Intensity Shoulder Workout #1

Exercise	Weight	Reps	Sets
Behind-the-neck	95	10	1
military press	135	10	1
	185	10	1
	205	6	1
	225	4	1
Upright rows	135	10	1
	155	10	1
	165	8	1
	175	6	1
DB lateral raise	25	10	1
	30	10	1
	35	10	1
	25	10	1

High Intensity Shoulder Workout #2

Exercise	Weight	Reps	Sets	
Standing barbell	135	10	1	
presses to the front	185	8	1	
	205	6	1	
	225	4	1	
DB Arnold presses	75	10	1	
	85	10	1	
	100	8	1	
Reverse Flyes	30	10	4	superset
superset with				
cable upright rows	150	10	4	

Triceps Training

High Intensity Triceps Workout #1

Exercise	Weight	Reps	Sets
Close-grip bench	185	10	1
	225	8	1
	275	4	1
French curls	65	10	1
	85	10	1
	100	8	1
	110	6	1
DB triceps	25	10	1
extensions	30	10	1

High Intensity Triceps Workout #2

Exercise	Weight	Reps	Sets
French curls	80	10	1
with one DB	100	8	1
overhead	100	6	1
Dips (between two	2 plates	12	1
benches w/ weight	3 plates	10	1
on your lap)	4 plates	8	1
strip	3 plates	6	1
	2 plates	4	1
	1 plates	4	1
Pushdowns	150	10	1
	160	10	1
	160	10	1
strip	130	10	1
	110	8	1
	100	6	1

Summary

- Even though I suggest no more than 12 sets per body part I sometimes perform well over that. Once again, your level of bodybuilding will determine how many total sets you should perform. I considered myself an advanced bodybuilder where my muscles could easily handle the additional sets and intensity.

- On my last set of a particular exercise, I usually perform a light set to finish with "perfect" form. I like to contract the muscle hard, holding and squeezing for almost a full second.

- I do not count my warm-up sets as full sets. I only account sets where I exert myself. For example, for weighted pullups, my warm-up set is without weight and with squats, my warm-up set is with 135. Both of these warm-up sets I perform with ease, so I do not count them.

CHAPTER 14

Overtraining and Injuries

Overtraining and Injuries_____

Overtraining

There are several ways to overtrain: training too many days
per week, performing too many sets for certain body parts,
training a body part too many times per week, or training too
many body parts per workout. However you overtrain, it can
lead to injury and other undesirable results.

The most overtrained muscle groups are chest and biceps.
One problem with overtraining chest is that other muscle
groups are neglected. For example, performing 15 to 20
sets of chest two to three times per week is overtraining. As
a result, the chest overpowers the rest of the physique causing an imbalance of strength and muscle size. This imbalance, quite noticeable on young bodybuilders is known as
forward head rounded shoulder. This is where the shoulders
slouch and *round-off* in the front, giving that *gorilla* look. Not
only is it unappealing, it also causes irreversible postural
problems.

The biceps are a very small muscle group that do not need to
be worked frequently with multiple sets to grow. Too many
people perform 12 or more sets of biceps three or four times
per week. That's too much! Train biceps once a week performing six to eight sets. Vary your exercises with preacher,
barbell, and dumbbell curls. Remember that even though you
don't train biceps directly, that they still work hard when
working other body parts. For example, the biceps work
when performing back and shoulder exercises such as
pullups, bent-over rows, seated rows, and upright rows.

The problem with overtraining a small muscle group or any
muscle group with too many sets and frequency, is that the
muscles don't have time to recover. Muscles actually tear
when you lift. The soreness you feel following a workout is a

result of tiny tears in the muscles. If you do not allow proper time for these tears to rebuild, you will continuously break down the muscle fibers and interrupt the growth process. I don't recommend total body workouts for those looking to increase muscle size. Using heavy weights and performing multiple sets for each body part in one workout can lead to overtraining and injury. The body is not capable of with-standing that type of wear and tear on the muscles, tendons, and joints. Total body workouts are recommended for those who just want to firm up using light weights and performing very few sets for each body part.

You can also overtrain certain muscle groups by the way you group them. For example, I don't recommend training chest and shoulders on the same day. As mentioned before, the chest requires a lot of work from the shoulders, especially during bench presses. Training shoulders immediately follow-ing chest would be difficult.

You may want to reconsider training back and biceps or chest and triceps in the same workout. The biceps work hard when training back, and the tries perform a lot of pushing for the chest. In both cases, the biceps and triceps can be easily overtrained. *(See Chapters 2 & 4 for more on grouping body parts.)*

Shoulder Injuries

Another problem with overtraining the chest is the risk of shoulder injuries. How many times do you see young body-builders grab their shoulder after a set of bench presses? It could very well be those 15 to 20 sets of chest three times per week.

In order to fully comprehend shoulder injuries, you need a basic understanding of the shoulder joint and the muscles surrounding it.

Muscles surrounding the shoulder:

The rotator cuff muscles: Most people think of the rotator cuff as some type of object or *cuff* imbedded somewhere in the shoulder. The rotator cuff consists of four muscles beneath the scapula where most lifting related injuries occur.

- Supraspinatus
- Teres Minor
- Infraspinatus
- Subscapularis

Any injury to the rotator cuff muscles results in restricted shoulder movements. Movements away and to the side of the body such as a lateral raise, or overhead movements such as a military press will commonly cause pain.

The supraspinatus, infraspinatus, and the teres minor, are known as the *SIT* muscles of the rotator cuff because they sit directly on top of each other.

The **supraspinatus** runs directly under and straight through the acromion *(a bone on the top of the scapula.)* Picture a long hose fitting tightly through a small bridge. The arc of the bridge would be the acromion and the floor of the bridge would be the humerus. The supraspinatus is the hose that fits tightly through the bridge, not allowing much room for

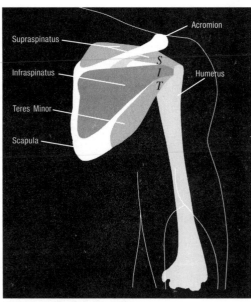

Rotator cuff, posterior view

inflammation. The location of this muscle is **very important** in understanding shoulder pain because the supraspinatus is the

278

most commonly injured muscle of the rotator cuff. Inflammation of the supraspinatus muscle and tendon is the single most common cause of shoulder pain.

The **infraspinatus** lies behind the supraspinatus. The **teres minor** lies directly behind both the supraspinatus and infraspinatus. The **subscapularis** lies in front of the shoulder and is the only one of the four rotator cuff muscles not capable of being physically touched through the skin.

The other more obvious muscles are the deltoid muscles, the anterior, medial, and posterior heads, or simply, the front, side, and back of the shoulder (*see shoulder diagram in Chapter 3*). These muscles usually don't get injured. They help stabilize the shoulder joint. That's why it is important to work all three heads of the shoulder.

Tendinitis

Tendinitis is chronic irritation and inflammation of the supraspinatus caused by continuous trauma that eventually leads to impingement.

Impingement

Impingement occurs when the supraspinatus gets so inflamed that it reduces the space for it to pass underneath the anterior edge of the acromion. Remember the analogy of the hose running through the bridge. The hose swells and reduces the space in the bridge causing severe pressure and pain. Micro-tears or trauma to the supraspinatus causes inflammation. This condition is known as the *rotator cuff impingement syndrome*.

The Rotator Cuff Impingement Syndrome has four common stages *(Ardheim, Daniel D., D.P.E., Modern Principles of Athletic Training):*

Stage I

The beginning stages of these injuries are curable and predominate in young athletes and weightlifters. The following are common symptoms in the early stages:

- Aching in the shoulder after the activity. *(Many young body builders complain of aching shoulders after bench pressing.)*
- Tenderness over the top of the shoulder.
- Pain during movement to the side and away from your body especially past 90 degrees, as in a lateral raise.

Stage II

- Spreading of pain to the biceps.
- Worsening of shoulder pain at night.
- Thickening of the rotator cuff muscles.
- Development of scar tissue as a result of the micro-tears.
- Limited range of motion during arm movements.

Stage III

- History of shoulder pain and problems.
- Tears to the rotator cuff muscles.
- Increased shoulder pain at night.
- Surgery sometimes needed to repair.

Stage IV

- Obvious weakening of the shoulder, especially during abduction movements such as a side raises.
- Pain is much worse during exercise and at night.
- Surgery usually needed to repair.

Treatment and Prevention of Shoulder Injuries

Before Workouts:

Warm up the upperbody before lifting. A good warm-up is any type of rhythmic arm movement for about five minutes such as:

- Nordic Track
- Aerobic rowing machine
- Airdyne Bike or any bike where the arms are involved.

During Workouts:

Start with light weights and modify the exercises that cause or have potential to cause shoulder pain. For example, if the bench press hurts your shoulder, try a closer grip on the bar. This may relieve stress from the shoulder.

Try to listen to your body. It gives you warning signals before disaster strikes. Pain or discomfort usually precedes injuries such as pec tears. I know; my body talked to me before I tore my pec. During a very heavy set of dumbbell bench presses I felt a torque in my right pec. I finished the set unharmed, but decided to perform another set even heavier, ignoring the warning signal. During that set, I again felt the torque, but decided to work through it. As a result, I tore my pec one week before a contest. Luckily it wasn't that serious where I wasn't able to compete.

If it hurts, don't do it. You should be able to determine between a good pain and a bad pain. A good pain is the pump and burn you feel in the muscles during an exercise. A bad pain is when you feel a sharp pain or discomfort in your muscles and or joints. An example of a bad pain is a sharp pain in your knees during squats, or a sharp pain in your shoulder joint during behind-the-neck shoulder press. In both of these examples, you can decide not to perform these exercises and try to resume them another time, or modify them. When squatting, you can try a wide stance with your toes out to alleviate pain from your knees. You can perform overhead presses to the front rather than behind your neck. The following chart shows alternatives to exercises that commonly cause pain to the shoulder joint.

Exercises	Alternatives
Shoulder Exercises	**Alternatives**
Behind-the-neck press	Presses to the front Dumbbell overhead press
Chest Exercise	**Alternatives**
Barbell bench press Incline barbell press Dips Flyes	Dumbbell bench press Flat bench dumbbell press Decline press Machine flyes
Back Exercises	**Alternatives**
Behind-the-neck pulldowns	Pulldowns to the front Pullups

After Workouts

Stretch the upperbody *(see Chapter 15, Stretching)*.

Apply ice to the shoulder to reduce inflammation. Be sure to apply in 15 minute intervals. You do not want to cut the blood circulation to the area by leaving the ice on too long. Do apply heat after the workout. Heat will inflame the muscles even more. Heat can be used during the warm-up stages. If pain persists, over-the-counter medication such as naproxen sodium, acetaminophen, ibuprofen, or even plain aspirin can help reduce the inflammation. If this doesn't help, try resting for about one week. Lay off the weights; your body may just need a break. If pain persists, then see a doctor. He may have to refer you to a specialist.

Ice vs Heat

Recent studies have shown that ice is effective for muscle strains, pulls, tears, inflammation, tendinitis, and related injuries. Ice has proven to heal four times faster than heat. Use ice within the first 36 hours after the injury. The best form to use is regular ice cubes from your freezer. Ice packs do not stay cold long enough. Remember to apply ice in 15 minute intervals to avoid circulation problems.

Use heat to warm up muscles before exercising with either a heating pad or by using a rubbing compound.

Other Common Lifting Injuries

Pec Tears to the pectoralis major are usually caused from bench pressing with heavy weights and extending too far down with dumbbell flyes. These tears vary in severity. The worst case is when the pectoralis major tears completely off the bone, requiring surgery to re-attach it. This type of tear is usually accompanied by discoloration, disfigurement, and extreme swelling where the chest and biceps meet. You may need to refrain from bench pressing for at least six months following a pec tear depending on the severity of the tear.

Lower back injuries are also very common with people who overtrain with weights. Most of these injuries are disc related. A disc is a jellyfish-like cushion between each of the 24 vertebrae of the spine. They act as shock absorbers when the spine experiences uncommon pressure, such as lifting weights.

There are three types of disc problems:

- slipped disc
- ruptured disc
- degenerative disc

Slipped Discs occur when they move from their position and protrude and compress a nerve.

Ruptured Disc: When the jellyfish breaks, the jelly gets squeezed out. The discs lose their shock absorber ability and the vertebrae move closer together causing nerve problems. The vertebrae impinge on nerves causing extreme pain. The uprooted nerve becomes elongated and pressures against adjacent bone. A ruptured disc leads to a degenerative disc.

Degenerative Disc: As the jelly gets squeezed out, the size of the disc diminishes.

As you move down the spine, the vertebrae and discs gradually increase in size to support more body weight. Discs in the lower part of the spine undergo more weight-bearing stress and are more likely to slip or rupture.

If you suffer from chronic low back pain, avoid exercises such as heavy squats, dead lifts, and bent-over rows. Substitute with exercises such as leg presses, back raises, and one-arm rows.

Bodybuilding Mistakes

Six weeks before my last contest, I pulled and strained my back to a point where I could not get in and out of bed. One week before the same contest, I tore my pectoral muscle causing swelling that disfigured my chest.

What was happening to me? I was overtraining!

There was no need to perform heavy deadlifts and bent-over rows six weeks before a contest causing undue stress to my lower back. There certainly was no need to perform 130-pound dumbbell presses one week before my contest.

The biggest fear that a bodybuilder has is losing size. As you get closer and closer to a contest, your body is more susceptible to injury because you are probably eating less, losing weight, and training harder. You won't be able to lift the same amount of weight as you did earlier in your training because of the weight loss. Lifting heavy weights prior to a contest can result in muscle pulls and tears, strained joints, lower back problems, and other injuries.

Bodybuilders need to overcome the fear of losing size weeks before a contest. Sacrificing some muscle mass and strength during precontest is sometimes necessary for the complete defined look. You should still lift heavily, but not as heavy as you did off season. If you continue to train hard and eat well during precontest training, you will not lose any significant size.

CHAPTER 15

Stretching

Stretching

Stretch after your workout when your muscles are warm. Stretching cold muscles prior to your workout can be very difficult and ineffective.

There are two basic types of stretches, ballistic and static. Ballistic stretches require bouncing and jerking the muscles to stretch them. This type of stretching is not recommended because it can cause severe muscle pulls or tears. Instead, do static stretching where you hold stretches for at least six to eight seconds.

Flexibility is important for weightlifters and bodybuilders as well as other athletes. Stretching can prevent injuries because it keeps muscles from pulling and tearing and also strengthens tendons and ligaments.

Stretching allows muscles to lengthen. The longer your muscles, the more capable they are of growing. It also increases the muscles' ability to work through a fuller range of motion. Because of limited flexibility, many people have difficulty performing flyes and pullovers, two chest exercises that require a full range of motion for maximum effectiveness.

The term, *muscle bound* refers to those who have short, tight muscles and usually find it difficult performing everyday tasks, such as putting on a shirt or reaching for a high shelf. Weightlifters and bodybuilders can become muscle bound if they don't stretch properly and become flexible. Being muscle bound not only can prevent you from performing everyday tasks, but can also affect your appearance. People who are tight in the shoulders and chest have a tendency to slouch. Rather than exposing a well-built chest and shoulders, they show bad posture by slouching. Lifting weights can enhance your physical appearance, but without proper stretching, you may defeat the purpose of reshaping your body. For the optimum shape and health of your muscles, stretch after every weight training workout.

Stretching can be enjoyable and more effective with a partner. Your partner can stretch your muscles while you lie back and relax. Muscles are easier to stretch when you are relaxed. Breathing deeply while you stretch can help you relax and get the most benefit from the stretches.

Communication plays a big role when using a partner. While being stretched, let your partner know when to stop with a verbal *que* such as, *OK*. When you are performing the stretching, ask your partner when you should stop, by simply instructing, *tell me when.* When you are being stretched, it is important that you feel the stretch in the intended muscle. You should not feel pain during the stretches.

A partner can also assist with an innovative stretching technique called PNF stretching. PNF is short for proprioceptive neuromuscular facilitation, also known as the contract/relax stretch. The muscle is isometrically contracted for about six to ten seconds and then stretched. Although you can perform this type of stretching alone, it is much more effective with a partner. For example, during a hamstring stretch, press your leg against your partner's shoulder for the six to ten second isometric contraction and then relax as your partner stretches your hamstring by pushing your leg forward *(see photographs on the following pages).* You will find that PNF stretching allows the muscle to stretch farther than usual. The concept is complex involving the central nervous system and motor learning, but it works.

Rather than rest between sets of exercises, stretch the muscle group that is being trained. For example, when training legs, stretch the quadriceps between sets of squats or stretch the hamstrings between sets of leg curls. For the upperbody, stretch the lats when training back or stretch the chest and biceps with one single stretch between sets of flyes *(see photographs for upperbody stretches).* Stretching between sets can greatly reduce injuries and enhance the shape of the muscles.

Hamstring Stretch: While sitting on the floor, extend one leg out and the other tucked in as shown here. Grab your calf under the extended leg and pull your chest towards the extended knee and hold. Try to keep the extended leg straight; do not allow it to bend.

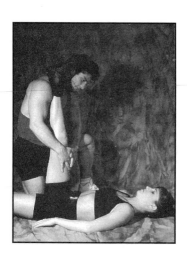

Hamstring Stretch with a Partner: When stretching your partner, position yourself on one knee or where you are most comfortable. Place your partner's ankle on your shoulder and your hands *above* your partner's knee, not on it. From this position, push their leg forward keeping only a slight bend in their knee. Ask your partner if they feel the stretch in the hamstring. If yes, then hold the stretch for at least six to eight seconds. For the PNF stretch, have your partner push their leg on your shoulder for six to eight seconds. That's the isometric part. Then tell them to relax and slowly push their leg forward until they tell you to stop. The person being stretched, should relax and take deep breaths. The leg that is not being stretched should be flat on the floor. The head and back should also be flat on the floor.

Quadriceps Stretch Lying:
Lie on your side with one arm extended, supporting your head and the other grabbing your ankle. Pull your ankle back until you feel a stretch in your thigh keeping the other leg slightly bent and relaxed as shown above.

Quadriceps Stretch Standing:
While bracing yourself on something sturdy such as a pole, grab the top of your foot keeping the other foot flat on the floor. Pull your foot to your buttocks while leaning forward and hold.

Hip and Buttocks Stretch:
To stretch the right side, place your right leg over your left. Support your weight with your right arm by placing your right hand on the floor. Push your left elbow into right thigh below the knee until you feel a good stretch in your right hip and buttocks. Hold the stretch for at least six seconds before switching sides. For best results, twist your body the opposite way that you push.

Hip and Buttock Stretch with a Partner:

When stretching your partner's right side, hold their left shoulder down by pressing it gently. Grab their left ankle or calf and extend it across their body, and hold. To prevent their

right leg from moving, position your right foot in front of their right leg as shown in the photograph.

Calf Stretch:

Lean against something sturdy such as a pole keeping one leg in front and the other behind. Bend the forward knee and lock the rear knee. Lean and push until you feel a stretch in the rear calf. Be sure that the rear foot is flat in order to feel the full stretch.

Upper Back Stretch:

When stretching the left side, hold on to something sturdy with your left hand. Bend at the waist and push your buttocks out. Sweep your left leg behind your right leg and lean to your left.

Lower Back Stretch:
Lie flat on your back grabbing under your knee as shown at left. Pull your leg to your chest keeping the other leg flat on the floor.

Abdominal Stretch:
With your hips resting on the floor, push up with your arms until they are extended. Be sure that your hips remain on the floor and look up as shown at right.

Chest Stretch with a Partner:
When stretching your partner, place your hands or arms inside your partner's elbows. Pull their arms back until your partner instructs you to stop. For the PNF stretch, have your partner clamp their arms forward as you resist them for six to eight seconds. Instruct them to relax and then slowly pull their arms back.

Chest and Biceps Stretch:

Brace your wrist against something sturdy such as pole at shoulder level. Lean into the pole and away from your arm and hold.

Chest and Biceps Stretch with a Partner:

When stretching your partner, grab both arms above the wrists and below the elbows. Pull the arms back and hold. You can also feel this stretch in your shoulders.

Triceps Stretch:

To stretch your right triceps, grab your right elbow with your left hand behind your head. Pull the right elbow and hold. You can also perform this stretch against a pole as shown in the far right photograph.

Triceps Stretch with a partner:

Push your partner's elbow behind and across their head while supporting them with the your other hand. For the PNF stretch, instruct your partner to push against your hand as you resist. After six to eight seconds of isometric contraction, instruct your partner to relax and then slowly push their arm back across their head.

CHAPTER 16

Contest Preparation

Choosing a Contest _____

When searching for a contest, The National Physique Committee (NPC) offers the most. It offers contests for all levels and ages:

- Teen Men and Women
- Open Men and Women
- Masters Men and Women
- Mixed Pairs

If you are a drug-free bodybuilder, you can choose a contest that tests for steroids. The NPC sponsors many "drug-free" contests. Drug testing at an amateur level usually entails a lie detector test or urine sample. "Drug-free" does not necessarily mean that the competitors on stage have never used steroids. Some contests prohibit steroid use within the last one to five years.

The NPC is the largest bodybuilding federation in the country. It sponsors many amateur contests nationwide including drug-free contests. It sends out more written literature and receives more media and television coverage than any other bodybuilding federation.

In order to compete in an NPC contest, you need to be an NPC member. Write to:

NPC
P.O. Box 3711
Pittsburgh, PA 15230
(412-276-5027)

Being an NPC member will keep you updated on most local, regional, state, and national bodybuilding contests as well as other events. The NPC will send you a free issue of the *NPC News*, published by the National Physique Committee of the USA. The *NPC News* includes:

- Interviews and articles with famous bodybuilders
- Tips on training and nutrition
- Advertisements for posing trunks, supplements and bodybuilding wear

If you are a college student at a university, check with the intramural sports department—they may stage a bodybuilding contest that you may not even know about. Starting at a college level is a great way to begin competing in bodybuilding. This is how I got started. At one time, Rutgers University held one of the largest contests in the country. It started as small intramural event attracting only a handful of competitors and spectators. It eventually grew to draw crowds of 3,000 fired-up students, parents and local spectators (see Chapter 20).

If your college does not sponsor a bodybuilding contest, and has an intramural sports department, take the initiative and start a bodybuilding contest at your school. Go to the college gyms and sign people up. Present your school and fellow students with a well-organized proposal. Be prepared with a place, potential date and time, judges, crowd control, advertising, sponsors from local businesses and gyms—especially gyms; they would love the publicity. Try tanning salons, fraternities, beauty salons and barber shops for sponsors and advertising.

Planning is Everything

The first thing to do when preparing for a bodybuilding contest is find yourself a planner with a monthly and daily calendar with space to prioritize daily tasks. A planner that includes space to log your daily caloric intake, workout schedule and space for notes, would be even better. Use this planner for the duration of your contest preparation.

Locate your contest date on your calendar and mark it. Count back the number of weeks until your contest. This monthly example shows one of my contests held Saturday, April 30, 1994. I knew that on April 23, I was one week away from my contest. April 16, two weeks away. April 9, three weeks away. On April 2, four weeks away from my contest, I started tanning. I knew that on April 24, I should start decarbing and that on April 27, I should start carbing up (see the following sections for more details on carbing and decarbing).

Sun	Mon	Tues	Wed	Thurs	Fri	Sat
					1	2 4 weeks AWA x START TAnning
3	4	5	6	7	8	9 3 weeks away
10	11	12	13	14	15	16 2 weeks away
17	18	19	20	21	22	23 1 week away
24 DeCARB •increase protein •increase water	25 DECARB	26 DecARB	27 CARB UP POSE	28 CARB UP POSE	29 CARB UP POSE	30 ✗ Contest DAY ✶

April / 1994

©1994 Power Writings Printed in U.S.A

The time you have to prepare for the big day will determine the detail of your plan. September, October, November, and December were my muscle building months. January through April were my precontest preparation months. *(See Eat to Build in Chapter 4.)*

If you have time for the building phase, then mark the first and last day of the building phase on your calendar. Hopefully you have allowed at least three to four months to build. If you only have two to three months, then follow the building phase for those months. If your contest is two to three months away, then go straight to the precontest phase. Do not panic if you feel that you are not big enough to compete. Most bodybuilders win contests for being *ripped* not big. Big does not win contests, ripped does. Proper planning can help you enter a contest ripped.

For my first Mr. Rutgers contest in 1988, I weighed 175 pounds. I lost 35 pounds in about one month and placed second in the middleweight division. In 1989 with a year of additional planning, I won Mr. Rutgers weighing 164 pounds, losing over 40 pounds in three and a half months. My improved planning skills helped me lose the weight and prepare for my contest more efficiently. Losing 35 pounds in one month as I did in the 1988 contest was not good planning.

Precontest planning includes changing your eating habits and training plan, starting intense posing sessions, and adding some finishing touches to your physique.

You will need at least two to three months or eight to twelve weeks for the precontest phase. During this phase, most of you will need to lose weight. Changing your eating plan will usually require some weight loss in order to be competitive. Use your planner to log important precontest tasks. The following section on *Precontest Dieting* details important tasks to log in your calendar.

Recapping The Initial Plan

- Obtain a planner.
- Locate contest date and mark it.
- Count back the number of weeks you have until your contest day.
- Locate and label months for building phase.
- Locate and label at least two to three months for precontest preparation.
- Log important precontest tasks discussed in the Precontest Dieting section of this book.

Daily Planning

Daily planning includes using your planner to prioritize, organize and carry out your daily tasks. Without a plan, the everyday priorities in your life may conflict. These may include, preparing for your contest, studying, attending classes, working, and social events. Whatever your priorities may be, I highly recommend using a planner.

The diagram shows an example of a day planned, using my planner.

Date: 2/12/94

✓	Things To Do	Appointments
✓	Train legs	Early A.M. 5:30 meet Ron
✓	Prepare English Assig	To train legs
	mail Letters	8:00
	Talk To John)	9:00
	About Rent }	
		10:00
	Call Prof. Smith	
		11:00 English class
	Food shopping	
		12:00 Prof Smith
	Prepare meals)	
	For Tomorrow }	1:00
		2:00 NAP
		3:00 aerobics/Bike
		4:00 WORK
		5:00
		6:00
		7:00 LAST Meal
		Late P.M.

Plan with consistency.   Schedule your workouts and meals at the same times each day. For example, if you are a college student and have English class every Monday and Wednesday at 11:00 a.m., schedule your workouts every Monday and Wednesday at 3:00 p.m. and your meals at 5:00 p.m. Consistency allows you to be proactive by planning for the entire week or month. This prevents conflict with your training and eating schedule.

Being proactive will also help you avoid missing meals and workouts by having a contingency plan ready.   For example, after reviewing your planner, you notice a history exam logged at 9:00 a.m.. You want to study at the library from 8:00 a.m. to 9:00 a.m., but the only problem is that you usually go back to your dorm room for your second meal at 8:00. Rather than having to skip a meal, prepare it the night before and take it with you. There is nothing worse than sitting in class or at work feeling hungry.

Documenting and prioritizing your daily tasks will also help you with your contest preparation.   Using the example on the previous page, you urgently need to speak with Professor Smith about a grade and you know that his office hours are from 10:00 a.m. to 1:00 p.m.   From your daily planner, you realize that you have time to contact him at 12:00 noon. Cross reference your daily schedule and your list of things to do.   Seeing what the whole day looks like in advance will help put you at ease, especially when you are training. The last thing you want to do is forget to do something important during the day and remember it while you are training.   This can ruin the entire workout and day. Check off your tasks as you accomplish them. Seeing a check next to your tasks will put you at ease and give you a feeling of accomplishment.

Planning Your Meals & Workouts

I found it most helpful planning my meals the night before. My refrigerator and shelves were always supplied with food because I planned my food shopping every Saturday. The night before, you can look in your refrigerator and cabinets to see what is available to prepare for the next day. If you eat some of your meals in a cafeteria, get a meal schedule to help you plan.

Plan your meals by documenting the times of your meals, the number of calories, carbohydrates, protein, and fat you plan to consume. *(See Nutrition in Chapter 6 and the following section on Precontest Dieting for more details.)* Budget your calories by evenly allocating them throughout the day. For example, you have budgeted 2000 calories for the day and scheduled five meals with the last meal at 8:00 p.m. You should have a good idea that no meal should exceed 400 calories: (400 X 5 = 2000).

Use the example below as a guide to document and plan your meals and budget your calories. *(For more sample diets and using an exercise log, see Chapters 2 & 6.)*

Date: _MondAY April 4_

Exercise Log				Food Diary			
Aerobic Activity: Bike				**Food**	**Cal** **Carb** **Prot** **Fat**		
Calories	**Distance**	**Time**		6:00 AM oatmeal 1 serv	105	25	3	2
400	6 miles	30 min		Banana	100	20	0	0
Muscles Worked: Chest/Bies				3 egg whites/	60	0	10	0
Exercise	**Wt**	**Reps**	**Sets**	9:00 AM 1 large Potato	300	60	6	0
Bench Press	135	10	1					
	225	10	1	11:30 AM Tuna 6 oz	300	2	45	2
	275	8	1	Rice 3 serv	300	69	9	0
	315	6	1	Broccoli	20	5	0	0
DB Incline								
Press	100	10	1	2:30 PM oatmeal 2 serv	210	46	6	4
	110	8	1					
	115	6	1	4:30 pm Vegetable Salad	300	69	0	0
	120	4	1					
DBFlys	50	10	1	7:00 PM 2 chicken Breasts	300	0	50	6
	60	10	1	1 cup Pasta plain	420	80	14	2
	65	8	1					
				8:00 pm 3 Rice cakes	105	21	3	0
Pullovers	100	10	3					
				TOTAL	2820	397	146	16
Barbell Curls								
	95	10	1		56%	21%	6% 0	
	105	10	1					
	115	8	1					
	125	6	1					
Preacher Curls								
	85	10	1					
	105	10	1					
	115	8	1					

Planning your workouts entails developing a training schedule for each week, knowing what body parts to train, and what exercises to perform, before you get to the gym!

The training schedule should include a well thought-out plan of the body parts to be trained for each day:

Weekly Training Schedule

Mon	Tues	Wed	Thurs	Fri	Sat
chest biceps	back triceps	quads only	off	shoulders hamstrings	resume Monday

Planning workouts ensures that all body parts are worked at least once a week and that the muscles to be trained are grouped logically for best results. For example, grouping chest and biceps rather than chest and triceps will ensure a great triceps workout on Tuesday. The chest requires a lot of work from the triceps because of the pushing movements involved. If you trained chest first and then triceps in the same workout, your triceps may be too tired to get a good workout as a result of heavy chest exercises.

Notice in the training schedule above:

- A large muscle group is trained with a small, allowing efficient workouts for each body part. Training two large muscle groups in one workout can be difficult if you want to build size and lift heavy. Your goals for contest preparation, will also determine the grouping of body parts.

- You would not want to train triceps on Monday and then chest on Tuesday. The triceps would be sore and fatigued from Monday's workout and would affect your chest workout on Tuesday. As a result, you would not be able to train chest intensely. You also want your triceps to rebuild after a vigorous workout. Working them again on Tuesday for chest would disrupt the rebuilding process and result in overtraining.

- Training legs with any other body part is totally out of the question. See my leg workouts and you will see why.

- I allow at least two days between my back and leg workouts. The lower back works hard when performing back exercises such as bent-over rows and deadlifts. Training legs the next day, or the day after could prove to be difficult because of a sore and fatigue lower back. The same goes for training legs one day and back the very next day. Not only may you find this difficult to do, but it also may result to injury.

Knowing what exercises to perform before you get to the gym will help save time and allow you to experience a more focused workout. You do not want to *wing* your workouts. Knowing what exercises to perform may not be enough for a well-planned workout. Have a contingency plan for the exercises you have planned. For example, you plan to perform bench presses for your first chest exercise, but all the benches are being used. Don't wait for a bench and waste time. Have an alternate exercise planned such as dips. This will keep you moving through the workout without any delays. If you have dumbbell incline flyes scheduled after dips, but all the incline benches are being used, plan on performing decline flyes instead.

Crowds are something you want to avoid. Waiting for equipment or having to use contingency exercises can be counter productive. Check your planner for a better training time when the gym is less crowded.

Precontest Dieting

On January 2, 1989 I weighed 213 pounds. By mid April, I weighed 167 pounds ready to compete in the middleweight class of the AAU Mr. New Jersey Bodybuilding Contest. Although I gained too much weight off season and may have slightly over dieted for my contests, I followed a good plan and won contests. The weight loss was gradual, two pounds per week without sacrificing much muscle. If I were to do it all over again, I would have tried to stay closer to my contest weight during the off season. I would have stayed around 190 pounds, having only to lose about 20 pounds rather than 40 to 50 pounds.

BEFORE: *1988, at 175 pounds during contest time.*

AFTER: *One year later, almost 10 pounds lighter.*

Through my years of competing as a middleweight, I could have weighed as much as 176 pounds. In my first bodybuilding contest, the Mr. Rutgers Contest, in 1988, I decided to come in at the top of the weightclass at 175. I placed second. I lost 38 pounds from 213 pounds. The following year, I competed at a body weight of 167 pounds, eight pounds lighter, and won my weightclass at the AAU Mr. New Jersey and the overall Mr. Rutgers Title. As the photographs show, I looked better and harder at 167 pounds. I gave up some size, but I was the *most ripped* bodybuilder on stage! The following year I packed some more muscle on my frame and competed near the top of my weight class at about 174 pounds, maintaining a ripped physique.

The point is, if you want to win a contest, then you better learn how to diet right! I have judged and witnessed contests where third and forth place finishers could have easily won if they would have dieted a little harder and smarter.

Precontest dieting requires planning for your contest date *(see previous section on Planning).* This requires reducing your consumption of fat and carbohydrates, increasing your protein, and depending on your body weight, decreasing your total caloric intake.

Consuming smaller and more frequent meals will help increase your metabolism and ensure more efficient use of your calories. I have trained bodybuilders that actually increased their calories because of their super fast metabolism, but most of us are not as fortunate. Even though they ate more, they still lost body fat and gained muscle.

Get your calendar out now and prepare to plan! All my contests were held in mid April. The Mr. Rutgers Contest was always the second Wednesday of April. I started my precontest dieting January second. You want to allow at least three months or twelve weeks for precontest dieting regardless of how much you weigh.

Below is a breakdown that will help you plan for the last three months of precontest dieting:

12 weeks
- cut fats
- decrease carbohydrate intake
- increase protein
- increase or decrease caloric intake
- add 20-30 minutes of aerobics at least 3 days per week
- train twice a day

6 weeks
- cut all dairy
- cut all fruit
- cut all breads
- increase water
- adjust calories to weight & fat loss goal
- increase aerobic to 30 minutes three to four days per week
- start posing
- supplement with vitamins

6 full days prior to contest
- decarb
- increase protein
- increase water

3 full days prior
- carb up
- cut sodium
- maintain water consumption
- limit protein

Day of Contest
- carb up
- decrease water slightly
- eat carbs only, no protein.

The first thing to do is cut out your fats and rely on fats naturally found in healthy foods such as chicken and oatmeal.

During the building phase your fat intake should be about 15 to 20% of your calories. For precontest dieting, many body-builders reduce their fat intake to about 10%. For example, if you consume 2000 calories, only about 200 of those calories should be from fat.

In addition to reducing your fat intake, you should also reduce your carbohydrate intake. Try to stick with complex carbohy-drates such as rice, past, and potatoes and eliminate simple carbohydrates such as fruit, juices and sugar. Cutting back on both fats and carbohydrates will naturally decrease your caloric intake. Counter this decrease of calories with an increase of protein. This will help keep most of your muscle while reducing fat.

Increase your protein by one additional meal. This will equal about 30-50 grams of protein depending on the source and quantity. You should be consuming at least three protein meals per day. You can add a can of tuna which equals about 45 grams of protein. *(Protein consumption is dis-cussed thoroughly in the Nutrition chapter.)*

How much weight you need to lose will determine your plan. Modifications in your eating are necessary as you change to precontest dieting. I knew I had to lose over forty pounds, so I immediately cut my calories from about 4000 to 3000 calo-ries per day in the first week. I had a precise idea of how much to cut my calories by using my food diary from the previous year. I knew from the previous year, that decreas-ing my calories to 3000 in the first week, would result about a five pound loss. I then gradually decreased my calories to 2500 for weeks two through four, 2000 calories for weeks five through eight, and then to 1800 calories during weeks nine through twelve. After the initial five pound loss, I would lose about two pounds per week. For the remaining two or three weeks, I decreased my calories anywhere from 1400 to 1600 a day.

Everyone experiences a fluctuation of weight and needs to adjust their diets accordingly to how their bodies react. If you find that you are losing too much muscle or too much weight too fast, increase your calories. On the other hand, if you need to lose weight and find that you are not losing enough, then you are probably not cutting back enough on your fats and or total calories. By the end of the first month, I wanted to weigh less than 200 pounds, a loss of about 10 pounds. I easily reached my goal from following my plan.

If you need to lose only 10 pounds for a contest, then plan to lose only one pound per week. If you do not need to lose weight, you will still need to lose fat. You can probably maintain or in some cases increase your calories due to the addition of aerobic exercise, double training sessions a day, posing, and the decrease in fat intake. The aerobics and double workout sessions will help you burn more calories and increase your metabolism. The decrease in fat will ensure your body to efficiently use the quality calories from the additional complex carbohydrates and protein.

How often should you weigh yourself?

Weigh yourself every day and document it on your calendar because you will need to make changes in your diet depending on how your body reacts to the changes. Be sure to weigh yourself at the same times each day since your body weight fluctuates during the day. You may weigh less in the morning and more at night.

The Sixth Week

The sixth week before a contest is a living hell; it was for me. At this stage, you should cut out all dairy products, breads, and fruits. Use your calories as efficiently as possible by consuming only complex carbohydrates and protein. Cutting out breads will help you reduce carbohydrates and sodium. Eliminating dairy and fruit will give you a more "ripped" look by removing water between your skin and muscle. Since dairy products are high in sodium, eliminating them will prevent water retention.

Now that you have decreased or in some instances increased your calories, decreased fats and carbohydrates, increased protein, and eliminated dairy and fruit, you should start seeing some drastic changes in your body. You will see your skin and veins appear closer to your muscles from the elimination of fat and water.

Water

Drink water only. Don't waste your calories on juices and soda unless they are calorie and sodium free. You want to save your calories for muscle building food. For example, rather than drink a glass of orange juice, a simple carbohydrate with about 100 calories, eat half of a baked potato instead. Complex carbohydrates are used efficiently and stored in the muscles. Also, drinking juice or any other substances with high acidity and sugar can interrupt the digestion of protein and carbohydrates.

I have seen bodybuilders make the big mistake of drastically decreasing or even eliminating water consumption as their contests drew nearer. Rather than decrease your water, you should increase it as the contest nears. The reasoning is simple: As you get closer to your contest, you are eating less, reducing sodium, cutting dairy, and increasing exercise.

You need more water in your system to replace the foods you eliminated that normally contain water. Just about all foods contain some water and as you decrease your food intake, you reduce your water intake.

What if you are eating more?

With the reduction of sodium and fruit and your increase of exercise levels, you still need to replenish your body with water. Your level of exercise increases with the double sessions and the addition of aerobics and posing. As your level of exercise activity increases, you perspire more, and when you perspire more, you lose more water. Your body is about 75% water. What do you think will happen when you cut your water? You will be cutting your throat! If you have planned properly, you won't need to do anything drastic before your contest. I was always ready to compete about one month before every contest.

Decarbing

Decarbing is when you gradually decrease your carbohydrates in order to bring your body in a state of ketosis. This is when your body is deprived of carbohydrates and is capable of absorbing two to three times more carbohydrates and water to your muscles than normal.

Normally, your body is capable of metabolizing about 30 to 40 grams of carbohydrates per hour. In the state of ketosis, it is able to absorb about 100 grams per hour.

You need to plan six full days prior to your contest day because you need three full days to decarb and three full days to carb up. For example, if prejudging starts at 8 a.m. Saturday, the day of your contest, then start decarbing at 8 a.m. Sunday, six days before your contest. You will gradually cut your carbohydrates for three full days before carbing up.

How do you know how much to cut your carbohydrates?

How well you planned and documented your food diary will determine the answer to this question.

From using my food diary, I always knew that during last six weeks, my highest carbohydrate day was about 350 grams. I also knew that my average daily carb consumption was about 275 to 300 grams. On day six, I cut my carbohydrates in half, from 300 grams to 150 grams. On day five, cut to 100 grams, and on day four I maintained 100 grams of carbohydrates. Some bodybuilders decarb to zero carbohydrates; that means consuming no carbohydrates for one or two days. I think this is a little dangerous and unnecessary, especially if you planned properly.

How hard you diet and train will determine how low you will need to decarb. In some of my contests, I was ready to compete six weeks before the contest. All I needed to do was cut my sodium. For my last contest, I maintained 150 grams of carbs for three days and then carbed up. If you are in great shape several weeks before the contest, you really do not want to do anything drastic. This process can help you compete by appearing harder and tighter on stage, but it will not make or break you. Either you look great or you don't. The safety feature about decarbing is that you have three full days to carb up.

Carbing Up

After three full days of decarbing, you need three full days to carb up. When carbing up, it's important that you gradually increase your carbs throughout the three days and that you don't overeat! If you overeat you will "overcarb." That is consuming too many carbohydrates in the three days resulting to water retention. As a result, you will appear "puffy" rather than hard. Remember, it is better to undercarb than to overcarb. You would rather look a tiny bit flat than puffy.

Carbing up requires five or six small carb meals each day. As a rule of thumb, each carbohydrate meal should rarely exceed more than 400 calories or 100 grams of carbs. How well you documented your carbohydrate meals in your food diary will determine the success of this tedious process. You may think that a bigger bodybuilder can carb up more than a smaller one. That may not be true, because the smaller bodybuilder may have a faster metabolism than the larger one. If the larger bodybuilder's biggest carb day was only 300 grams of carbohydrates, then he should not be consuming too much more than that.

Look in your food diary and locate your highest carb days within the last six weeks of your precontest dieting. If your highest day was 300 grams of carbohydrates, then you should start with about 300 to 350 grams for day one of the carbing up process. Each meal should be about 50 to 60 grams of carbohydrates which is equivalent to about two baked potatoes. Be sure to allow about two hours between each meal. Continue carbing up until you reach your limit for the day.

On day two, consume more by increasing the number of carbohydrate meals rather than the size of each meal. Using the same example, consume 400 grams of carbohydrates on day two and 450 grams on day three.

Drink about one glass of water with each carb meal. Again, do not restrict your water intake until the day of the contest. Also, keep your protein to a minimum by allowing one or two small protein meals each day of your carbing up process. Be sure those meals consist of either chicken or turkey, no egg whites because of their sodium content.

You can expect to lose three to four pounds when decarbing and gain about three to four pounds when carbing up. Leave yourself some room to carb up. For example, the middleweight class has a limit of about 176 pounds. I wanted to come in at the top of my weight class for my last contest. I made sure I weighed about 170 pounds before I started carbing up. This allowed me a six pound gap to carb up and not worry about exceeding the 176 pound limit.

During the last three days, you should be posing hard and looking for changes in your body. If you notice that you are looking a little soft and puffy appearing to be retaining water, then you are probably carbing up too much and overeating. On the other hand, if you notice that you are still flat and your muscles are not filling in, then you are probably not carbing up enough. Also check the scale, be sure that you are not drastically gaining or losing weight.

Foods for Carbing Up

The first two days you should be carbing up with complex carbohydrates only! My favorite foods for carbing up were baked potatoes and rice. I ate very little pasta, but I did occasionally add it for variety. An average carb meal consisted of two baked potatoes or two servings of rice every two hours with an occasional protein meal in between. Try to eat protein separate from your carbohydrate meals. You do not want to mix your carbohydrates and proteins when carbing up because you may interrupt the process of glycogen entering the muscles. Also, do not carb up with foods high in sodium such as breads.

The morning of your contest wake up early and continue to carb up mixing complex and simple carbohydrates. I usually enjoyed some bananas, plumbs, and rice cakes with all fruit jelly. The fruit will be a treat if you followed this plan. You will not have consumed any simple carbohydrates in the last six weeks.

The theory behind consuming simple carbohydrates the day of the contest is that they help bring out some vascularity.

The sugar from the fruits helps bring out the veins more. Carb up until prejudging starts but be very careful. You do not want to polish off a bottle of all fruit jelly. Again, you do not want to over eat and appear bloated on stage not being able to strike an abdominal pose.

Sodium

The last three days before the contest, you want to restrict your sodium intake. Egg whites and tuna fish have a lot of sodium. Eat chicken and turkey only. Even low-sodium tuna contains enough sodium to result in water retention. Remember, if you have dieted hard and properly, your body will be very vulnerable to any foods high in anything. Once again, when carbing up, do not use foods like breads because of their high sodium content.

Precontest Training

Precontest training and dieting are carried out simultaneously. My precontest training and dieting started three and a half months or 14 weeks prior to the contest date.

Precontest training requires changing your workouts to define and shape the body into contest form. This includes:

- Varying your exercises and training techniques
- Increasing the number of sets and reps
- Training twice a day
- Incorporating aerobic exercise
- Posing

Changes in your workouts include varying your exercises and training techniques. I used a lot of supersets and strip sets during precontest training. *(See chapter on Training techniques.)*

I increased my reps and sets and used lighter weights when necessary. I increased my reps to a range of 12 to 15. You can continue using heavy weights and use techniques that require lighter weights and higher repetitions such as supersets and strip sets. For example, when training chest, start with three sets of heavy bench presses and strip the forth set. You can do the same with weighted dips. Use heavy weights for the first three sets and strip the last set. After bench presses and dips, superset incline presses with dumbbell flyes. If you are supersetting, you will need to use lighter weights since you are pounding the same body part with two different exercises without a rest.

Six weeks prior to my contest, I trained twice a day, three days of the week. Since I added aerobic exercise, posing, and tanning to my regimen, I found it difficult to get everything done in one workout. I would train heavy, or large body parts in the morning and train light, or smaller body parts at night. For example, I trained back in the morning, posed for 20 minutes, and finished with 30 minutes of stationary bike. I came back at night and trained triceps, abs, and calves and then tanned for 30 minutes. I trained twice a day only three days of the week. The other days I trained only once a day.

During precontest training, I used a lot of cable work for my upper body. Cables help isolate the targeted muscle groups because of the constant resistance on the negative and positive movements. For example, when performing heavy barbell upright rows, you will have a tendency to lower the bar quickly without concentrating on the negative movement. With cable upright rows, you constantly feel a muscle burn because of the constant stress on the shoulders throughout the entire range of motion.

Varying your exercises can help fine tune the body into contest shape. For chest, you can use cable cross overs, cable flyes, or pec-dec flyes.

Chest

Cable Crossover: Alas! This is what you've been waiting for. Did you ever think you would see me performing this exercise? Well, I did during precontest training when no one was using the cable machine. And I do now, occasionally, if the gym is empty on my chest day. So if you're going to do these, do them right!

Attach a handle to each side of the high pulleys on the cable cross over machine. Grip both handles and position yourself to the center of the floor between the cables. Position one foot forward as shown in the photographs. This will allow for a better stretch compared to your feet being together. You can start with either your arms apart or together. If you start with your arms together:

- Slowly open your arms with your elbows slightly bent.
- Allow your arms to move away from each other in a circular motion until you feel a good stretch in the chest and pause.
- Squeeze the cables across your chest as if hugging a tree, maintaining the same bend in your elbows.
- Slightly cross one hand over the other when squeezing your chest, or simply have your hands meet in the middle.
- If you can't maintain a circular motion with only a slight bend in the elbows, throughout the entire range of motion, then the weight is too heavy. Remember, this is a shaping exercise that requires light weights.

Cable Flyes can be performed on any bench positioned between the cable crossover machine. For best results, use an incline bench. The incline bench allows for an increased range of motion because the cables travel a farther distance from the floor to your chest as apposed to using a flat bench.

Attach a handle to each side of the low pulleys. Grip both handles and lie on the bench. Perform a flye using the same form as with dumbbell flyes. Be sure to select a weight that will allow for a full range of motion. Once again, this is primarily a shaping exercise performed with lighter weights and higher repetitions.

When lowering the weight, your arms should open out and wide with a slight bend in the elbows. This will guarantee a great stretch in your chest. The positive movement is more challenging. On the way up, squeeze the cable handles together using the same wide motion as on the way down keeping a slight bend in the elbows.

Pec-dec Flyes: If your gym has a pec-dec, you can use it for variety. Be sure to position the seat high where the arm pads line-up with your chest. This will give you leverage and prevent you from using your shoulders. Open your arms *slowly* allowing a great stretch in your chest. After pausing for a quick second, bring your arms together, squeezing your chest, keeping your elbows on the pads. A spotter can be very helpful during this exercise to help you squeeze out those last few reps.

Back

Cable One-Arm Row: The toughest part of this exercise is maintaining good form. Stand with your feet close together, far enough away from the weight stack so that when you lower the weight, it doesn't slam the other plates.

When you pull:

- Maintain the same bend in your knees.
- Throw your chest out and squeeze both shoulders back.
- Arch your back.
- Keep your left hand on your left thigh.

Start with your knees slightly bent and your buttocks out. If you are working your right side first, position your left arm on your left thigh for support.

Pulldowns:

One of the rare times I perform pulldowns is during precontest training. Otherwise I prefer pullups. Pulldowns can be performed either behind the neck or to your chest. I prefer pulling down to my chest. Performing them behind the neck sometimes hurts my shoulders. For variety, I also change my grips. In the third photo, I'm using a reverse grip.

Performing pulldowns to the chest works more of the outer part of the back. Be sure to pull the bar on an angle rather than straight down. Do this by leaning back slightly and pulling the bar to the top of your chest. After squeezing the back for one full second, slowly raise the bar until your arms

Pulldown Tips:

- Pull your shoulders back and down. Do not shrug your shoulders.
- Throw your chest out.
- Keep your elbows out.
- Arch your back.
- Squeeze and hold each repetition.

are fully extended getting a good stretch. Notice the full extension in the first photo.

Stiff-Arm Pulldowns: This exercise mimics a pullover. Instead of lying on a bench, you are standing. Another difference is that your arms are stiff during this exercise where with pullovers, they're slightly bent. When performed properly, stiff-arm pullovers target the outer part of your lats.

 This was usually a finishing back exercise, but I also used it to superset back.

Start with your palms and fingertips only, on a short, straight bar. Don't grip the bar. You don't want to work your arms. You will have a tendency to want to use your triceps, but don't. Remember this is a back exercise. *Pull* the bar down to your thighs keeping your arms locked or *stiff*. Squeeze your

Tips when performing stiff-arm pulldowns:

- Use a light weight.
- Don't fully grip the bar. Your palms and fingertips only rest on the bar.
- Keep your arms locked. Don't bend your arms.
- Keep your back arched and chest out. Don't round your back.
- Squeeze your back as you pull the bar down to your thighs.
- Slowly raise the bar back keeping your wrists forward.

back as if you were performing a seated row. Also remember to keep your back arched and chest out. You may also have a tendency to want to round your back to pull down the weight. Don't! Keep your back arched! On the way up, *slowly* allow the bar to rise feeling a good stretch in your back. To prevent the bar from slipping off your *hands (since you are not gripping it)* curl your wrists forward as you raise the bar.

It's very important to concentrate on working your lats. Think about pulling and lowering the bar with your back. This is a time to put your mind in your muscle. If you do it right, you will feel an incredible burn in your back. Be sure to use a light weight.

Shoulders

Cable Upright Rows: I get a real good burn with this exercise. I like supersetting these with dumbbell lateral raises or barbell upright rows. Using the low row pulley, attach a short bar for your grip. Use the same form as with barbell upright rows. Be sure to raise the bar up and away from your body rather than straight up keeping your elbows out. I recommend using a light weight for this exercise to allow a full range of motion. Perform barbell upright rows with heavy weights.

Cable Lateral Raises: Follow the same form as with dumb-bell lateral raises. You will need to grip the opposite side cables to perform this exercise. For example, you must grip the right side low cable with your left hand and vice versa. Be sure to keep your wrists down and elbows slightly bent when raising the weights.

Cable Reverse Flye *(for the rear deltoid)*: When performed properly with light weights, this exercise can really isolate the rear part of your shoulders. From a kneeling position, grab a handle attached to a low row pulley. Laterally pull keeping your torso straight. Notice the slight bend in my elbow in the second photo. Try not to fully extend your arm. You will be working your triceps instead of your rear deltoid.

Other Shoulder Exercises

Anterior Deltoids
Dumbbell front raises
Cable lateral raises

Medial Deltoids
Barbell front raises

Posterior Deltoids
Seated rows with a rope:
Seated rows are usually performed for back. Using a rope and pulling high, will work the rear deltoids.

Tips for good form:
- Use a very light weight.
- Keep a slight bend in your elbow.
- Keep your torso straight.
- Don't shrug your shoulders.
- Squeeze the back of your shoulder and hold for a full second.
- S*lowly* lower the weight maintaining a slight bend in the elbow.

Triceps

Triceps Pushdowns: There are numerous ways to perform this exercise, below are a couple:

Pushdowns Using A Rope: If you have access to a rope, use it for that extra range of motion and incredible burn! Usually, when performing pushdowns, your arms should be pinned to your sides. But with a rope, you can allow the arms to deviate from your sides for that extra range of motion on the negative movement.

- Maintain a slight bend in the knees.
- Keep your back arched.
- Keep your chest out and your shoulders down.
- Don't shrug your shoulders!

Once you fully extend your arms, try spreading the rope apart and squeeze your triceps. Focus on pushing the rope through your body rather than pushing straight down to the floor.

Single-Arm Reverse Grip Pushdowns: This exercise targets the back of the triceps. I like to either grab the side of the cable machine with my non-working hand as shown in the photographs or keep it on my waist.

Begin by gripping a handle with your palm up. Pin your arm at your side with your elbow bent at about a 90 degree angle. Push straight down towards the floor keeping your body upright with your chest out. Do not cheat by leaning forward. The only thing that should be moving is your elbow. At the end of the movement, squeeze your triceps and return your arm to the 90 degree starting position.

Biceps

Cable Preacher Curl: Position a preacher bench in front of a low row cable machine. Attach a bar to the low row pulley and use the same form as with regular preacher curls shown in Chapter 3. Notice that I don't sit on the bench, but rather lean into it. This helps with leverage and allows for a better stretch when lowering the weight.

Concentration Curl: Sit on the end of a flat bench. Starting with a dumbbell in your left hand, position your left triceps inside your left thigh and fully extend the arm as shown in the first photograph. Curl the dumbbell, pushing your arm inside your thigh. Before repeating, fully extend the arm.

Concentration Curl Tips:

- For leverage, stay on your toes rather than with your feet flat on the floor. This will help you pump out those extra reps. You can press your thigh into your arm as well as your arm into your thigh.
- Keep your chest out.
- Don't slouch over, or this will decrease the range of motion.
- Use your right arm positioned on your right thigh for additional leverage and support.

Quadriceps

Sissy Squats: Sissy Squats are not for sissies! These squats look easy, but are very difficult to perform. When good form is use, this exercise is excellent for defining the quadriceps.

Start on your toes holding on to something sturdy such as a squat rack. In the photos, I'm holding on to the leg press. Your other arm should be across your chest holding a light plate. In the photos, I'm holding a 10 pound plate.

Slowly squat by leaning back, arching your back and coming up on your toes. When your body is almost parallel to the floor, come back up.
- Be sure to stay on your toes throughout the entire range of motion; do not come back to a flat footed position.
- Do not stand straight up. As soon as you come up, go back down.
- The plate across the chest is used for form as well as added intensity. It should rest on your chest without you holding it there. If it falls, you are standing too straight up rather than leaning back.

Leg Extensions:
I always thought of leg extensions as the hammer and chisel for defining the legs. They're great to superset with squats or leg presses. The main thing to remember is to hold and squeeze each repetition for one full second before slowly lowering the weight. You can vary the position of your toes by pointing your toes in for the outer thigh and out for the inner thigh.

Hamstrings

Stiff-leg Deadlifts: In the first edition of my book, I included this exercise in Chapter 3, where I discuss basic exercises. Well, over the years, I have changed my mind. It isn't a basic exercise, quite the contrary. It's a very difficult and complex exercise. I don't recommend this exercise for beginners or anyone that is not looking to compete in a bodybuilding contest.

I have to admit, I performed this exercise religiously during precontest training. But unless you really know how to properly perform this exercise, you greatly risk injuring your lower back. Since I don't compete anymore, I rely on lying standing leg curls for developing my hamstrings.

But if you are going to perform this exercise, do it right!

Take a shoulder width grip. I like grabbing the bar with one hand over the bar and the other hand under the bar. In the photos, I have an underhand grip with my right hand and an overhand grip with my left. This grip helps me keep the bar close to my body as I lower and raise it.

The initial movement is to stick your buttocks out, with *locked* knees and a slight arch to your back. These two movements alone should immediately stress the hamstrings. From here, slowly bend over keeping your legs locked and slowly lowering the bar with your arms straight. Focus on lowering the bar through your legs rather than straight down. Keep the bar as close to your body as possible until you reach the bottom where you will move the bar away from your body for an extra stretch. Notice the stretch in my hamstrings in the second photo.

Once you have completely stretched your hamstrings, slowly start straightening your body without bending your knees, keeping the bar close to your body as possible.

The following charts show examples of my precontest training workouts:

Example #1 using supersets and strip sets for chest:

Exercise	Weight	Reps	Sets
Barbell bench press	135	12	1
	225	10	1
	275	8	1
	315	6	1
Weighted dips	1 plate	10	1
	2 plates	8	1
	3 plates	6	1
(strip set)	3 plates	6	-
	2 plates	6	-
	1 plate	6	-
	none	6	-
Dumbbell incline press	100	10	1
	85	10	1
	75	10	1
	65	10	
Supersetted w/cable flyes	35	15	1
	40	12	1
	40	10	1
	35	12	1

Summary of Example #1

- Notice I continue to use heavy weights to help keep my size. I perform a warm-up set of bench presses with 135. With a short rest between sets, I perform three more sets gradually increasing my weight.

- I perform weighted dips heavy and then strip the weight. I start with one 45 pound plate tied to my waist and increased to two and three plates respectively. The last set is performed with three plates and then stripped.

- I perform six reps with three plates and immediately take off one plate.

- I perform another six reps with two plates and take off another plate. Then perform six more reps with one plate, take off the last plate and finally perform my last six reps of dips with no weight.

- Incline presses are performed with moderate weight with supersets of cable flyes. First I perform a set of incline presses and immediately perform a set of flyes and repeat twice more. I decrease the weight from 100 to 85 to 75 as I superset presses with cable flyes.

Example #2 using staggered sets for chest and back:

Exercise	Weight	Reps	Sets
Pullups	no weight	12	4
(staggered sets)			
Bench press	135	12	1
	225	10	1
	275	8	1
	315	6	1
Dumbbell incline presses	100	10	1
	110	10	1
	120	8	1
	130	6	1
(staggered sets)			
Dumbbell one-arm row	90	10	1
	100	10	1
	110	10	1
	120	10	1
Seated rows	180	10	1
	200	10	3
(staggered sets)			
Cable crossovers	60	15	3

Summary of Example #2

■ Pullups and bench presses are staggered. First I perform a set of pullups, and immediately perform a set of bench press. I take about a 15 second rest after the bench presses and repeat for a total of four sets. I increase the weight with bench presses, but continue performing pullups with no weight.

■ Dumbbell incline presses and dumbbell one-arm rows are staggered. I increase the weight with both exercises. I can still lift heavy because while my chest rests, my back works, and vice versa.

■ I perform my last staggered set with seated rows and cable crossover:

■ Notice that I did not increase the weight with either exercise because by this time, I am very tired and want to maintain proper form with high repetitions.

Example #3 using staggered sets for back and triceps:

Exercise	Weight	Reps	Sets
Pulldowns	180	12	1
	200	10	1
	210	10	1
	220	8	1
(staggered sets)			
French curls	100	12	1
	110	10	1
	120	10	2
Bent-over rows	135	10	1
	185	10	1
	225	10	2
(staggered sets)			
Lying triceps extensions	100	12	4
Single cable one-arm row	60	15	1
	70	12	1
	80	10	1
	70	10	1
(staggered sets)			
Pushdowns w/rope	100	15	3
(strip set)	100	6	1
	80	6	1
	60	6	1

Summary of Example #3

- Pulldowns are staggered with French curls.

- Bent-over rows are staggered with lying triceps extensions.

- Cable one-arm rows are staggered with pushdowns using a rope.

- Pushdowns with a rope are much more difficult than regular pushdowns with a bar. It's important to use a light weight to squeeze the triceps at the bottom of the movement for a full range of motion. I then finish pushdowns with a grueling strip set. The last set of pushdowns I start with 100 pounds. After performing six reps, I strip the weight to 80 pounds, perform another six reps and then strip the weight one last time and perform my last six reps.

Example # 4 supersetting shoulders with strip sets:

Exercise	Weight	Reps	Sets
Dumbbell overhead press	75	10	1
	90	10	1
	100	8	1
	110	6	1
Cable upright rows	90	15	1
	100	12	1
	110	10	1
(strip set)			
	110	6	-
	90	6	-
	70	6	-
(supersetted)			
Dumbbell lateral raises	35	12	1
	40	10	1
	40	8	1
(strip set)	40	6	-
	25	6	-
	20	6	-
Single-arm cable reverse flyes	30	15	3

Summary of Example #4

- Notice that I do not superset dumbbell overhead press. I like performing this exercise with heavy weights. I usually like to start with a basic muscle building exercise using heavy weight.

- I superset cable upright rows with dumbbell lateral raises and strip the last set of upright rows.

- I like finishing shoulders with cable reverse flyes with light weight and strict form.

Example # 5 using supersets and strip sets for quads:

Exercise	Weight	Reps	Sets
Squats	135	20	1
	185	20	1
	200	20	1
(strip set)	200	10	-
	185	10	-
	135	10	-
(supersets)			
Leg extensions	80	10	3
	100	6	-
	80	6	-
(strip set)	60	6	-

Note: Squats are supersetted with leg extensions.
The last set of squats and leg extensions is stripped.

Leg press	5 plates	15	1
	6 plates	10	1
	7 plates	6	1
(strip set)	7 plates	6	-
	6 plates	6	-
	6 plates	6	-
(supersets)			
Sissy squats	25 lb. plate	10	4
Hack squats	1 plate	10	1
	2 plates	10	1
	3 plates	8	1
(strip set)	3 plates	6	-
	2 plates	6	-
	1 plate	6	-

Summary of Example #5

- Squats are supersetted with leg extensions. I keep the weight with leg extensions at 80 pounds during the supersets with front squats. The last set of front squats and leg extensions is stripped.

- Leg presses are supersetted with sissy squats. I use a 25 pound plate resting on my chest for sissy squats.

- I perform three sets of Hack Squats gradually increasing the weight. I start the last or fourth set with three plates and then strip the weight.

Final Preparations _____

Final contest preparations include, tanning, posing, shaving, and oiling the body. Choosing the right posing trunks and having a good hair style are also important. Although these may seem trivial, they may make a difference in your appearance on stage.

Tanning

Nothing is worse than a great physique on stage that's not tan. It's like Van gogh deciding not to paint a master piece that he planned and worked on for months. A tan brings out the shape of the muscles and the vascularity of the veins.

Whether you tan indoors, using a tanning bed, or outdoors, do it gradually. Plan your tanning as you would your dieting. You wouldn't try to lose 10 pounds one week before your contest. Similarly, you shouldn't try to get tan in one week. Start tanning at least one month before your contest, 20 to 30 minutes, four or five times per week. This will prevent peeling and long exposures to tanning beds and the sun. To help avoid peeling, massage your body with baby oil or lotion at least once daily. Planning ahead and gradually tanning will give you the best and safest results.

Outdoor Tanning

Although a suntan is actually damage to your skin, it's a very amazing process. The skin's cells react to sunlight by vibrating against each other. The friction of the cells causes a natural form of inflammation that results in redness in the form of a sunburn. When exposed to the sun's rays for a prolong period of time, skin cells vibrate too rapidly, causing them to destroy each other. This causes skin damage. When skin cells die, the skin sheds. When the skin peels, we are actually shedding dead damaged skin.

If you choose to tan outdoors, be certain to protect yourself with a sunscreen. Regular use of a sunscreen can reduce your risk of some forms of skin cancer by almost 78% *(Johnson & Johnson Guide to SunSafety, Straight Talk About Family Suncare, 1994).*

What is SPF?

Sun Protection Factor (SPF) tells you how much longer you can stay in the sun without burning using a sunscreen versus using no protection. For example, SPF 15 means that if you normally start to turn red in ten minutes, you can stay in the sun 15 times longer before turning red. The amazing thing about SPF is that it actually tricks your skin's cells not to vibrate. The cream itself has little to do with shading your skin from the sun.

For bodybuilding preparations, you can choose SPF 4 since you do not totally want to block the sun and still be well protected.

When choosing a sunscreen, there are some basic qualities to look for:

- UV barrier system
- PABA-free & chemical free
- Moisturizer
- Sweatproof and waterproof

Using a product with the UV barrier system will protect your skin from the sun's ultraviolet rays, the UVA and UVB rays. The UVA rays were once considered as *safe* tanning rays. Studies have shown that the UVA rays are just as harmful as the UVB rays. Although UVA rays do not cause the same short-term sunburn as UVB rays, they do penetrate deeper into your skin causing more long-term damage. The UVB rays, known as the tanning rays, are responsible for most sunburns. There are many brands of sunscreens that do not offer the UV barrier system to protect you from skin cancer. So be sure to read the label.

PABA is a sunscreen chemical ingredient that is irritating to the skin. There are quality sunscreens available without PABA. Also use a sunscreen containing moisturizers to help keep your skin soft and smooth.

Use a product that is sweatproof and waterproof so you don't need to reapply it every time you sweat or get wet.

Indoor Tanning

Many of us will need to resort to an indoor tanning bed. If you choose this method, start gradually, 20 to 30 minutes, four to five times a week, at least four weeks before your contest.

You can also use a sunless tanning lotion in addition to indoor and outdoor tanning. A sunless tanning lotion promotes a safe tan without the harmful rays of the sun and also moisturizes your skin. You can purchase a sunless tanning lotion in pharmacies and GNC stores.

These products work with your skin's natural proteins to safely provide a tan in just a few hours. They stimulate your skin to produce more than its normal amount of melanin. Melanin is a dark brown/black pigment that produces color in living skin cells. It protects your skin from the sun. Your normal levels of melanin will determine the darkness of your tan as a result of using a sunless tanning lotion. People with higher levels of melanin will see better results. In order to achieve a deep tan, reapply the product every few hours.

If you want to get extra dark a few days before your contest, you can use a product such as ProTan. It's a dye specially made for bodybuilders that you apply with a small brush.

On the first night, apply three coats allowing each to dry before reapplying. On the second night, apply two cotes following with two last coats on the morning of the contest. In order to prevent the coats from washing off in the shower, you must only rinse off and pat yourself dry with a towel. If you stay in the shower too long, or wash your body thoroughly, you will wash off the dye.

It is very important to rinse off in the shower the morning of the contest after applying your last two coats. This will avoid an orange looking appearance. Also, be sure to shave thoroughly before tanning and dying.

Shaving

Removing all hair from the entire body can be challenging. A good tool to use is an electric razor. In the past, I tried using a regular razor, but too much hair and skin got caught in the razor. If you are really hairy, I wouldn't recommend any lotions to remove hair. You can also consider waxing.

Oil

Before stepping on stage, you want to be sure the right amount of oil is on your body. You will be perspiring on stage under the hot lights, so you do not want use too much oil.
Oil and dye running off your body can take a judge's focus away from your physique.

For best results have someone apply the oil on you, one body section at a time. For example, start with the legs. Once the legs are complete, work on the torso. Do not try to oil the entire body at once. The person applying the oil should start with a small amount of oil in each hand. After rubbing both hands together, they should be sure that no oil drips from their hands. If it does, they are using too much.

After the entire body is completely oiled, test for drips. Stand under bright lights back stage and look for running oil. If there is excess oil on your body, dab it with a dry towel.

I found that regular baby oil works fine. You do not need to spend additional money on any special kind of oils.

Posing Trunks For Men

Choose a solid color! Judges in the past have refused competitors on stage with multi-colored trunks. As a result, competitors in the past had to purchase Superman underwear to compete. This incident was probably the most ridiculous thing I have ever witnessed in bodybuilding, but well worth the laugh.

Through the years, I have used several colors from red to black. Use a color that compliments your physique or one that you feel comfortable with. Be sure the trunks fit you well. You do not want them hanging off your buttocks or squeezing you to death either.

Posing Suits for Women

You want to choose a solid color that compliments and fits your physique. *Muscle & Fitness Magazine* has a great selection of suits to choose from.

Hair

Men should wear their hair short for contests. That may sound ironic coming from me. If you noticed my hair in this book's contest photos you'll no what I mean. Short hair will make you appear bigger. If your hair is thick and puffy like mine was, it will overshadow your physique. If it is long in the back, tie it in a ponytail. Women should wear long hair up. You do not want your hair covering your back muscles.

The Day of The Contest

Most bodybuilding contests start early in the morning about 9:00 AM. Get there early because weigh-ins usually start at about 7:00 or 8:00 AM with prejudging immediately following. I have seen people show up late and not compete. If you are competing in a NPC contest, the first thing you need to do is check in at the judge's table and present your NPC card or purchase one there. All NPC contests require that you register for the contest at least one month in advance. Anyone that shows up to the contest unregistered will not be allowed to compete.

The night before, make a check list of the things you will need to take with you. See the example below:

NPC Registration Card
Music TAPE (CASSETTE) TWO COPIES!!!!!
Extra Pair of Posing Trunks
Rice cakes
Jelly
Other carbing up food
Water
Towel
Protan (In case it wears off from prejudging)
Oil
A Big Car to take home your trophy.

Your weight class will determine what you will do following weigh-ins. If you are a light or bantam weight, you will need to immediately start pumping up back stage since you are the first to compete. I was a middle weight, so I relaxed until the light weights were finishing their one minute posing routines.

After prejudging is over, you need to return at night about 6:00 p.m. Here is the kick, at this point you still don't know if you will get to pose in front of your friends later at night. In NPC contests, there are usually well over 10 competitors in each weight class and only the top five get to pose for the night show.

If you make it to the night show, you will pose for one minute to your selected music. The top five competitors of each weight class get trophies and the first place finishers of each weight class pose down against each other. The pose-down between the winners of each weight class is similar to the compulsory round during prejudging where the judges compared the competitors pose for pose. The winner of that round is the overall winner of the contest.

Pumping Up Back Stage

In the past, I used towel resistance exercises or light dumbbells to pump up. The only problem was that I rarely got a good pump. Posing after a good training is when I experienced my best pumps. So before stepping on stage, I made sure to use intense exercises with moderate weight to pump up back stage. You are somewhat limited depending on the weights available back stage.   Be sure to break a sweat before stepping on stage. Being nervous before stepping on stage prevented me from getting a good pump. This was another good reason to experience a mini-workout before competing. It would help me break a sweat, release tension, and pump up.

CHAPTER 17

Posing and Judging

Posing and Judging

You have trained intensely and prepared diligently for the big day. Dieting has made you sacrifice the more enjoyable aspects of life for the last several months. Your tan looks great on your hard and ripped muscles. Now, you find yourself on stage ready to strike a pose in front of a team of judges.

How well you present yourself on stage can make a huge difference on how you are judged. Take it from me, in my first contest, the 1988 Mr. & Ms. Rutgers Bodybuilding Contest, I weighed 175 pounds and was the biggest and hardest middleweight on stage. Somehow I found a way to lose my weight class to a smaller and less muscular competitor. Not to discredit the winner, because he looked great, but I lost the contest because I did not present myself well. On the other hand, the middleweight winner was the best poser on stage.

Practice, Practice, Practice

How well you plan and prepare determines a successful presentation. Preparation, or lack of it, will show on stage. Start practicing at least six to eight weeks before your contest. I practiced immediately following my workouts. I really got into it, because after a workout, I was extraordinarily pumped. I was lucky because my gym had a private posing room with mirrors and lights, where I evaluated myself from all angles.

Posing is an exhaustive workout. You'll sweat profusely from flexing and holding poses. Practice every round of the three segments on the following pages. Also practice poses from both sides when applicable and hold each pose for several seconds before relaxing. On stage, you will tire from holding poses for several seconds under the hot lights. So be prepared for a workout of your life!

Posing between sets during your workouts can enhance the shape and definition of your muscles as well as help you practice your poses. For example, when training back, flex your lats between sets by performing a front double lat spread. Hold the pose for six to ten seconds and repeat until it's time for your next set. Another example is practicing your side chest poses between sets of chest exercises. You can do this for all your body parts. First you need to learn the poses, so read on.

Main Points on Contest Posing:

- Know the three posing rounds of a bodybuilding contest.
- Learn how to stand on stage during the symmetry round.
- Learn the eight mandatory poses.
- Plan a one-minute posing routine.
- Choose music for your one-minute posing routine.

Three Posing Rounds of a Bodybuilding Contest:

- The Relaxed Round or Symmetry Round.
- The Muscularity Round or Compulsory Round .
- Presentation/one minute of free posing.

All three rounds take place during prejudging where all competitors have a chance to show their physiques in front of a team of judges. Prejudging usually takes place in the morning directly following weigh-ins. Prejudging filters the top competitors of the contest of each weight class. Because NPC contests are so large, only the top five to seven competitors from each weight class get a chance to pose at night.

Weight Classes

The size of the contest will also determine the number of weight classes. The Mr. & Ms. Rutgers Contest, my first bodybuilding contest, had only three weight classes, light, middle, and heavyweight, for both men and women. Other larger contests such as the NPC Mr. New Jersey included a bantam weight and light heavyweight in addition to light, middle, and heavyweight. Some contests are judged according to height rather than weight. All NPC contests are judged by weight classes as shown below.

Bantamweight: Up to and including 143¼ pounds.

Lightweight: Over 143¼ and up to and including 154¼

Middleweight: Over 154¼ and up to and including 176¼

Light Heavyweight: Over 176¼ and up to and including 198¼

Heavyweight: Over 198¼

The poses, rules, and procedures are the same for both men and women. The only time you will see a difference in posing between men and women is during the free posing round, which is discussed later in this chapter. For the symmetry round, the competitors stand in line across the stage and wait for instructions from the head judge.

Symmetry Round

Webster's dictionary defines symmetry as, *balanced proportions, beauty of form arising from balanced proportions: correspondence in size, shape, and relative position of parts...*

This is the first and probably the most important round of a bodybuilding contest. A general assessment is made of the overall balance of musculature while standing in semi-relaxed position. This includes a series of turns to view the body from the front, sides, and rear as shown in the photographs. The judges asses total muscularity and symmetry, that is the balance of each muscle group in relation to other muscle groups. You may have seen bodybuilders with unbalanced physiques. For example, bodybuilders with may large pectorals and biceps with small shoulders and triceps. The classic example of lacking symmetry is a bodybuilder with a huge upper body and underdeveloped legs.

Amateur bodybuilder Scott Bauman practices his symmetry round poses two months prior to his contest date.

The symmetry round in my opinion is most important because it's the first time judges lay eyes on you. This is where they start shuffling and moving bodies. They group the best competitors at center stage. Some bodybuilders may be overlooked during the symmetry round before they even get to flex a muscle. Scrap paper is first used by the judges for a rough placement of the competitors. The placements usually change a few times on a judge's scrap paper before a final decision is made on the score card. For example, a judge might place you first after the symmetry round and change you to second after seeing you in the compulsory and free posing rounds. From my experience, if a judge has you placed first after the symmetry round that placement usually stands. Final changes are usually made after seeing the top competitors in all three rounds during prejudging.

The symmetry round starts with an entire weight class of competitors on stage in numerical order. If there is enough room to line up all the competitors from a weight class across the stage, then the judges will immediately start shuffling bodies around for comparisons. If there is not enough room on stage, then they break the class into two or more groups. From here, they choose the best, say five competitors from each group and combine the top ten or so competitors to form one group. Eventually, the judges choose only the top five or seven competitors to return for the night show.

The head judge first instructs the competitors to stand in a *relaxed* position facing the seven judges directly below the stage. This is the first symmetry round pose, standing in front of the judges in a *semi-relaxed* position. Even though the head judge directs you to stand relaxed, that does not mean you stand relaxed. You should be standing on stage with your heals together and somewhat flexing your entire body. There is a fine line between standing relaxed and actually posing. You want to look *hard* without showing effort. Your arms should be slightly away from your body rather than straight down to your sides with your shoulders back and chest broad. I have seen judges scold competitors for posing during the symmetry round.

From here, the head judge instructs, *a quarter turn to the right*. It never fails; I usually see at least one competitor turn to the left. There is no excuse for this. During this round, you will always be asked to turn to the right first. If you practiced enough, you will automatically turn to the right without even thinking about the judge's instruction.

The left side of your body will be facing the judges with your right shoulder slightly, and I repeat, slightly flexing the right side of your chest. Scott Bauman demonstrates this well in the photos below. Your left arm that is facing the judges should be slightly flexed to show your triceps. Once again, there is a fine line between flexing your muscles and standing relaxed. I have always had a good grasp of that fine line. I always looked *hard* and tight on stage, but didn't look like I was struggling to do so. Only practice and experience will perfect this.

In this position, it is very important to look straight ahead! Do not look at the judges. You should be looking at the back of the competitor's head in front of you, assuming you are not the first person on line. Although the head judge will instruct you to have your feet together, your left foot should be ever so slightly in front of your right.

The judge again instructs, *quarter turn to your right*. Your back should now be facing the judges as shown in the third photograph. Once again, your heals should be together with your toes slightly pointing out. Your back should be slightly spread as if performing a lat spread. But again, do not exaggerate the spread. Keep your arms slightly flexed at your sides. Flex your hamstrings and your glutes by gripping the floor with your toes.

After the next quarter turn, the right side of your body will be facing the judges as shown in the last photograph. You will do exactly the same as in your first quarter turn when the left side of your body was facing the judges.

The last quarter turn, will have you facing the judges once again. You are now ready for the compulsory round.

Compulsory Round

There are eight mandatory poses you will need to learn:

- Front Double Biceps
- Front Lat Spread
- Back Double Biceps
- Rear Lat Spread
- Side Chest
- Side Triceps
- Abdominal Pose
- Most Muscular

Practice and learn the eight mandatory poses. You can use this book and photographs of bodybuilders in magazines such as Muscle & Fitness®, Flex®, and Iron Man®. I taped pictures on my mirror where I practiced my poses. I can still remember mimicking pictures of Bob Paris, Shawn Ray, Lee Labrada and others. I studied the photos and posed simultaneously. Understand and observe the location and position of all your bodyparts including your fingers and toes on every pose.

Once you have become familiar and comfortable performing these poses have photographs taken of yourself performing all the poses. Compare your photos with pictures from your favorite bodybuilders and from this book. This book shows the basics and some variety of the mandatory poses. Use friends familiar with the sport to critique you. Take notes for every pose and log areas where you need improvement. I used bullet notes right under the photographs as shown in this chapter.

Following the symmetry round, the judges will start moving you around, usually arranging the best competitors to center stage. Try to remember the number pinned to your posing trunks and listen carefully for the head judge. He may very well call your number and instruct you to move.

Any of the judges may direct you to perform any one of the mandatory poses. Try to be the first to strike the pose and the last to relax. Hold your pose until they tell you to relax. From here, the judges will continue to move everyone around until satisfied with the results of their score cards.

Once you have become familiar and comfortable performing these poses, have photographs taken of yourself performing them. Look for compatibility with your photos and use this book's photos and descriptions as a guide. Use friends familiar with the sport to critique you. Take notes on every

pose and log areas where you need improvement.
Following the symmetry round, the judges will start moving
you around, usually arranging the best competitors to center
stage. Try to remember the number pinned on your posing
trunks and listen carefully to the head judge—he or she may
very well call your number and instruct you to move.

The judges may direct you to perform any one of the mandatory poses. You want to be the first to strike the pose and
the last to relax. Hold your poses until they tell you to relax.
From here, they will continue to move everyone around until
they are satisfied with their scores.

Front Double Biceps: This is a very popular pose that shows your muscularity from a front view. Start all poses from the bottom up. Your feet and legs should be in a good position to strike and hold a pose. There are several ways to position your legs and feet as Scott, Denise, and Vincent show in the photographs. If you are a beginner, start with your feet slightly apart with your heels together, toes pointed out, and your knees slightly bent. Once you get the hang of it, you can experiment with your legs. Denise has one leg extended while Scott has one leg in front of the other. Find out what works for you.

Scott Bauman, Denise Marsh and Vincent Burke all strike winning front double biceps poses.

- ■ Flex your arms over your head at about 45 degree angles.
- ■ Curl your wrists forward.
- ■ Flex your chest as well as your biceps.
- ■ Flare out your lats.
- ■ Suck your stomach in and expand your rib cage.

Front Lat Spread: Although called front lat spread, this pose also shows off you chest, shoulders, and arms. Once again start with your feet in a good position. Vincent shows the most basic foot and leg position with his heels together and toes out with his knees slightly bent.

The front lat spread: Denise Marsh, left, extends one leg; Diana Cimato, center, shows her excellent calf development; and Vincent Burke displays basic form with his heels together.

- Suck in your stomach, take a deep breath, and spread your the lats.
- Flex your chest and biceps.
- Squeeze your waist with your thumbs and index fingers with your hands in a "fistlike" position.
- Don't forget to flex your legs.

Back Double Biceps: This pose shows the muscularity of the entire back of the body including the hamstrings and calves. The judges will sometimes specify that you extend one leg back to flex the calf. If the head judge does not specify, then you can choose several options. You can extend one leg back facing the judges, extend one leg to the side as Jeannine shows in the photo, or cross one leg over the other as Vincent shows in the other photo. If you do extend one leg back, be sure to flex the calf by planting the ball of your foot on the ground and raising your heel. Also, flex the hamstring as well by keeping the extended leg slightly bent using the floor as resistance.

Left: Vincent Burke strikes a back double biceps with his left heel extended back and to the right.

Inset: Jeannine Fisher extends her left leg to the side.

- Be sure to arch the back hard and flex all the muscles of the lower back.
- This pose will differ from the front double biceps pose. Rather than positioning the arms slightly forward, you will be squeezing them back while arching the back to flex all the muscles of the upper and lower back.

Rear Lat Spread: This pose will show the judges the width and thickness of the entire back. Again, the head judge will specify the position of the legs.

- As with the front lat spread, use your thumbs with your hands in a fist to grab and squeeze in the waist and spread your lats as wide as you can.
- While flexing the lats, squeeze and flex your arms as well. From the rear, your triceps will stand out when tightened.

Vincent Burke shows great back development during a rear lat spread.

Vincent Burke and Jeannine Fisher demonstrate basic right and left side chest poses.

Side Chest: You may be given a choice to strike this pose from the right or the left side of your body. Be ready to pose from either side because sometimes the judges will want to see it from both sides. Keep in mind which side you will pose when given the choice.

Right Side Chest: If you choose or are instructed to perform a right side chest, then the right side of your body should be facing the judges.

- Position the ball of your right foot (with your toes raised) in the center of your left foot.
- Press your right leg, (which will be your forward leg) into the left leg. This will give an illusion of one bigger leg from being compressed against the rear leg.
- Your right leg should be slightly bent as shown in the photos.
- Your left leg should also be very slightly bent, but less bent than your right leg.

Scott Bauman shows some creativity in his leg positioning during a left side chest.

With your right palm facing up grab your right wrist with your left hand. Tuck and squeeze your right arm into the right side of your body flexing the right bicep and right side of your chest.

Your left arm should also be tucked into the left side of your body flexing the left side of your chest. Even though you are posing a *Right Side Chest*, you are still posing and flexing the left side of your chest as well.

- Do not to shrug your shoulders.
- Bull your chest out with your shoulders back and down.
- There should be minimal space between your arms and your body. Keep your arms closed tight to your body.

Be sure to show all the judges your post by slowly moving from left to right and right to left with your feet in position. Your torso is the only thing that should be moving. For the left side chest, do exactly the same as with the right side chest. The only difference is that the left side of your body will be facing the judges.

Side Triceps: Once again, the judges may request to see this pose from both sides. From my experience, the judges have always given the competitors the choice. They usually say, *side triceps of choice.* You can pose your triceps one of two ways, with your arm extended, or behind your back. Regardless of which way you pose your triceps, your feet and

Vincent Burke displays two styles of the side triceps pose: to the left with arm extended, and right with arm behind the back.

legs should be positioned the same as if you were performing a side chest pose. If you're lucky, they will ask you to strike a triceps pose immediately from your side chest. In that case, you won't even need to re-position legs.

1. **Arm Extended**: With the left side of your body facing the judges and with your legs in position, simply extend your left arm down towards the floor as if you were performing a push-down with one arm. Your right arm should be in the same position as if you were performing a left side chest except that you won't be holding your left wrist. Be sure to use your right arm to flex the right side of your chest as Vincent demonstrates in the first photo.

2. **Arm Behind Your Back:** With your body in the same position, put your arms behind your back as if getting hand-cuffed. Grab your left wrist with your right hand. Flex your left triceps by fully extending it as if performing a pushdown.

- Be sure to pull your left shoulder back. This will show your chest as well as your triceps.
- Do not shrug your shoulders.
- Show all the judges

Abdominal Pose: For the compulsory round, the head judge usually instructs the abdominal pose with both hands over your head and with one leg extended. Rather than clasp your hands together as if you were praying, grab one of your wrists instead. This will force you

Frank Melfa, left, and Vincent Burke display basic Abdominal poses with one leg extended.

to reach farther back behind your head, exposing more of your midsection. This will also leave little room between your arms and head. Your forearms are actually pressed behind your head rather than your hands.

The leg of your choice will be fully extended directly in front of you. Don't forget to tighten it as well as extend it. You are not just posing your abs; you are also posing your chest, biceps, and legs.

- Be sure to place your toes on the floor with your heal slightly raised.
- The rear leg should be slightly bent and visible for the judges.
- From here, take a deep breath in and squeeze the abdominals gradually and slowly letting out the air you sucked in.
- Be sure to flex your biceps, chest and front leg.

Most Muscular Pose: This is the last of the mandatory poses that shows off your entire muscularity. There are several ways to strike this pose. The following photographs show some of the most common ways. You can choose any variation of this pose during the compulsory round. Notice that in all four photos that one leg is extended out in front.

Frank Melfa
displays the Crab

Frank Melfa

Vincent Burke

Scott Bauman

1)The Crab is probably the most familiar of the most muscular poses. The crab reminds me of Lou Ferrigno on the TV series, *The Incredible Hulk.*

With one leg extended in front of you, flex both arms across your body as if performing a cable cross over for the chest and squeeze every muscle in your body.

2) My favorite most muscular is performed with both hands on the hips with one leg extended in front and modestly squeezing all my muscles.

3) Another way to perform this pose is with one hand on the hip and the other across the body as Vincent Burke demonstrates in the third photo from the left.

4) Scott Bauman deviates from the norm and grabs his wrist to display his most muscular.

Facial Expressions: The way you present yourself can determine whether you win the

contest or just place. Facial expressions are important when posing. I have seen too many competitors struggle on stage and it shows through facial expressions. You have to feel like a winner on stage. You need that winning smile! A modest smile is enough to let everyone know that you are confident on stage. Posing should appear effortlessly. Don't shake your head or clench your teeth, unless it's a viscous clenching like in my most muscular pose. If you have properly prepared for your contest, you should have no problem with confidence and presentation.

Holding Your Poses: Once you strike a pose at the judge's command, hold it until instructed to relax. You want to be the first to strike the pose and the last to release it. This way, all the judges can see you. If you release to quickly, you can be easily overlooked. Also be sure to show all the judges your physique by slightly moving your body from left to right without leaving your position.

Stay Tight and Never Relax: When the judge directs you to relax, that means stand with your hands to your sides and release the pose. It doesn't mean looking down and slouching over. You want to stand tall and hard with your arms slightly flared, semi-flexing all the muscles of the upper body. Grip the floor with your toes to flex your legs.

One Minute of Free Posing

This is what all bodybuilders dream of doing! This is where you show your personality and passion for bodybuilding. Professional bodybuilder Bob Paris explains, "Perhaps the most artistic aspect of bodybuilding is the free posing round."*

Remember, you are still in prejudging. You won't be allowed to use music until the night show, assuming you make it that far. But you are FREE to do what you want for one minute. Just don't show your buttocks or modify clothing on stage. I have seen judges disqualify competitors for lifting up their trunks to show off their ripped glutes.

You have the opportunity to show the judges how elegantly, intelligently, and creatively you can transition from one pose to the next. Bob Paris adds, "I don't seek applause during my posing; I want people to be engrossed with their mouths open throughout the whole thing."

You want to show the judges a variation of your best mandatory poses with a personal touch. The following photographs show Vincent Burke and I, demonstrating a variety of creative poses incorporated in our posing routines. Notice how Vincent likes to pose from the floor, where I prefer posing on my feet.

* Reprinted by permission of Warner Books, New York, from Beyond Built, ©1991, Bob Paris

Planning Your One-Minute Routine

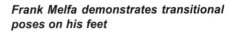

Frank Melfa demonstrates transitional poses on his feet

Judges really look for transition, how artistically you flow from one pose to the next. If you have a friend at the gym that can help you with posing, take advantage. There's no substitute for one-on-one instruction. You can learn transition by attending bodybuilding contests or watching them on TV.

The first thing to do is prepare a list of poses you will be using for your routine. Try to include some mandatory poses as well as your own creative ones. Then practice your transition. If you have access to a camcorder, have someone tape you, so you can observe yourself. Be sure to practice with and without music. Remember, during prejudging, no music is allowed. You can hum your song while you pose to help you flow during your routine.

I also practiced my posing routine in my mind: I would play the music that I selected for the night show while lying down with my eyes closed, mentally going through my routine.

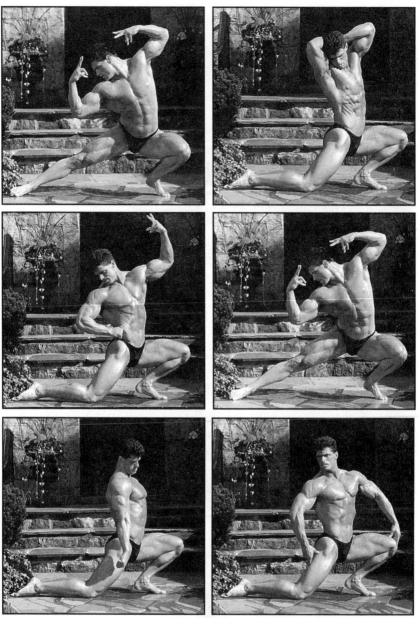

Vincent Burke demonstrates transition from the floor

Be sure to keep your routine to one minute; no longer! The judges will cut you off at one minute regardless where you are during your routine.

Vincent Burke demonstrates transition on his feet

Selecting your Music

Only the competitors who make the final round at night use music. In most contests only the top five to seven competitors from each weight class pose at the night show. Unfortunately, because of time restrictions, all competitors can not pose at night in front of their family and friends.

Select music that compliments your physique and personality. Be sure it's music you feel comfortable with. You may be competing in your first contest and will be plenty nervous. Using music that you feel comfortable with can help you relax. Do not rely on your friends to pick your music. They didn't spend the grueling hours in the gym; you did. They didn't diet for the contest; you did.

Select a couple of songs you think you may want to use and practice your routine to them. Choose the one most suitable for posing. The music's beat should allow you to strike and hold poses and allow transition.

How the Judges Select the Winner

When prejudging is over, the judges have already selected the top five or seven competitors from each weight class in order of placement.

When you step on stage, the panel of seven judges starts the process of elimination using scrap paper. After the symmetry round, the judges already have a good idea of the top competitors. The compulsory round and the free posing round will eliminate any doubt of placement. The judges do not have much time to perform this task. After they have gone through all their scrap paper and maneuvering competitors, the judges record their final tally on their score cards.

The judges assign numerical placings with points. For example, a first place vote equals one point; a second place vote equals two points, etc. The lower the score, the better. The competitor with the lowest score wins. In the example provided, Smith has three first place votes, three second place votes, and one sixth place vote. This initially adds up to 15, but the judges drop one of the highest and one of the lowest scores to eliminate inconsistencies. His new score is now 8. The competitor with the most first place votes does not always win. In the example, Jones has four first place votes and loses to Smith. Smith pulls it off with his second place votes.

Example of a score sheet:

NPC Mr. New Jersey				
Mens Middleweight				
Contestant **Name & Number**	**Judges** 1 2 3 4 5 6 7		**Total** **Score**	**Place** **Number**
Smith #3	1 1 1 2 2 2 6		8	1
Jones #6	4 4 7 1 1 1 1		11	2
Johnson #5	3 3 3 3 4 3 2		15	3

The high and low scores are eliminated to prevent inconsistencies. In the example, judge number seven scores Smith with a 6. It's obviously inconsistent with the other judges' scores of 1's and 2's.

Similarly, Jones probably didn't deserve a score of 7 from judge number three. Therefore, it's eliminated. To balance his score, a first place vote is eliminated as well.

Johnson is clearly the third place finisher, while his high and low scores of 4 and 2 are eliminated.

CHAPTER 18

Bodybuilders:
Artists and Athletes

Bodybuilders: Artists and Athletes_____

Michelangelo's *The Creation of Adam*

Bodybuilders are athletes that participate in a unique sport that most people have little understanding. In the August 1992 *Muscle & Fitness* article, *Athlete Artist or Sex Object?*, K.R. Dutton and Ronald S. Laura, Ph.D., explain, *"Bodybuilding was more clearly seen as a sport thanks in great part to the International Federation of Bodybuilders."** They explain the serious context for bodybuilding as a sporting activity governed by strict rules of judging and presentation.

Bodybuilders prepare and train vigorously to compete against other bodybuilders in their weight class. The competition is fierce; a bodybuilder can compete against 20 or more other bodybuilders. Only the best bodybuilders are selected to portray their sculpted bodies. The others go home, and train for the next competition *(see Chapter 17, Posing and Judging).*

Bodybuilding is sometimes confused with the sport of weightlifting. Weightlifters compete on the basis of who can lift more weight for specific exercises such as the bench press, deadlift, or squat. Most weightlifters do not have aesthetic physiques. They rely on bulk to lift heavy weight. A good portion of this bulk is located around their waist. You will notice that many weightlifters are heavy around the waist

* Reprinted with permission of *Muscle & Fitness Magazine,* August 1992

and have little resemblance to body-builders.

Bodybuilding is an art form as well as a sport. Dutton and Laura add, *"the minimally clad display of the muscular physique can be related to the world of art."** Choreographed posing routines portray the beauty and aesthetics of a sculpted body. The transition from pose to pose combined with the graceful, sleek muscles make for a tranquil and moving phenomenon. Perhaps the best poser in bodybuilding history, Bob Paris, explains, *"I see posing as a theatrical display."***

Michelangelo's *David*

LEFT: *Amateur bodybuilder Luke Canestri resembles a Greek god, as if chiselled from stone.*

RIGHT: *Vincent Burke artfully displays his sculpted body with a passionate pose.*

* Reprinted with permission of *Muscle & Fitness Magazine*, August 1992
** Reprinted by permission of Warner Books, New York. From *Beyond Built*, ©1991, Bob Paris.

Some of the most beautiful paintings and sculptures ever created portray the muscular, human body. Michelangelo's, *The Creation of Adam,* painted on the dome of the Sistine Chapel, and his incredible muscular sculpture of David are classic examples. They wonderfully portray the human body with beautifully sculpted muscles. David gave the idea of a hero, the defender of a just cause. It comes to no surprise that a powerfully built icon represents the qualities of an idol.

If Auguste Rodin were alive today, he would have plenty to sculpt. He would have appreciated the similarities between his sculptures and bodybuilding. I never noticed until I stepped foot in the Rodin Museum in Philadelphia. I couldn't believe the striking similarities. I love the position of the hands most. Rodin was intrigued by hands as you can see from his sculptures shown below and on the next page.

CHAPTER 19

Sex and Bodybuilding

Sex and Bodybuilding

I have always found it ironic that because bodybuilders take pride in their physical appearance that people perceive them as being unintelligent. I still remember meeting people for the first time. This was when I was much bigger, weighing well over 200 pounds. After a discussion with someone I had just met, I would always hear how impressed that person was with me. As if to say, *I didn't expect anything intelligent from that bodybuilder guy.* Thanks to Arnold Schwarzenegger that all changed. Not only is Arnold intelligent and a great actor, he is also a sex symbol. That's one stereotype about bodybuilders I don't mind!

Can a leaner, more muscular body result in a better self-image and sexual performance?

The Psychological Factor

A good argument is made for people who exercise and have well-developed physiques. They have better self-images and therefore make better lovers.

As a former personal trainer, I have trained hundreds of people with low self-images because of the great dissatisfaction with their bodies, including high-level executives. When you feel good about yourself and know you look good, there is a greater chance you will perform better during sex as well as other components of your life. Dr. Marvin S. Hausman, MD, seems to agree. In an October 1992 article in *Muscle & Fitness Magazine, Why Bodybuilders Are Better Lovers,* he writes, "Increased body awareness leads to enhanced self-image and increased ability to interact socially and therefore, sexually."

Visualization

We are preprogrammed and genetically inclined to learn systems of visual stimulation. These stimuli activate our hormonal responses that lead us to sexual activity. The brain sends a message and hormones react. There is no thought process involved. Men are known to be more visual than women. There is no doubt about it. Look around you, bill boards, porno tapes, magazines, sex TV, all featuring beautifully toned women with large breasts. Advertising executives rely on man's visual stimuli to sell products.

A recent study found that male college students were more likely to choose hard-core pornography over women who predominantly preferred soft core or chose not to view it at all. How many times have you caught your partner staring at a lean, well-built physique? Does a man think about looking at a woman? No, he reacts. There is no time to think about it. This may be a sad excuse for men, but it holds some merit. Anthropologist, Donald Symons, PhD, explains in his book, *The Evolution of Human Sexuality (Oxford University Press, 1979)*, "The inclination to stare is a part of a male's sexuality." He explains that a woman's waist is a major desirable factor for men. His studies concluded that there is a preferred woman waist-to-hip-ratio for men consistent to the hourglass shape explained in Chapter 1. Women are considered to be more sensitive to touch than to site, but are still inclined to choose muscle over flab. Dr. Warren Farrell, PhD, author of The Myth of Male Power *(Simon and Shuster, 1993)* explains that a woman uses cues that indicate a man's status. For example, a man's height, dress, and movements help indicate a man's status. A man moves with more confidence if he is well-built than a man who is overweight.

The Physiological Factor

Increased muscle tone, body temperature, and blood flow, all results of exercise, lead to more hormonal circulation that stimulate physical responses. An erection requires about seven times the regular blood flow levels to the penis. Viagra, the new "sex" pill for men increases blood flow to the penis. Sexual desire in males depends on their flow of test-osterone. In his October 1992 article in *Muscle & Fitness Magazine, Why Bodybuilders Are Better Lovers,* Dr. Marvin S. Hausman, explains, "There is no question that sexual desire and behavior in the human male depends on some threshold or minimum amount of circulating testosterone." Bodybuilders do not require that much of an increase to perform because of their naturally high levels.

The Genetic Factor

Recent studies show that sexual attraction is linked to genetic factors as well as psychological ones and support a theory that physically fit people are more sexually desirable than those who are overweight.

Anthropologists and psychologists have agreed that genetic sexual behavior links human adaptation to the environment. Physical attraction to hard bodies has evolved as an adaptation to our competitive and predatory behavior. Why else do people obsess with losing weight and getting into shape? Even the most intelligent populations commit to their physical appearance. Many corporations have gyms in their office buildings. Top corporate executives initiate decisions of this magnitude. Companies with fitness facilities have experienced a reduction in health care costs, absenteeism, with an increase in productivity.

Since primitive man, Darwin's theory of survival of the fittest has proven itself time and again. Primitive man stayed alive by adapting to its physical and competitive environment. Those who failed to compete, died. Only the strong survived by hunting for food. Today we continue to fight for position as we struggle through the journey towards upward mobility. And being in good physical condition is a major component of that journey. Given that, get to the gym. Enhance your sex life and work performance!

CHAPTER 20

The Mr. & Ms. Rutgers Bodybuilding Contest

The Mr. & Ms. Rutgers Bodybuilding Contest

I made my bodybuilding debut in the 1988 Mr. & Ms. Rutgers Contest, where I took second place in the middleweight class. Kurt Faurenbach won the middle weight class with a well-polished physique and posing routine. That year featured the biggest heavy weight in the history of the contest, 6 foot 3 inch 240 pound Jimmy Ray shown in the photo below at left. Jimmy Ray was big and hard, but lightweight, Adam Eisman, shown in the photo at far right, prevailed with symmetry and a ripped physique for the overall Mr. Rutgers title. The crowd of over 2800 spectators agreed with the results, but you can be the judge.

Mike Duffy, the first Mr. Rutgers.

From left to right: 1988 winners, heavyweight Jimmy Ray, middleweight, Kurt Faurenbach, and overall winner, Adam Eisman.

Kathy Adamenko defeated Tory Masonis in the women's heavy weight division and went on to win the 1988 women's overall title.

In 1981, a Rutgers senior by the name of Bob Falcone founded the contest as an experimental intramural event.

The contest attracted little interest that year with a hand full of men, no women, and about 50 curious spectators. From 1981 to 1992, The Mr. & Ms. Rutgers Bodybuilding Contest grew to become one of the largest in the country.

At left: Gail DeRisi shows her dedication to Bodybuilding, competing with a broken leg at the 1983 contest.

1982 featured Mike Duffy and Barbara LaSpenosa, the first students to win the Mr./Ms. Rutgers Contest. Mike went

At right: 1983 Mr. Rutgers, Robert Plevy.

on to win other prestigious bodybuilding titles and later returned to judge the 1989 Mr. & Ms. Rutgers Contest.

Eight men and six women took the stage for the 1983 contest where Robert Plevy and Sonia Cruz won the overall titles. The 1983 contest introduced a memorable competitor, Gail DeRisi. Gail contributed a great deal to the contest over the years with MC appearances, TV commentating, and helping students with posing, dieting, and other contest preparations. But it is Gail's second place finish in the 1983 competition for which she will be most remembered. Gail gave true meaning to the word, *competitor* by hobbling on stage with a cast on her broken foot! Gail explained, "I had been a spectator of the very first Mr. & Ms. Rutgers Contest and vowed that I would compete. For one year I trained. I was ready, and then it happened. I turned my foot over in Modern Dance Class and fractured my foot." With a cast on her leg, her father commented that maybe no one would notice. There was no

Renee Feldman, 1985 Ms. Rutgers.

doubt in her father's mind that Gail would compete. "So I did," said Gail and the rest is history.

Fred Keifer and Jan Allen won the prestigious title in 1984, witnessed by another record-breaking crowd.

The 1985 contest featured a bit of controversy concerning the overall men's title between Richard Allen, and John Festa. The bigger Allen apparently beat the more symmetric Festa for the title. Renee Feldman took the women's overall title. Renee went on to win other prestigious NPC titles.

The fifth annual competition highlighted the massive middle weight, Eric Brumskill. Eric defeated light weight Jeff Behar for the overall title. Apparently, both competitors weighed the same, but made the contest more interesting by competing in different weight classes. Ellen Scepansky won the overall women's title with combination of muscle, dance, and gymnastics. This contest was the first of three times that 1988 overall men's winner Adam Eisman stepped on stage.

1987 Ms. Rutgers women take the stage.

In the above photos: 1987 Ms. Rutgers winner Laura Halpin demonstrates creativity during her posing routine.

By the 6th annual competition, it was evident that the Rutgers show was increasing in popularity. It attracted a respectable number of men and women that took the stage in front of a panel of judges and a crowd of more than 1500 spectators!

This year exhibited one of the most popular woman competitors in the history of the contest, Laura Halpin. Laura demonstrated her wonderful physique with incredible symmetry and an exciting and creative posing routine. Her brilliant mix of gymnastics, theatrics, along with her elegant, muscular physique earned her the overall title. Laura's physique was so appealing, that her photograph appeared on the front page of many local newspapers. This year also featured a 210 pound heavy weight, Chris Brasko who beat venerable competitors such as Adam Eisman and Steve Mennela took the overall title. Also, the first student

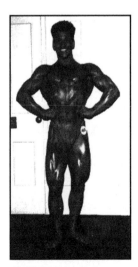

1987 Lightweight runner-up, Steve Mennela.

1988 Mr. & Ms. Rutgers Winners, Adam Eisman and Kathy Adamenko with judge Ron Capodanno.

pairs exhibition took place and brought the crowd to their feet with exciting choreography and creativity.

In 1989, the year I won the Mr. Rutgers title, the contest was a nationally recognized event attracting almost 100 competitors and a captivating and electrifying crowd of almost 3000!!

The person responsible for the success of the contest was The Mr. & Ms. Rutgers coordinator, Anthony Doody. Mr. Doody's stage efforts captivated the audience. This included special effects such as an electrifying light show, dry ice, a music system that would have put any night club to shame, and other creative stage props. Tony also employed top amateur guest posers, MCs, and National Physique Committee President, John Kemper as the head judge. The contest also received television coverage on local cable channels.

Winning the 1989 Mr. Rutgers title was very exciting for me. I was determined to win the contest by training hard immediately following the 1988 contest. I improved my diet, training techniques, posing routine, and overall stage presentation. I never missed a workout, or cheated on my diet for one full year! I was in much better shape than the previous year. On

1988 women competitors including Tori Masonis at the far right.

contest day, I weighed 167 pounds, eight pounds lighter than the previous year. I knew I would have some respectable competition from Dwayne Butler, the thick and defined light weight. Dwayne was coming off an impressive showing at the NPC Mr. New Jersey contest.

The 1990 contest was bigger than ever. Another capacity

Frank Melfa middleweight runner-up at the 1988 Mr. Rutgers contest.

crowd of over 3000 students again packed the Rutgers *Barn*. The overall titles that year went to Rich Refi, and Kristin Fless. Rich, at six feet one inch, found it difficult to pack muscle on his tall frame. Through hard training and strict dieting, Rich packed enough muscle to beat every man on stage. Rich and I enjoyed a few leg workouts that I'm sure he will never forget. Rich later came back to guest pose for the 1991 competition. Kristin competed in the contest for her third year before finally capturing the title in 1990. Through the years, Kristin's physique matured with shapely muscles that clearly sepa-rated her from the rest of the competi-

1989 Mr. & Ms. Rutgers winners Frank Melfa and Lori Keenan with Judge Ron Capodanno

tion. She literally turned the crowd upside down by performing exotic poses on her head.

The following year featured a wealth of bodybuilding talent. Andy McGurr, who went on to win the Mr. Rutgers title, Peter Antonakis, the middleweight winner, and lightweight Scott Bauman. Andy looked as if someone had actually carved him from stone. He gave new meaning to the word, *ripped*. Diana Cimato, a transfer student from Indiana took the overall women's title. She demonstrated excellent calf development and was not afraid to show it.

The 1992 Contest was host to some controversy. I not only trained the overall winner, Peter Antonokis, but also judged the contest. The judging was close between Pete and light-weight winner Scott Bauman, but the symmetry and stage presence clearly went to Pete. Scott was probably the biggest lightweight ever. To let you in on a little secret, the judges had scored four votes for Peter and three for Scott. The head judge, Ron Capodanno wanted to make certain that there would be no controversy. As a result, he asked Vince Sferra, a respectable name in bodybuilding, to place his vote. His vote made Pete the unanimous winner.

Second place finisher, Joseph Farese was competing in his forth Mr. & Ms Rutgers Contest. He had made obvious improvements every year. Joe commented, "I didn't reach my goal of winning Mr. Rutgers, but through hard work and perseverance one can reach lofty goals and live a healthy lifestyle." Joe later went on to win natural contests. There was a certain pride seeing Joe presented on posters in several gyms as a natural, bodybuilding champion.

1989 Lightweight winner, Dwayne Butler, shows great muscularity.

Bodybuilding 101

By 1990, the Mr. & Ms. Rutgers Contest became such a prominent event, that Rutgers University offered BODYBUILDING 101. In a way, it was similar to other classes at Rutgers. You had to register for it, a syllabus was used, attendance was taken, and it ran for an entire semester. It differed significantly from any other Rutgers courses. You received no credit for it; it was not held in a classroom or lecture hall, but in the Rutgers gym, better known as the *Barn.* You can be sure that the Rutgers students who attended came to learn, and learn they did. The 1990 contest held the most well prepared bodybuilders I had ever seen through the years. Not only were they physically prepared, but also well rehearsed on stage. They presented themselves with chiseled bodies and outstanding posing routines.

1990 Mr. & Ms. Rutgers, Rich Refi and Kristin Fless

The course was taught by Dr. Vincent Sferra. Sferra's credentials were very impressive. He had been a practicing chiropractor at the time for three years, finished first place in the light heavyweight division at the prestigious Mr. New Jersey contest in 1988, and weight-trained for 17 years. The class covered everything such as training principals, nutrition, and posing techniques. Those who attended the classes found themselves with obvious

Middleweight winner Chris Roberti captivates the crowd at the 1990 contest.

advantages over those who did not attend. Sferra agreed, "Those who attended, finished proportionally better than the rest of the competition."

The Mr. & Ms. Rutgers Bodybuilding Contest was consistently held on a Wednesday night in early April. This avoided conflict with spring break, midterms, and weekend events. The prejudging started at about 5:00 p.m. where the symmetry, muscularity, and presentation rounds took place. These three rounds followed the same procedures as most contests (*see the Judging and Posing chapters for more details*). The winners of each weight class were chosen at prejudging. At about 7:00 p.m., the night show started. Here, the big difference between The Mr. & Ms. Rutgers Contest and any other contest was demonstrated.

A record breaking crowd of 3000 students, family and friends.

The following is a conversation between the contest coordinator, Tony Doody and Rutgers student and bodybuilder, Steve Mennela right before the start of the 1989 Mr. Mrs. Rutgers Contest:

STEVE: *"Tony, I think it's time. Everything ready?"*

TONY: *"Yes, all set . . . God, would you look at this crowd!"*

STEVE: *"There's nothing like it."*

TONY: *"Take a deep breath. OK . . .*

1991 Mr. & Ms. Rutgers, Andy McGurr and Diana Cimato.

Each night show started with loud and vibrant music bringing the enthusiastic crowd to its feet. As the music blasted, a slide show of past Mr. & Ms. Rutgers competitors projected the walls of the gymnasium to help tease the crowd to an uproar. Then the competitors would take the stage and each strike a pose in the midst of a prism of lights and smoke emulated by dry ice. Now the crowd is going wild and the stage is starting to shake.

The night show segmented the men, women and mixed pairs by weightclasses. The men were divided into three weightclasses: light, middle, and heavyweight. The women were divide into two classes, light and heavyweight.

	Men	**Women**
Lightweight	under 158 lbs.	under 114.5 lbs.
Middleweight	158-178 lbs.	—
Heavyweight	over 178 lbs.	over 114.5 lbs.

1992 Mr. and Ms. Rutgers, Peter Antonakis and Lisa Plasters.

From left to right: 1991 Lightweight runner-up, Steve Rosen, 4-year competitor and 1992 Middleweight runner-up Joseph Farese, and 1992 Lightweight winner Scott Bauman.

A mixed pair is formed with a man and woman from any of the weight classes. The judges look for muscularity and symmetry. Their physiques must compliment each other, and their posing routines must gracefully join the two as one. Their poses

1992 Men's posedown with Pete Antonakis (left) and Mark Rossman (right) in the forefront.

should flow incessantly to their selected music. The mixed pairs were the first competitors to take the stage followed by the women. After a brief intermission, the men light weights take the stage, followed by the middle weights and finally the heavyweights. Between segments, guest posers sometimes appeared at several of the contests. I had the honor of guest posing at the 1990 contest along with Mr. Greece! I was a little nervous about my guest posing appearance for a couple of reasons.

"Posing must be entertaining, and why not?"*–Bob Paris. Frank Melfa, below, and Rich Refi, right, return to the stage for their guest posing appearances at the 1990 and 1991 Mr. Rutgers contests.

PHOTO BY WILLIAM DEJIANNE

One, I didn't think anyone would remember me from the previous years. Two, I thought Mr. Greece, who was much bigger than me, was going to steal the show. Much to my surprise, I received welcoming cheers and jubilant ovation that I will never forget. It was probably one of the best moments of my life! Mr. Greece received a modest array of cheers, but nothing like mine.

The Mr. & Ms. Rutgers contest uniquely differed from any other contest because all competitors had the exciting opportunity to pose in front of their friends and family. At the 1992 Mr. & Ms. Rutgers contest, there were over 20 light weights alone. At any other contest, only the top five competitors pose at the night show because of time restrains. That goes to show how well organized this contest was. It was planned to the minute.

Each competitor from each weight class posed for one minute to a song they each selected. Following the one minute routines of each weight class, the top three of each class received trophies for their efforts. As in any contest, the winner of each weight class poses for the overall winner.

Posing

You may have realized that posing is one of my favorite topics to write about. Posing at the Mr. & Ms. Rutgers contests was very entertaining indeed. All competitors displayed their own unique posing styles. Some were very serious, creative, acrobatic, and sometimes even amusing.

Amusing you ask? One thing I learned in bodybuilding is that Rome wasn't built in a day. Stepping on stage, for the first time, at the 1988 Mr. & Ms. Rutgers Contest, was extremely awkward for me. I love looking back at those photos. They never fail to bring a smile to my face. For example, look at my less-than-graceful front double biceps pose in the photo above. I have learned to laugh at myself.

But then I practiced, and I practiced, and practiced some more.

Then finally it all started to come together. Nothing is better than striking a winning double biceps!

The following photographs show the variety of ways the Rutgers competitors displayed their physiques on stage. Many of the poses shown below are variations of the mandatory poses during the compulsory and free posing rounds *(see Chapter 17 for more posing details)*. Poses during the free posing and mixed pairs rounds are much more creative because there are no instructions from the judges, so anything goes! So let's take a final look at a decade of bodybuilding at Rutgers University.

From left: Allison Denny, 1992; James Gaeta, 1989; Joe Petriello, 1992 Heavyweight winner; and 1992 Mixed Pairs Chris Wahlers and Shannon Lesnevich.

Kathy Adamenko kicks her way to a victory.

From left: 1989 Lightweights Michael Maiorino, Glen Firestone and Chris Trochiano hit their front lat spreads as competitor Jimmy Eng looks on from behind.

To the far right, Deana Degrace and Shannon Lesnavich display their front double biceps in the competitive 1991 Heavyweight class.

From left: 1992 lightweights Rich Alverez, Scott Bauman, Larry Hau and Laurence Laudicina. 1989 Lightweights, from left, Kelly Jacobs, Linda Gavazzi, Kristin Fless and Mary Fellner.

From left: Heavyweights Charlie Halado, 5th, Don Orrell, 1st, and John Kudrick. 1989 Mixed Pairs, from left, Larry Faljean with Kristin Fless and Stephen Braccioforte with Diane Drago.

Back Stage at The Barn

Some people wonder what takes place back stage at a bodybuilding contest. The visual things are noticeable such as, pumping up, waiting for the last minute to practice your posing, and applying oil to your body. However, the most significant and interesting parts of the back stage experience are the mind games. For the Rutgers competitors, back stage was our home. Many of us at one time or another visited the Rutgers Gym, better known as the *Barn*.

It would be safe to say that many of us did most of our training there. It was amusing to train and prepare at the Barn, especially a few months before the Mr. & Ms. Rutgers Contest. Everyone wondered who was competing that year. We asked ourselves what the chances were to place and bring home a trophy, or even win the overall title! *Me, Mr. Rutgers? It can never happen.* I was just looking not to embarrass myself.

I remember my first year preparing for the 1988 Mr. Rutgers. Not only was it my first bodybuilding contest, it was also my first year at Rutgers. I didn't know many people. I wasn't familiar with the contest or any of the competitors. I had no idea what to expect. There was always a lot of chatter in the gym. I spoke to no one because I knew no one. I always felt that I didn't belong and that no one even knew I was alive. I'm sure we all shared that anxiety one time or another. So much so, that many decided not to compete at all. I know many competitors that planned to compete, but dropped out weeks before the contest because the anxiety was just

In 1989, Kelly Jacobs uses her back-stage time efficiently as she performs pushups and gets oiled simultaneously.

too much. But those of us who finally made it back stage the night of the contest knew what anxiety was all about. You look around the room. Your heart starts racing as you hear the 3000 plus crowd roaring. You ask yourself how many competitors are in your weight class. Or better yet, you ask your friend, you know, the one that helps you with the oil, as if they should know. You can't find your water. Your friend, whose only responsibility is the oil, but finds a way to lose it. You forgot to bring a spoon for your jelly. Your hair looks terrible and your posing trunks don't fit. What else could go wrong?

Who can forget that wonderful smell? What a combination: oil, sweat, tanning sprays, food, body odor (from not showering for days to prevent your tanning products from washing away) and of course the worst possible gas you can possibly imagine. Eating all those carbs almost made us smell inhumane. Howard Stern would have had a field day talking about that smell. Yeah, we looked healthy, but we sure didn't smell healthy!

Most competitors would strip down one hour before stage time and begin warming up. Not me. Not only did I try to relax, as shown in this photo, but I also never revealed anything. I enjoyed making people wonder how I looked and what I was thinking. I just sat back, closed my eyes and thought about my posing routine. Did that mean I wasn't nervous? Absolutely not!

Sure I was nervous, but never showed it. Another thing I learned about bodybuilding, *it's never in the bag!* I was never sure I was going to win. For example, in 1988 when I placed second in the middleweight class, I remember people telling me back stage that I was a cinch to win my weight class. Well, as you already know, I didn't.

You better believe that back stage during the 1989 Contest, I wasn't taking anything for granted. I was just recuperating from a disappointing showing at the NPC Mr. New Jersey Contest the weekend before the Rutgers Contest. Not only wasn't I sure about winning the contest, I was depressed, nervous, hungry, grouchy, tired, and anxious. Bodybuilding, what a great sport!

Mr. & Ms. Rutgers Bodybuilding
A Decade of Champions

1st Annual (1982) Mike Duffy
Barbara LaSpenosa

2nd Annual (1983) Robert Plevy
Sonia Cruz

3rd Annual (1984) Fred Keifer
Jan Allen

4th Annual (1985) Richard Allen
Renee Feldman

5th Annual (1986) Eric Brumskill
Ellen Scepansky

6th Annual (1987) Chris Brasco
Laura Halpin

7th Annual (1988) Adam Eisman
Kathy Adamenko

8th Annual (1989) Frank Melfa
Lori Keenan

9th Annual (1990) Rich Refi
Kristin Fless

10th Annual(1991) Andy McGurr
Diana Cimato

11th Annual (1992) Peter Antonakis
Lisa Plasters

The Student Bodybuilder_____

How on earth did we find time to attend classes, prepare and eat meals, train twice a day every day, perform aerobics, tan and pose, study, and work? Not only is bodybuilding a demanding sport, it can also be expensive, especially for a college student. We incurred expenses such as: food, bodybuilding supplements, gym memberships, tanning salons, tanning products, and even hair cuts.

Did you ever try training at a college gym? How about waiting in line to get in the gym? Once you finally got in the gym, you hand to wait in line to use the equipment. We put up with it because most of us could not afford a membership anyplace else.

What were we supposed to eat from the school cafeteria?

What about sacrifices like missing parties, spring break, drinking beer, eliminating fatty foods? This also meant abstaining from basic college staples such as pizza, ice cream, and chocolate! And how about dating and sex? Shall I more appropriately say, eliminating dating and sex! No wonder why I was grouchy all the time. I was rotten to everyone including my friends, family, and class mates. I even got into a fist fight in the gym, which really wasn't my fault. But you can read about that later.

Wow! How did we do it? In this chapter, I take each of these issues and talk about how student bodybuilders handled these everyday dilemmas as student bodybuilders.

Attending classes was one of the more difficult things for a student bodybuilder. Being attentive in class can be a challenge when you felt tired, grouchy, sore, HUNGRY, and lacking energy, to mention just a few wonderful things. I could never sit still and pay attention in class for more than 15 minutes. The worst part was the anxiety of knowing that I had to return to the gym for a second grueling workout of the day. If I was real unfortunate, it would be a leg day. Nothing is worse than training legs when you are famished and tired. Training legs takes every ounce of energy left in you if you trained with the same intensity I did.

Diana Cimato, 1991 Women's Overall Ms. Rutgers Winner experienced some anxiety in the classroom herself. "I was only one month away from my contest," she explained, "there I was, sitting in class wondering how I was going to get down to 105 pounds. If I didn't fall asleep in class, I would be reading my food diary rather than the class lessons."

Diana also found time to study and maintain her grades. "I had no social life. While everyone was out partying, I was studying."

Bodybuilding and Good Grades?

Although I was not very successful in class, I did find time to study. Since I did not party from September to April, I found plenty of time to study on weekends. What I missed in class I made up studying. My grades did not suffer at all. In fact, they improved. I found that during my three years of body-building at Rutgers, my spring semester grades were consistently better than my winter and fall grades.

Kathy Adamenko, 1988 women's overall winner and Kurt Farenbach, 1988 men's middle weight winner agreed. They both experienced their best semesters at Rutgers while preparing for the Mr./Ms. Rutgers Contest.

Kurt, who lived in a fraternity house, explained, "I gave up drinking and stopped partying. It freed up all my time to study." When asked about planning, he replied, "I planned every move, everything I did was planned to the minute. I set goals and achieved them and bodybuilding was one of them."

Kathy remembered her tough schedule, "I was dancing, attending classes, participating in my sorority, and lifting weights. I had to plan or else I would be lost."

Peter Antonakis, 1992 Mr. Rutgers, explained his priorities: School, lifting, sleeping, and eating. When I asked him about his social life he answered, "None."

I also credit bodybuilding for my improved planning skills and ability to stay focused. I learned to budget time and money, write things down, and set long and short term goals. Most importantly, I achieved the goals that I set for myself.

After you finish reading this book, you will realize how much planning goes into bodybuilding. Hopefully this will help you realize the importance of planning, not only for your fitness goals, but for other goals in your life. *(Also see the section, Planning Is Everything, in the contest preparation part of this book.)*

Bodybuilding Dreams?

If anxiety did not dawn on us in class, it caught up to us in our subconscious.

My worst dream was getting on stage with hairy legs because I forgot to shave! Another common one was not being tan. But FOOD was the ultimate nightmare. I used to dream about eating pizza and feeling guilty about it in the morning.

Diana recalled: "My worst bodybuilding dream was that someone was forcing me to eat something fattening."

Eating in Class

I remember one time being hungry in class. It was time for a ricecake break, but I was too tired to leave the classroom. In the middle of American Literature I whipped out a ricecake and started chomping on it. Anyone who has ever eaten or heard someone eating a ricecake knows how noisy they can be. So there I was, *crunch, crunch, crunch*, savoring one of those rare moments of my day. The next thing I know, the professor has the nerve to interrupt class and ask me if I could chew on a piece of bread instead. If only he knew that I hadn't eaten a piece of bread in 12 weeks! I answered him simply, "I wish." Bread is one of the many foods you eliminate before a contest because it contains salt and sugar.

Diana recalls her embarrassment about eating tuna fish in class, "It smelled so bad, but I had to get my meal in."

Another rice cake story took place at the computer center on the Rutgers campus where I was typing a paper when it came time for a ricecake meal with all fruit jelly. As I was taking my first bite into a ricecake, one of the workers ordered me to stop eating in the room and referred me to a sign that read, NO EATING OR DRINKING IN COMPUTER ROOM. Of course I saw the sign, but I figured since he was drinking a soda and eating his healthy potato chips that it was OK for me to eat my ricecakes. He warned me about damaging the computer with the jelly if it spilled onto the key board. I asked him what he thought would happen if his soda would spill onto the key board. With an audience of about 20 people, he told me he had the money to pay for the computer should he damage it. I guess he wanted everyone know that he came from a wealthy family. It didn't explain why he was working in the computer room for three bucks an hour. Anyway, he asked me if I could afford to pay for the computer if I were to damage it. I of course had just enough money left to purchase my next bottle of amino acids and distilled water.

By this time I already ate my second ricecake. Now he was fuming. He threatened to call security and have me removed from the room. Now things were really getting hot as I continued chomping my second ricecake. I was going to tell him to try and remove me from the room, but by this time the other computer worker nicely asked me if I could finish eating outside. I acquiesced. The irony of this story is that after I won the 1989 Mr. Rutgers Contest a few months following that incident, I later bumped into him. His tone changed dramatically. He must have congratulated me about twenty times and kept on telling me how great I looked.

Preparing Meals

Rubber Chicken?

"I microwaved everything" recalled Kathy Adamenko, 1988 Overall Ms. Rutgers Winner. "I relied on my microwave for fast cooking. My schedule was just so busy, that I never had time to cook. I had to eat rubber chicken all the time, because that's what it tastes like after the microwave." I also weighed everything to the "mili ounce." Nothing I ate went without being weighed first."

I prepared everything with ricecakes. My last ricecake story took place at a local Grand Union. The last thing on my shopping list was ricecakes. I looked down every aisle and could not find ricecakes. Only a bodybuilder can understand the importance of a full supply of ricecakes during contest preparation. I was thinking about what kind of supermarket did not sell ricecakes. What was the world coming to? I thought as I walked up to a cashier and asked her where the ricecakes were. She told me to look in aisle eight. I was already in aisle eight, but I went back.. Who knows? I thought, could have missed them. Much to my dismay, I still could not find the ricecakes. I then proceeded to ask a customer service representative where I could find the ricecakes. He also instructed me to aisle eight. I thought it possible to have walked by them a second time. So once again, I tried aisle eight only to be disappointed once again. By this time I totally refused to accept the fact that they probably ran out of rice cakes. I was in denial. I had about three workers in the store looking for ricecakes. Finally it occurred to me that I was going to leave that store without ricecakes. In a crazed state of hunger and frustration, I yelled in the middle of the store: "I can't believe that a supermarket can run out of ricecakes!"

Hard dieting and training can lead to this type of behavior. I drove just about everyone crazy, especially my family and friends.

Abnormal Behavior?

One thing I hated was fitness and diet questions from my family and friends. Driving home from one of my contests after a disappointing showing, my brother-in-law, who was notorious for dumb questions, didn't let me down:

"Frank, I was thinking, what's better for you, 1% milk or 2% milk?"

My reply: "Hey Marcelo, what's better for you one bullet in your head or 2 bullets in your head?"

My 5:30 a.m. Experience

I trained early morning at 5:30 a.m. at Ron Capodanno's Gold's Gym. I had the entire gym to myself every morning; it was great not having to wait for equipment. Most of the guys that worked out there were considerate about equipment anyway. If they knew you were training for a contest, they would get out of your way and give you first choice. Of course there are always those exceptions:

There were some people in the gym at 5:30 a.m. Most were considerate except for one individual. I was about two weeks away from the Rutgers contest. My training routine involved moving quickly from one exercise to the other, then it happened.

Someone told me that he did not appreciate me "hogging" the equipment. I told him to give me a break because I was training for a contest and that he was training to look good for his girlfriend. He did not appreciate that comment very much, but I didn't really care. If any of you has competed, you know how grouchy you can get. Anyway, I remember I was supersetting shoulders with upright rows and lateral raises. When I completed my upright rows, I immediately ran for the dumbbell rack to perform my lateral raises. Guess who I accidentally bumped into? You have to believe me, the last thing I wanted to do was get into a fight at 5:30 in the morning when the only energy I had was to train. He pushed me pretty hard when I bumped into him. I found myself face to face with this guy. In a split second time I was considering to let the issue go or just punch him out. Well, I chose the latter; I punched him out. I could not believe it. He went down like a ton of bricks. One second he's in my face, and then he's on his knees in *lala* land. I thought I killed the guy. As he sat on the floor in a daze, I went back to performing my lateral raises, not wasting any more time. That was the funny part; I never even broke stride. As soon as he went down, I immediately went for the dumbbells. Now that is staying focused! Of course, that was not the end of it. The next thing I know I'm getting tackled into the dumbbell rack during my set of lateral raises. Once he tackled me, I just laid there. I was too tired to get him off and he wasn't doing anything to me anyway. Two other guys at the gym pulled him off me and I once again continued with my lateral raises. I didn't even remember what the guy I punched out looked like. He could have been there the very next day and wouldn't have even known. I did notice a big scratch across my back during a posing session, but it was not noticeable during the contest.

Frank The Flounder

Six weeks before my last contest, the 1990 NPC Mr. New Jersey, I was in pretty bad shape. During those six weeks, I had already dropped 45 pounds, pulled my back out, and tore my chest bench pressing with 135 pound dumbbells.

I ate plenty of fish for dinner and trained early morning at 5:30 a.m. I pulled my back out and could not dress and undress without being in pain, especially putting on and taking off my shoes. To save time and pain, I avoided the repetitious task of dressing and undressing. So I didn't shower as often as I should have and slept with the same clothes including shoes that I wore for dinner. I sometimes even slept with my weightlifting belt. I would wake up fully clothed, eat a quick breakfast and go to the gym unknowingly smelling like the previous night's flounder. The smell was on my clothes and would come out of my pores when I perspired in the gym. Unbeknownst to me, I used to stink up the gym and the posing room. About one year later, I went to the same gym and it smelled like fish. When I commented about the odor, Tori Masonis, a former Rutgers Bodybuilding competitor, told me it almost smelled as bad as when I used to come and stink up the gym. I was kind of embarrassed knowing that I smelled like fish that whole time and was never aware of it. I probably would not have done anything about it anyway. She also told me she used to go into the posing room and know I was there previously because of the strong smell of fish.

Sometimes I went straight to class from the gym. I can just picture me like Peppy Lapue, the cartoon skunk with this green aroma floating over me. I was so out of it I just did not care. I do remember people complaining of a fish smell in the gym. I kind of figured it was me, but I was just ignorant of it all. All I knew was that I had a workout to finish.

424

I also remember having to go to the chiropractor following my workouts because I had thrown my back out. I was still training, but not performing exercises the hurt my back. I remember sitting in a full waiting room in excruciating pain. Once again, I must have stunk up the entire waiting room. I noticed the secretary was very cute, but she avoided me at all cost. I later dated her and asked her if I smelled like fish when I came in for sessions. The only thing she said was, "Don't even get me started." I guess that was an understatement for yes. We never discussed it after that.

Cafeteria Food: What Can You Eat?

Depending on what contest stage I was in determined how useful the cafeteria food was. If I was in my bulking stage, I ate plenty from the cafeteria. On the other hand, if I was in the precontest stage *(about 12 weeks out)* not much was palatable.

In the building stage, I was consuming about four to five thousand calories a day. I was the first person in the cafeteria for breakfast every morning and I ate a lot:

Breakfast foods: cream of wheat, muffins, granola, cereals, eggs

Lunch foods: whole wheat bread with boiled eggs, turkey breast without gravy, salads, and fruit

Dinner foods: (same as lunch)

When I had to cut 40 pounds to compete at middle weight, there was not too much from the cafeteria that I could eat since I cut out all fats, breads, and fruits.

For breakfast, I cooked my own oatmeal or cream of wheat. The cafeteria always had either salt or margarine in theirs. If you lived in a dormitory, you had to use the dorm kitchen, which wasn't that convenient especially when it was on the first floor and you lived on the fifth floor.

Before salmonella was a health problem, I use to drink about six to eight egg whites per day. That was so easy: no cooking or cleaning.

For lunch, I had some type of carbohydrate with a can of tuna. Usually, I had some rice, pasta, or even oatmeal. Yes, oatmeal. I mixed a can of tuna with hot oatmeal which tasted pretty good, almost like stew. I cooked and prepared everything myself because the cafeteria never had plain anything. Between classes, if I had to eat in the cafeteria, I would make the biggest salad on campus. I used a variety of vegetables along with hard boiled egg whites and wheat germ.

Dinner, which consisted of either chicken or fish (usually flounder or haddock) with a baked potato or vegetables, I always ate in my dorm room or my off campus house.

Bodybuilding Expenses

Bodybuilding did get expensive, especially for a college student who can make five dollars last an entire week. How many of us paid well over $300 for a meal plan at one of the Rutgers Dining Halls only needing to spend more money on real food? I remember how expensive chicken and fish were to buy. Pasta, potatoes, vegetables, and hot cereals were relatively inexpensive, but still an additional expense. Ricecakes did get expensive when purchasing three or four bags at a time. The all fruit jelly was twice as expensive as regular jelly and contained half as much.

Amino acids and other supplements were not cheap either. A bottle of 100 amino acids sold for an easy thirty dollars. When instructed to take five to seven pills after every meal, how far do you think that bottle went?

I budgeted my money by logging monthly expenses and income. After figuring how much money I would need, I added about 20% to that total, to avoid underestimating my costs. I then proceeded to save the money needed to cover the expenses. Saving money was not that big of a problem without beer and pizza expenses.

Through my years of Rutgers Contest preparation, I managed to get some breaks to cut down on some of my costs.

The first break came when I was tanning for my first Rutgers Contest in 1988. I knew would eventually need a hair cut for the contest when one of the hair dressers offered to my cut hair for free. He told me it was good publicity for him. He ended up cutting my hair for the first contest for free and every time else after that.

Luckily, Gold's had a tanning booth right in the gym. Ron Capodanno, who helped me tremendously with my preparation gave me a deal on tanning sessions. He only charged me $20 for 10 sessions.

Another expense was the dye to paint your body, called Protan®. This product cost about twenty dollars a bottle. One time, a friend spilled the entire bottle. He caught hell from me because I warned him over and over to be careful.

I lived in a dorm room when preparing for The 1988 Mr/Ms Rutgers Contest and worked at the gym on campus for minimum wage. It was my only source of income at the time. It was a very convenient job. The gym was directly across the street from my dorm and I also had access to it anytime. I even used the aerobics room to practice my posing. The only problem was that it did not have enough equipment. It lacked necessary leg equipment such as a leg press. I was forced to bus over to the College Ave Gym where I waited on line for at least a half hour to use the gym. Once I got in, most of the equipment was being used anyway. I hated waiting for equipment. It really put a damper on my training intensity.

The following year, I knew I had to join a gym in order to properly prepare for the 1989 Mr/Ms Rutgers Contest. I did not have the money to do it. I remember sitting in my off campus house trying to think of a way to join a gym. At that moment, two of my friends came into my room a gave me a gift certificate to the local Gold's Gym. It was the best and most useful gift I had ever received.

The worst part of my morning workouts was knowing I had to return later that day for a second session. My second session was not as strenuous as the morning one. It included a 30 minute aerobic session on the bike, a brief abdominal workout, a short workout training small body parts such as biceps, triceps, or hamstrings, and a posing session. Although the second session was not as physically taxing as the first, I still had to drag myself either from class or from my apartment to the gym.

Sacrifices

My New Years Resolution for 1988 was to compete in the Mr. Rutgers Contest and stop drinking. I thought that I would never be able to give up drinking. All through high school and my first two years of college, I used to look forward to drinking from Thursday through the weekend. At first it was very difficult. While everyone else was drinking and having a good time at parties, I was either in my dorm room doing schoolwork, or in the gym training. This was not how I envisioned a college student having fun.

Initially, I thought that drinking would be the biggest sacrifice, but I later found that limiting my food intake was the toughest. At first, I cut out all my fats but was still eating large quantities of healthy food. But when I had to cut my calories from

5000 to about 1400, drinking beer was the furthest thing from my mind.

I was hungry all the time. Food was all I ever thought about, even in my subconscious. At one time, I used to consider an erotic dream to be sexual, but when I had to sacrifice eating, I considered an erotic dream eating pizza with extra cheese. It's funny how I always took food for granted. I would sit in the cafeteria and ask everyone how their food tasted. I always told everyone that when I was through competing, I was going to eat whatever they were eating.

Another hang-up was asking people what they had for dinner when they went out to eat. It was funny. Someone would be trying to tell me a serious story about how they got into a fight with their girlfriend in the restaurant and all I could think about was what they both had ordered for dinner. I had to know everything: the drinks, appetizers if any, the main entree, and desert.

My worst encounter with food was in an elevator with a Domino's pizza man. I remember that moment too well: The aroma was seeping through the cardboard box, I could smell the sauce and cheese; my mouth was watering and I was getting very pissed off. Good thing he got off at the next floor or he would have ended up like my friend at the gym. I really thought that this person was there to purposely tease me. I must say that I never once cheated during any of my contest preparations.

Most of us spent more time in the gym than any other place, at least three to four hours six to seven days per week. Renee Feldman, 1985 winner commented," I was in the gym every day, never missing a work out."
After lifting for about one hour and a half, we still needed to perform 30 to 40 minutes of aerobic exercises such as: stationary bike or stairmaster. Practicing our posing routines

required at least another half hour. Tanning utilized another 20 to 30 minutes.

Painting Experiences

Two nights before one of my contests, my roommate was supposed to help me dye my body with Protan. You usually dye yourself two to three days prior the contest to get that real tan look. It's extremely difficult to paint those hard to reach places on your own. Much to my dismay, he wasn't coming home and I wanted to go to sleep, but I needed to be dyed. So I called a female friend of mine. I explained the situation to her and told her that I needed her to dye me. She agreed and came over. When getting painted, I could never reach the entire back of my body. I needed some help. I lay on my stomach, on a towel, on the kitchen table wearing only my posing trunks, while a friend or roommate painted me.

Well, there we were, she, rubbing my body with a paint brush, I, barely awake, enjoying the caressing. The next thing I know she stopped painting. I asked her what was wrong. She told me that she was too "turned on" to continue! I told her to forget it because I didn't have the energy. She finished painting me and went home. Believe it or not, it's the truth.

Index

431

Bibliography

The author acknowledges the following references used in preparation of this text:

Arnheim, Daniel D., D.P.E., A.T.C. *Modern Principles of Athletic Training*. Boston: Times Mirror/Mosby College Publishing, 7th ed., 1989.

Balch, James F. MD, Balch, Phyllis A. C.N.C. *Prescription for Nutritional Healing*. Garden City Park, New York: Avery Publishing Group Inc. 1990.

Burden, Sheldon O., MD. *Sexual Fitness*: *Muscle & Fitness,* March 1993:42.

Brumberg, Elaine, *Take Care of Your Skin*. New York: 1st ed., Harper Perennial, 1989.

Cadena, Bryant. *Are You Gaining Muscle and Losing Fat? Muscle Media 2000*, issue number 36, 1993.

Davis, F.A. *Taber's Cyclopedic Medical Dictionary*, Philadelphia: 17th ed.

Dobbins, Bill. *Rachel Today: Muscle & Fitness*, August 1992: 101-103.

Doheny, Kathleen. *Get A Grip on Body Fat: Men's Health*, 1994.

Dutton, K.R. and Ronald, Laura, PhD. *Athlete, Artist, or Sex Objects: Muscle & Fitness*, August 1992: 110, 181.

Farrell, Warren, PhD. *The Myth of Male Power.* Simon & Schuster, 1993.

Hausman, Marvin S., MD. *Why Bodybuilders Are Better Lovers: Muscle & Fitness*, October 1992: 146.

Hoppenfeld, Stanley, M.D. *Physical Examination of the Spine and Extremities*. Appleton & Lang, California: 1976.

Kennedy, Robert. *Rock Hard! Supernutrition For Bodybuilders.* New York: Warner Books, 1987.

Kennedy, Robert. *Savage Sets! The Ultimate Pre-Exhaust Pump Out.* New York: Sterling Publishing Co.,1989.

Lamar, Peter. *Anabolic Nightmare: Flex Magazine*, August 1987: 74.

Lamar, Peter. *If The Facts Don't Scare You, We Don't Know What Will: Muscle & Fitness,* August 1987: 75.

Luoma, TC. *Amino Acid Supplements: Do We Really Need Them? Muscle Media* 2000, June 1994: 53-55.

Med Text, Inc. *Clinical Pharmacology*, Boston, Massachusetts.

Paris, Bob. *Beyond Built: Bob Paris' Guide To Achieving The Ultimate Physique.* New York: Warner Books, 1991.

Paris, Bob. *gorilla suit: My Adventures In Bodybuilding.* New York, New York. St. Martin's Press, 1997.

Phillips, Nathaniel W. *Anabolic Reference Guide.* 6th issue, Golden, CO: Mile High Publishing, March 1991.

Phillips, Nathaniel W. *Natural Supplement Review.* 2nd ed., Golden, CO: Mile High Publishing, July 1991.

Prentice, William E., Ph.D., A.T.C., P.T. *Rehabilitation Techniques in Sports Medicine.* Boston: Times Mirror/Mosby College Publishing, 1990.

Sieg and Adams. *Illustrated Essentials of Musculoskeletal Anatomy.* Gainsville Florida: Megabooks, 2nd ed., 1992.

Schlosberg, Suzanne, Neporent Liz, MA. *Fitness For Dummies*™ Foster City, CA. IDG Books Worldwide Inc., 1996.

Schuler, Lou. *Unlock the Power of Passion: Muscle & Fitness.* June 1992: 98.

Schwarzenegger, Arnold. *The Encyclopedia of Modern Bodybuilding.* New York: Firestone Books, Simon & Schuster 1985.

What's Your Type, Shape Magazine, August 1994: 79-87.

Sparkman, Dennis PhD. *Alcohol & Exercise: Muscle & Fitness*, February 1994: 178.

Strote, Mary Ellen. *Man: The Visual Animal: Muscle & Fitness*, February 1994: 166, 168.

Symons, Donald Phd. *The Evolution of Human Sexuality.* Oxford University Press, 1979.

The PDR® Family Guide To Nutrition And Health.™ Montvale, NJ. Medical Economics 1995,

Webster's Collegiate Dictionary, 10th ed., 1993.

Weider, Joe. *Nutrition & Training Programs, The Best of Joe Weider's Flex,* Chicago: Contemporary Books, 1990.